Shakespeare and the 99%

"The smartest, most original, and most useful book on Shakespeare and the politics of higher education I have seen in many years. *Shakespeare and the 99%* shows at once how vital Shakespeare can be for thinking through the structural inequalities of a debt-driven higher education system and how necessary Shakespeare's work remains to non-elite students, readers, and citizens increasingly alienated from the classrooms of ivy-clad academe. Writing from an unusually wide range of institutional positions and professional conditions, the contributors weave sophisticated theoretical analysis with situated personal detail in ways that neither float upward toward pious abstraction nor descend to the merely anecdotal. The result? An account of Shakespeare's work, in his world and in ours, that feels genuinely new; a style of criticism living up to the promise of critique and responding to the responsibility of pedagogy and accessibility; and a model for committed humanities scholarship in the twenty-first century."

—Henry S. Turner, *Professor of English, Rutgers University, USA*

"An incisive, invigorating critique of the promise of the humanities following the 2008 financial collapse and the rise of a debt economy, *Shakespeare and the 99%* offers startling answers to questions of what we can do with Shakespeare and what Shakespeare can do for us: his plays engender and combat political cynicism; they bolster and dismantle the divisions of class, race, and gender structuring higher education today. An avatar for tradition and lever for social mobility, Shakespeare, it turns out, may be our best, last hope for a revitalized and relevant liberal arts."

—Amanda Bailey, *Professor of English, University of Maryland, USA*

"*Shakespeare and the 99%* offers an engaging, provocative look at the profession and challenges readers to rethink Shakespeare's place in today's neoliberal university. An important call to action for Shakespeare studies, the collection challenges us to examine our roles as scholars and pedagogues in the twenty-first century."

—Louise Geddes, *Associate Professor of English, Adelphi University, USA*

Sharon O'Dair · Timothy Francisco
Editors

Shakespeare and the 99%

Literary Studies, the Profession, and the Production of Inequity

Editors
Sharon O'Dair
University of Alabama, Tuscaloosa
Tuscaloosa, AL, USA

Timothy Francisco
Youngstown State University
Youngstown, OH, USA

ISBN 978-3-030-03882-3 ISBN 978-3-030-03883-0 (eBook)
https://doi.org/10.1007/978-3-030-03883-0

Library of Congress Control Number: 2018961184

Cover credit: Lebrecht Music and Arts Photo Library/Alamy Stock Photo

This Palgrave Macmillan imprint is published by the registered company Springer Nature Switzerland AG
The registered company address is: Gewerbestrasse 11, 6330 Cham, Switzerland

To the memories of our working-class parents

To our working class-students

Acknowledgements

During the past fifty years academic writing and research has often responded to the zeitgeist—and helped to create it—by interrogating received understandings of gender, race, colonialism, the environment, ethics, and indeed of literature itself. *Shakespeare and the 99%: Literary Studies, the Profession, and the Production of Inequity* is no different and would not have come into being without the social, economic, and professional disruptions of recent decades and especially since the Great Recession of 2008.

Indeed, the essays included here originated in forums provided by the Shakespeare Association of America over a series of years and we wish to thank our professional organization and its past Executive Director, Lena Cowen Orlin, for offering places on the annual programs for the kinds of work represented here. At the 2016 annual meeting, Emily Isaacson and Greg Foran co-directed a seminar on "Part-Time Shakespeare" and we co-directed a workshop on "Working-Class Shakespeares: Shakespeare in Class and Class in Shakespeare." We are grateful to the all the participants and auditors in that seminar and workshop whose work, whether or not included in this volume, has contributed significantly to it. Building on that work, Deborah Uman and Sharon O'Dair co-organized a roundtable on "Shakespeare beyond the Research University" for SAA 2017, which the program committee selected as the Association's featured "Futures" panel. We are grateful to the program committee, to Deborah, and to the roundtable's participants, Denise Albanese, Katherine Boutry, Marisa Cull, Emily Isaacson, Fayaz Kabani, and Daniel

Vitkus, as well as to all those in the audience, whose commentary provided not just affirmation but valuable insight as we were producing this volume. We are grateful, too, that the SAA continues to support work in this vein, putting on the program for 2019 a "Futures" panel organized by Amanda Bailey, "Shakespeare and a Living Wage." We also acknowledge and thank the Modern Language Association for offering this topic as a panel at the 2018 meeting in New York City.

Sharon O'Dair would like to thank the Hudson Strode Program in Renaissance Studies in the Department of English at the University of Alabama as well as her colleagues in the Strode Program, with special thanks to her former assistant there, Nicholas Helms. Her department chair, Joel Brouwer, and her associate dean in the College of Arts and Sciences, Tricia McElroy, also deserve many thanks for their years of support. So, too, above all, does Carol J. Pierman, who deserves more than the many thanks I can give.

Sharon O'Dair

Timothy Francisco would like to thank the Office of Research, the Department of English, and his colleagues at Youngstown State University. Thanks also to Thomas J. Slagle for his work on manuscript preparation, and in helping to keep the project organized. Thanks always to Rex W. Fisher, partner in all things.

Timothy Francisco

Together we thank Palgrave's editor Allie Troyanos, her editorial assistant, Rachel Jacobe, and the anonymous reader of this collection for careful and thoughtful guidance.

Contents

Notes on Contributors

Denise Albanese is Professor of English and Cultural Studies and Director of the Cultural Studies Program at George Mason University. She holds a Ph.D. in English from Stanford University and has held multiple short-term fellowships at the Folger Shakespeare Library, among other honors. She is the author of *New Science, New World* (Duke 1996) and *Extramural Shakespeare* (Palgrave 2010). She has published many essays on early modern science, literary theory, Shakespeare, and contemporary education.

Mara I. Amster is Professor of English at Randolph College. She holds a Ph.D. from the University of Rochester. She is the editor of a two-volume facsimile edition, *Seventeenth-Century Texts on Prostitution: Essential Works for the Study of Early Modern Englishwomen* (Ashgate 2007), and is working on a project about women's work and prostitution.

Daniel Bender teaches at Pace University. His research focuses on innovative methods for the study of early modern literature. A recent article, "'appertaining to thy young days': The End of the Academe in *Loves' Labour's Lost* and A Curriculum for the Future" (2016), proposes a curricular fusion of life-skill training and traditional thematic analysis in the classroom. He is a member of Imagining America, an academic organization working on educational reforms.

Katherine Boutry is Chair of Language Arts and Director of the Creativity Studies Program at West Los Angeles College, where she regularly teaches Shakespeare and other canonical writers. She holds a Ph.D. in English from Harvard University. Boutry is a practicing screenwriter, with multiple teleplays to her credit; she is a member of the Writers Guild of America. Her academic writing includes several essays on creativity as a pedagogical practice and a writing textbook.

Marisa R. Cull is Associate Professor of English at Randolph-Macon College. She holds a Ph.D. from The Ohio State University and is the author of *Shakespeare's Princes of Wales: English Identity and the Welsh Connection* (Oxford 2014). Her current scholarship focuses on faces and facial expression in Shakespeare's histories.

Craig Dionne is Professor of Literary and Cultural Theory at Eastern Michigan University. He specializes in Shakespeare and early modern cultural studies. He is the author of *Posthuman Lear: Reading Shakespeare in the Anthropocene* (punctum 2016). He has co-edited *Rogues and Early Modern English Culture* (with Steve Mentz, University of Michigan Press 2005), *Native Shakespeares: Indigenous Appropriations on a Global Stage* (with Parmita Kapadia, Ashgate 2008), and *Bollywood Shakespeares* (with Parmita Kapadia, Palgrave 2014). He currently working on a book, *Shakespeare's Instincts: Ethology and Geological Time in the Early Modern Imagination.*

Doug Eskew is Associate Professor of English and Director of Writing at Colorado State University, Pueblo. Professor Eskew's scholarship explores the history of rhetorical theory as it intersects with a variety of cultural productions, from early modern English drama to the twentieth-century popular music and politics. His essays have appeared in *Early Modern Literary Studies*, *Cahiers Élisabéthains*, and *Exemplaria.*

Timothy Francisco is Professor of English and Director of The Center for Working-Class Studies at Youngstown State University. He has written essays on Marlowe, journalism pedagogy, and numerous journalism pieces on widely-ranging of topics.

Elizabeth Hutcheon is Assistant Professor of English at Huntingdon College. She has degrees from Georgetown University, Oxford University, and the University of Chicago. Her work has appeared in venues including *Shakespeare Studies* and *Comparative Drama*, and she is currently completing a book on *Shakespeare, Gender, and Humanist Pedagogy.*

Fayaz Kabani is Instructor of English at Allen University, an HBCU in Columbia, South Carolina. A first-generation student from a Ugandan refugee family, Kabani holds an M.F.A. and a Ph.D. in English from the University of South Carolina. His research interests include higher education, the practical humanities, and the social performance of masculinity in early modern drama.

Sharon O'Dair is Professor Emeritus of English and former director of The Hudson Strode Program in Renaissance Studies at the University of Alabama. She is the author of *Class, Critics, and Shakespeare: Bottom Lines on the Culture Wars* (Michigan 2000) and co-edited *The Production of English Renaissance Culture* (Cornell 1994). She has written dozens of essays on Shakespeare, literary theory, and English studies.

Rochelle Smith is Professor of English at Frostburg State University. She holds a Ph.D. in English from the University of Chicago. Her scholarship explores the interplay between drama and popular literature, with a focus on the broadside ballad. She directs the Frostburg State University Shakespeare Festival.

Daniel Vitkus is Professor of Literature and Rebeca Hickel Endowed Chair in Early Modern Literature at the University of California, San Diego. He holds a Ph.D. in English from Columbia University, is editor of *The Journal for Early Modern Cultural Studies*, and the author of *Turning Turk: English Theater and the Multicultural Mediterranean, 1570–1630* (Palgrave 2003).

Introduction: 'Truth in Advertising'—Shakespeare and the 99 Percent

Timothy Francisco and Sharon O'Dair

On September 17, 2011, hundreds of demonstrators marched into Zuccotti Park in Lower Manhattan, two blocks from Wall Street, in a collective action determined to call out the foundational inequalities of neoliberal corporate capitalism, a system in which, it was claimed, 1 percent of the population presides over one of history's greatest concentrations of wealth, while 99 percent increasingly struggle with precarity and poverty—despite living in one of the richest, most powerful, democratic economies in the world. From this initial occupation of a privately owned park, deliberately chosen for its proximity to the epicenter of American capitalism, hundreds, then thousands, then tens of thousands, of people joined in demonstrations that spread across the nation, and even the globe, to more than 80 countries, ultimately uniting hundreds of thousands in the mass action known as Occupy Wall Street and later as "Occupy."

T. Francisco
Youngstown State University, Youngstown, OH, USA

S. O'Dair (✉)
University of Alabama, Tuscaloosa, AL, USA

S. O'Dair and T. Francisco (eds.), *Shakespeare and the 99%*,
https://doi.org/10.1007/978-3-030-03883-0_1

From its beginning, Occupy Wall Street's organizers effectively exploited physical and virtual activism, the latter most visibly in the form of a participatory blog on Tumblr, *We Are the 99 Percent*, that engendered the slogan that became the rallying cry for the movement.[1] The introduction to this Tumblr makes plain the collective's intense dissatisfaction with an oppressive status quo:

> We are the 99 percent. We are getting kicked out of our homes. We are forced to choose between groceries and rent. We are denied quality medical care. We are suffering from environmental pollution. We are working long hours for little pay and no rights, if we're working at all. We are getting nothing while the other 1 percent is getting everything. We are the 99 percent.[2]

Our volume, predictably perhaps, does nothing to remedy these painful material conditions, nor does it offer any innovative solutions for darning the threadbare social safety nets that are now more forcefully than ever being unraveled by neoliberal capitalist ideology and policies.

Our first aim in this introduction, then, is to confront our appropriation of "the 99 percent," for as Denise Albanese rightfully cautions in her essay here, "[q]uestions of the criminally unjust distribution of wealth should not be transformed to questions of the cultural—of, for instance, unequal access to or veneration of Shakespeare—without a pause for reflection." To be sure, the yoking of basic human needs with what Albanese describes as "the cultural accouterments of a 'good' (i.e., bourgeois) life" warrants serious thought.[3] Yet from the beginning of the Occupy movement, the "99 percent" was a marker for a collection of experiences, morphing rightly or not, from statistical actuality to broad identity. Occupy Wall Street and its contiguous formulation of the 99 percent was, according to Ethan Earle, "From the start … a point of convergence for an incredibly wide range of critiques and viewpoints: big, small, radical, moderate, revolutionary, reformist—united mostly by a broad sense of injustice and converging in a public (physical and metaphorical) space where they knew they could express themselves."[4]

A frequent critique leveled through the Occupy movement was the failed promise of higher education, as, for decades, many of the 99 percent bought a bill of goods that access to the type of education for which Shakespeare has long been synecdoche *will* ensure at least some safe position in the distribution of wealth. In a post-Occupy assessment, and in an essay serendipitously titled, "The Winter of Our Discontent," Stanley Aronowitz explains one powerful reason why "students still march to institutions of post-secondary schooling and graduate professional training as if there are good jobs at the end of the slog." They march because "ideologies die hard": they "often precede and survive the conditions that produce and legitimate them."[5] At the same time, as Albanese notes, "the economic transformations that *were* the principal point of attack cannot but have left their mark directly and indirectly on publicly-funded educational institutions within which Shakespeare plays a large role."[6] One of the most visible of these economic transformations is government's defunding of public higher education, shifting the burden to the student "consumer," who now carries an average debt of around $30,000, thus magnifying the disappointment in finding there are few good jobs at the end of the slog.[7]

The anger resulting from the failure of an ideological promise of mobility through education looms large even in a cursory reading of more than five hundred posts on *We Are the 99 Percent*; disillusion with the debt economy of higher education is a recurring pattern. For example:

> ANOTHER COLLEGE GRADUATE WITH A BA (ENGLISH) WORKING RANDOM CLEANING AND BABY-SITTING JOBS (IF LUCKY) THAT TAKE ADVANTAGE OF YOUNG LABOR. BEEN APPLYING FOR JOBS (OVER 50) FOR THE PAST YEAR AND CAN'T FIND MORE THAN PART-TIME PIECE TOGETHER WORK WITHOUT BENEFITS. $20,000 AND GROWING LOANS AND ONLY JOBS I COULD DO WITHOUT EVEN NEEDING A DEGREE. I HAVE DEBT FROM COLLEGE AND NO JOB THAT PAYS ENOUGH FOR MY EXPENSES. SO MUCH FOR HARD WORK PAYING OFF. I AM THE 99 PERCENT.

As Ezra Klein notes, in many of these posts "college debt represents a special sort of betrayal. We told you that the way to get ahead in America was to get educated. You did it. And now you find yourself in the same place, but buried under debt. You were lied to."[8] Instead of getting ahead, or even simply landing on firm footing, too many students find they've bought entry into an unstable, precariat workforce, the antithesis of the entrepreneurial, innovative economy of opportunity promised by the neoliberal academy, with its incessant evocations of student "success" and agency in determining one's economic future.

This gap between promise—or public relations—and reality is addressed throughout this volume, and especially by Fayaz Kabani. The pull of mobility, of status, of a "career" not a "job," incentivizes additional debt and credentialing, and one can easily imagine a similar post to the one above by one of the legion of disillusioned PhD holders ("young labor"), desperately applying for tenure-track jobs ("over 50") while piecing together service-course, adjunct gigs that do not require the terminal degree and offer low pay and no benefits. One can easily imagine a post complaining bitterly about the continued overproduction of PhDs, pointing out that the shrinking number of tenure-track jobs go to graduates from a small number of elite PhD granting institutions.[9]

Occupy Wall Street, was, in fact, over-represented by under-employed college graduates carrying "substantial debt" and "deeply skeptical of the mainstream political system as a vehicle for effective social change," according to a study by Ruth Milkman, Stephanie Luce, and Penny Wells.[10] This may be because, as Jeffrey R. Di Leo explains, higher education has relied on widespread subscription to the promise of a democratic "knowledge economy," one that "would allow everyone [in society] to be a shareholder, an owner, and an entrepreneur." But the knowledge economy never could offer a place to everyone, and what has emerged instead and especially after the financial collapse of 2008 is a debt economy, a "social existence that is demarcated by debt, or alternately, credit." In this economy, students must rely on private creditors and "submit to the conditions dictated by shareholders, bondholders, and the owners of securities. These students form the groundwork of the indebted academe—and are its most repulsive consequence."[11]

As with Shakespeare's Bassanio and Antonio, social relations are lived according to interwoven, and chronic, transactions of debt and credit. For students and faculty in the neoliberal debt academy, Di Leo finds the "circle here is vicious: by going to college, students get themselves into debt. This, in turn, leads them to see education only as way to get themselves out of debt." And this understanding of higher education as a debt-driven enterprise both trickles down, and creeps up, as "decisions about higher education and its practices, policies, and mission are determined by the debt-credit relationship, not by the production of knowledge and reproduction of democratic values."[12] Instead, the academy enforces hierarchy and inequality by its policing of access and exclusion for students, and by its status economy for its practitioners. As Walter Benn Michaels explains, the replication of economic and class inequality is the very purchase of the university because the entire enterprise is built upon a neoliberal market philosophy of inimitability: "It's economically advantageous to go to Harvard, only because hardly anyone goes to Harvard."[13]

As the 99 percent operated as a "convergent metaphorical space" for laying bare the politics, and policies, of inequity and exclusion embodied by "Wall Street," so too in *Shakespeare and the 99%*, Shakespeare—the author, the plays, and the field—operates as a collective site for teasing out and making visible the complex, and often complicit, relations between literary studies as an intellectual discipline and the profession as a social organization, relations that result in a host of inequities across higher education, having to do with race, class, and gender but also with place, prestige, and resources. In so doing, such readings endorse Marjorie Garber's understanding of Shakespeare as what Michel Foucault calls an "initiator of discursive practices"; or, borrowing from cognition studies, the readings of Shakespeare's plays curated here work as heuristic analogies, exposing foundations of recurring struggles—the effects of capitalism, the breakdown of institutions, the oppression by a status hierarchy, to name a few—in order to posit hypotheses and offer critiques, for, as Jens Wilbers and Reinders Duit explain, "analogical transfer does not answer questions, it helps to ask questions."[14] In asking these questions, many of the essays here investigate the uneasy tension between scholarly imperatives that require the past to be ineludibly alien, and pedagogical imperatives of inclusion that often require the past to be anachronistically the same.[15] As such, this collection aims to begin, as Joseph North urges, to "work as the diagnostic element in a broader system of cultural intervention."[16]

The essays in *Shakespeare and the 99%* do not present a united front politically, pedagogically, or theoretically. Our scholars write from radically different positions—from tenured to ABD at the time of writing, from elite research institutions to comprehensive state universities, an HBCU, and an urban community college. What the essays share, what they reveal—and what we think is truly valuable—is a courage by the authors to question what they learned in graduate school about how to perform professional roles as scholars, pedagogues, and administrators; it's questioning that arises from their actual work lives in today's academy. Such questioning arises in part or at first, we think, because of the sometimes shattering but almost always disturbing dislocations experienced in moving from graduate school to a tenure-track position at an institution with far less status, prestige, and resources, including the resource of students. The dislocation is class-based; it is status-based; it's about the 99 percent and the 1 percent; and it is difficult to write about.

Emerging from the essays *is* a united front that interrogates the ideology of higher education in this country and of the graduate schools that produce most of the professors who staff its institutions of higher education. This is an ideology of the 1 percent, of the academic or intellectual 1 percent, too, and, as noted by Aronowitz, ideology covers over contradiction: higher education insists it is a meritocracy even as it relies on a bedrock of privilege, whether inherited (via family wealth or legacy admissions) or assigned (via affirmative action admissions or a calculus for diversity). Higher education promotes egalitarianism in society and particularly with respect to access to higher education, even as it reveals demonstrably unequal resources across institutions and demands competition from individuals, both faculty and students, for the financial and status rewards that accompany successful competition. All of this affects research and pedagogy, through the kinds of work allowed and rewarded, the foundations on which professional careers are built.

Ideology is valuable—it works—not just because it covers over contradiction, allowing adherents to live peaceably with themselves but also because it is so difficult to tear through the cover, to recognize the contradictions. In her essay, Marisa Cull uses the term "cultural anticipation"—from a study by Pamela L. Eddy and Jeni Hart—to describe this problem.[17] We are acculturated to anticipate a professional life like those of our professors, our mentors, but such a life is and has been for decades extremely difficult to achieve. Since jobs and therefore lives are far removed from those of mentors, both literally and figuratively, faculty undergo a difficult process to reconcile the disappointment or worse, the perceived or attributed failure, of not achieving it. The dislocating shock of moving from, say, the University of Chicago to a public regional university in Appalachia, does not easily spark critique of the ideology and the institutions that one has, in fact, just successfully negotiated. A new assistant professor must adjust, and adjust quickly, since her livelihood depends upon it. One must get on with one's work, put one's head down, literally. Too, and here's where the profession's status hierarchy proves especially effective, professors whether young or old find it difficult to question the judgments of mentors and colleagues with superior status, since they depended on them for a job and continue to depend on them for access to publication, grants, and other requirements of professional life.

None of this is new, and some elite professors—notably John Guillory—have offered stinging critiques of such "cultural anticipation."[18] As Sharon O'Dair explains in her contribution to this volume, "Guillory argued in the mid-1990s that the professional desire to teach graduate students, which is to say the professional desire to do research, is 'phantasmic', unachievable unless 'the number of graduate students … increase[d] geometrically'."[19] If someone of Guillory's intelligence and status has had no effect on the graduate school maw that twenty years later continues to overproduce PhDs and worse, if that is possible, continues to model a life of research and scholarship that is inaccessible to all but the smartest, most competitive, and luckiest of PhDs, one might wonder quite legitimately why the editors of this volume and indeed all of the contributors to it, think we may have more effect, or any. The reason, we think, is that our contributors offer distinct challenges to the model under which they were trained. They offer ways to reimagine scholarship, pedagogy, and indeed higher education based on perspective and experience gained on the ground of the 99 percent. And we encourage other colleagues to do the same. Further, though, sometimes the time feels right, and the past decade, since the Great Recession of 2008, since Occupy itself, has seen continued deterioration of society's institutions, including of higher education. Costs rise; students sink deeper into debt or do not graduate; colleges and universities impose neoliberal policy and management on faculty; everyone is angry and tense. On the streets in Los Angeles and New York, working-class people of color loudly protest gentrification that is led, they say, by artists, unhinging an article of faith among the cultured upper middle-class that art, that culture, that higher education, is always already progressive. Meanwhile, in the deindustrialized Rust Belt, dotted with smaller struggling cities for which gentrification seems a distant problem, and in rural communities across "fly-over country," the white working-class loudly protests at the ballot box against the political class they believe has pushed them aside. Such unhinging is mirrored in *Shakespeare and the 99%* by Fayaz Kabani, who argues that many first-generation college students would be served best not by a bachelor's degree but by schooling in the trades or in technical fields at community colleges. In various ways, the essays presented here attempt to reconceive political and social action for Shakespeareans, both outside and inside the academy, sensing that the status quo has not been working well.

Again, the essays do not offer one way to reimagine our work, although certain themes and movements do appear in many of the essays. The collection opens, appropriately we think, with two essays on alienation, as a theoretical and practical problem for both research and pedagogy. In "Identification, Alienation, and 'Hating the Renaissance'," Denise Albanese sets the tone for the collection by arguing that the alienating reading practices established in the 1980s, practices in which she was trained and in which she has been training her students, may have run their courses: reading against the grain, standing as suspicious of the text and its designs on us, and refusing to embrace unschooled pleasure may reveal a classed understanding of what high literacy means. There is, she argues, a disjuncture between the historical need in the 1980s for these alienating strategies among elite academics and the needs of today's students who do "not possess such literacy as an ancillary to inherited class privilege but rather [may] acquire … it through hard-won investments in literature as a site of positive value, and textual enjoyment as the fruit of hard work." Albanese, that is, turns the methodological dictum, "always historicize," toward our own theoretical and pedagogical praxis, moved to rethink her assumptions in part by a comment of one of her bright students, who quipped that her class had trained him "in 'how to hate the English Renaissance'."[20] Moves to make texts alien, she argues, may not be appropriate to left or radical critique in the early twenty-first century.

Often promoted to combat alienation is something called "the relevant" or the "accessible." As millions of students, regardless of ethnicity, entered college as the first in their families to attend, Shakespeareans labored to make the plays and the poems relevant to this cohort, accessible to this cohort, even though, as Mara Amster and Marisa Cull note in their respective essays, Shakespeareans, unlike colleagues in almost any area of literary study, are lucky to enjoy Shakespeare's prominent presence in the secondary schools, in community theater and festivals, and in popular culture. And indeed, Shakespeareans can easily supplement the deeply alienating, four-hundred-year-old texts with contemporary performance, with versions and revisions from across the globe, with parodies, with translations into modern English. All of this we do, hoping to make Shakespeare relevant or accessible. In his essay, "Shakespeare, Alienation, and the Working-Class Student," Doug Eskew takes issue with this nearly universal tendency and asks readers to consider the many ways in which alienation affects students such as his at Colorado State University, Pueblo, not all of them academic. Eskew insists that attempts to minimize alienation from the Shakespearean text is a losing cause: "A lot of the time (perhaps even 'usually'), a student's honest answer to this question of what Shakespeare means to people today is that Shakespeare doesn't mean much at all. Shakespeare is a requirement in school—that's it." Instead, he argues, we should pause to consider that the alienation working-class students feel from our subject, Shakespeare, can and should be good for their intellectual lives "if this kind of alienation presents a culture shock to students at the same time that it provides the intellectual methods of coming to terms with that shock." This sort of alienation does not need to be "cured or fixed"; it needs, if we may pun just a little, to be capitalized upon.[21]

In "The Whip Hand: Elite Class Formation in Ascham's *The Schoolmaster*, Shakespeare's *Love's Labour's Lost*, and the Present Academy," Daniel Bender offers a reading of Humanist education that surely would offer a culture shock to Eskew's students. Focusing on Roger Ascham's *The Schoolmaster*, Bender suggests that historical work on the Humanists, including recent studies attuned to contemporary theoretical requirements, fails to articulate fully—or, perhaps, whitewashes—the brutal, even violent and class-based nature of that education, an education designed to produce ministers of state with the rhetorical skills to silence popular dissent. The whip hand is directed by masters at boys themselves who then direct it, years later and metaphorically if not literally, at the commons who resist authority. Scholars' blindness to the social function of their work, the domination inherent in Humanist—and humanities—education, is no accident, and Bender urges colleagues to examine both research and pedagogy through this lens: how can professors, especially those at elite institutions, ensure they, too, are not enforcing the whip hand?

This question troubles Mara Amster, too. In "'instruct her what she has to do': Education, Social Mobility, and Success," Amster asks what Humanist education offered to women. In a compelling reading of two Kates, Petruchio's and Henry V's, Amster reveals an answer: to be wives, mothers, and household managers. The educations of each woman, regardless of how brutal or forced, do allow for social advancement; at the same time, their educations enhance the social standings or the egos of their mates, and of men generally. The question, then, isn't just what Humanist education offers to women in the Renaissance but whom do these educations serve, or serve in addition to the women themselves? In a clever and well-documented move, Amster shifts her focus to the first-generation students enrolled in the nation's elite colleges and universities in order to ask: who benefits from this sort of diversification in the nation's elite colleges and universities? Amster suggests (as will Kabani at length later in the volume) that, as in *The Taming of the Shrew* and *Henry V*, others beside the students also benefit. Today, Amster suggests, it is the institutions themselves and as importantly, the elite students who predominate at these institutions who also—and mainly—benefit.

"When I started writing this essay, in the summer of 2016, it felt like a different time," writes Elizabeth Hutcheon in her contribution to this volume, "Literature and Cultural Capital in Early Modern and Contemporary Pedagogy." Confident then that "I knew what was best for my students, that I could show them what kind of knowledge is important, and why," Hutcheon admits to just the kind of rethinking this volume attempts to capture: "Now I'm not so sure. That position feels like hubris." But even though her "own optimism … turned to ambivalence," thinking through it allowed her to realize that the "ambivalence is mirrored in Shakespeare." Shakespeare worries the value of education, from early plays like *Love's Labour's Lost* and *2 Henry VI* to late plays like *The Tempest* and *Pericles.* Nor does Shakespeare scant the class implications of that worry, but the result, Hutcheon argues, is that "Shakespeare teaches [us] that ambivalent benefits are still benefits."[22] It may be that this is where ethical thinking is most needed and at its best: how do we encourage students, whether undergraduates, graduate students, or faculty, to grasp ambivalence about their educations rather than an easily identifiable golden ring called success? As Matthew Stewart suggests in "The 9.9 Percent Is the New American Aristocracy," we haven't been doing a very good job of this: this newly solidifying American elite "may have studied Shakespeare on the way to law school, but we have little sense for the tragic possibilities of life."[23]

Three essays, by Katherine Boutry, Rochelle Smith, and Daniel Vitkus respectively, offer answers, both theoretical and pedagogical, and do so from very different institutional locations. Boutry's student population at West Los Angeles College is even less privileged than Eskew's at Colorado State University, Pueblo. West's students, she acknowledges, are usually not prepared for college-level reading and writing; they are burdened with jobs and responsibilities for children or parents; some are homeless. They want and need their courses to lead "somewhere quickly: either to transfer or to better employment."[24] And yet, in "Creativity Studies and Shakespeare at the Urban Community College," Boutry argues that her students, so very different from those literally in the

1 percent she taught as a graduate student at Harvard, are, in some very important ways, better equipped to understand Shakespeare than those children of privilege: their life experiences—the crises and constraints they tackle on a daily basis—allow them to persist with difficult reading and in time to grasp Shakespearean ethical dilemmas very, very well. Finding resources in an area of educational and psychological research called Creativity Studies, Boutry reads *King Lear* as an exercise in creative problem-solving, suggesting that students and faculty can find through their studies of the plays, creative ways to learn and flourish, despite constraints, in school and in society. There's no thinking outside the box, Boutry reminds her readers, without a box, and lowering expectations for this cohort of students because they live with constraints, within a box, is foolish.

Across the continent, Rochelle Smith teaches at Frostburg State University in western Maryland, a region whose fortunes have declined along with the industrial mining of coal. Some fifteen years ago, Smith began a small, predominantly pedagogical Shakespeare festival—a "cooperative project involving both our university and the area high schools from western Maryland, southwest Pennsylvania, and West Virginia." Smith's innovation was to bring college students—and not just aspiring secondary school teachers—to the high school classroom as mentors and facilitators. A striking success, Smith details this work in her essay, "Poverty and Privilege: Shakespeare in the Mountains," but she also assesses what it is about Shakespeare and his place in American life that allows or encourages this success. To Smith's community, even as it has changed, becoming poorer on the one hand and more culturally and ethnically diverse on the other, Shakespeare continues to offer great value to local constituencies. Elites may debate Shakespeare's still privileged place in a destabilized canon but, like Boutry, Smith finds that "the cultural capital attached to Shakespeare can have an unexpected pay-off in parts of the country where poverty is all too prevalent and 'privilege' something that often seems permanently out of reach. When high school students discover that they can read Shakespeare and even enjoy him, they start to wonder what else they might be up for." When college students—the mentors and facilitators—discover that they can teach and inspire, helping young people to examine texts alien to them, they, too, may start to wonder what else is possible in their own lives. Shakespeare "never underestimated any segment of his audience" and like Boutry, Smith thinks we should not, either. This is how Shakespeareans can "reach all of our own rich and varied publics," and become, if you will, public intellectuals in their communities.[25]

The Shakespearean text is difficult. But in addition, as Eskew puts it, Shakespeareans also ask their students "to learn a good deal about its context—the day-to-day minutia of life in Elizabethan and Jacobean England, its politics, foreign policies, ideological paradigms and contradictions, its specific histories and England's place in the European Renaissance."[26] This is the project of New Historicism, writes Daniel Vitkus, to make the Renaissance other, to "reconstruct the past in ways that defined that past as radically different." Difficult and different the past may be, but this history is not difficult to learn, unlike, say, nuclear physics or the higher mathematics. Knowing this, Vitkus asks us to use that historical knowledge today. In "How the One Percent Came to Rule the World: Shakespeare, Long-Term Historical Narrative, and the Origins of Capitalism," Vitkus upends methodological dogma, arguing for a reconsideration of historical metanarratives in the service of a project to upend the 1 percent. Shakespeare wrote when capitalism was beginning to emerge as an economic and ideological force; as Vitkus notes, it wasn't called that yet, but its powerful disruptive force was recognizable. If we want our research and our pedagogy to engage with "the current struggle against the power of the 1%, then we must focus on our linkage to Shakespeare's time through the continuous history of capitalism's expansion, from the end of the feudal order to the triumph of global capital today."[27] This is, in fact, easy to do, as Vitkus urges in his discussions of *The Merchant of Venice*, *King Lear*, *Coriolanus*, *Julius Caesar*, *Measure for Measure*, and *The Tempest*.

So why don't we do it? Or why don't more of us do it? One answer, probably the most important one, has been chimed already in this collection, and elsewhere, repeatedly, including by Shakespeare himself: education is part of the machinery that creates class difference and reproduces it, as Fayaz Kabani stresses in his essay for this collection, "Hal's Class Performance and Francis's Service Learning: *1 Henry IV* 2.4 as Parable of Contemporary Higher Education." Reading the tavern scene in which Hal tricks and mocks Francis the drawer, Kabani casts Hal in the role of a young, elite college student and Francis in the role of what Kabani calls the "new traditional student,"[28] the student like Boutry's—older, employed, responsible for others, overburdened, and underprepared. Colleges and universities want to enroll Hal, and they want students to want to be Hal. But not everyone can be Hal and not everyone wants to be Hal. In the early twenty-first century, social norms insisting upon the value of a bachelor's degree, the ubiquitous directive of "college for all," actually mis-direct personal and social resources to devastating effect: debt, disappointment, and failure for individuals; gaping needs in well-paying trades and technical jobs for society as a whole. Colleges and universities, too, pay a price: costs for campus amenities, from lazy rivers to gourmet food halls, and from support services to higher administration, including those administrators of faculty whose autonomy and remuneration continue to erode.

Of all the essays, Marisa Cull's "Place and Privilege in Shakespeare Scholarship and Pedagogy" addresses most directly the dislocation experienced in the move from elite graduate school to a tenure-track position in the hinterlands at an institution lacking in prestige and resources. Documenting problems of "fit" and comfort for faculty, as well as difficulties securing research funding or access to digital tools such as Early English Books Online, Cull argues that the profession itself has a 1 percent problem, which is to say that standards of evaluation and achievement in the profession—from the ability to compete for grants and fellowships to basic recognition and respect from peers—privilege faculty at elite institutions with abundant resources. Place isn't just physical location; it is also about professional status and how and whether they correlate. Cull nuances her argument, acknowledging that technology and a surrounding group of like-minded faculty—the result of overproducing PhDs for decades—ameliorate the frustrations many faculty feel, and yet Cull is able to offer valuable suggestions about how to prepare graduate students for life after the elite PhD and indeed to adjust some of the practices of evaluation and achievement within the profession to reflect the realities of colleagues who do not work at research universities, thus allowing more colleagues to contribute to and access our intellectual conversations.

In "Who Did Kill Shakespeare?," Sharon O'Dair alludes to Patrick Brantlinger's turn of the century apologia for English departments in order to contest the apologia. Like Albanese and Vitkus, though differently, O'Dair questions a tenet of academic orthodoxy, arguing that the universally praised opening of the canon has had some disturbing, even debilitating effects for professors of literature and especially for professors of early literature, including Shakespeare. In opening the canon, elites have slighted the literary, attenuating the distinctiveness of the field and undermining its authority and legitimacy, and further, with respect to Shakespeare and early literature generally, elites purposefully slighted the past in favor of the present. These moves, she contends, were doubtless made with noble intentions and early on were surely necessary, but, she demonstrates, their results do not affect those who promote them—the academic 1 percent. But they do very seriously affect the academic 99 percent of Shakespeareans, they who find themselves in departments of "English studies," where colleagues with no necessary commitment to literature or to literary writing dominate. Like Eskew, Boutry, and Cull, she asks colleagues at non-elite institutions not to underestimate students, who can in fact master the difficult writing that is literature, that is Shakespeare's. More subversively, she asks non-elite colleagues to consider that the research culture continually promoted by the academic 1 percent, the carbon-intensive research culture of trans-continental and trans-oceanic travel is dying, if not dead. And she asks non-elite colleagues to consider whether that culture is a principal source of our discontent and a potent generator of our declining prestige among the public and its representatives. Like others in this volume, O'Dair asks both for patience and for active engagement with the profession. Knowing that structures and norms do not change easily, she urges "professors of early literature teaching at non-elite colleges and universities to continue to think about ways to rescue themselves and their students from the perhaps unintended effects of forty years of democratization in access to higher education."[29]

Finally, and returning to our appropriation of the language of the Occupy movement, we recognize that a collection of academic essays is not social activism, even as we acknowledge that *We Are The 99 Percent* was both a discursive forum and an organizational platform, one that motivated the 99 percent to locate their experiences within systemic institutional inequities, and to initiate both conversation and action. Eight years after Occupy, little has been done to meaningfully dislodge the grip of the 1 percent (or more accurately the top 20 percent, which includes many of academia's 1 percent), on the bulk of capital and resources in either the United States' economy or the world's. Instead, from 2013 to 2017, for example, the share of wealth in the United States controlled by the 1 percent rose 3 percent, and to its highest point since 1962.[30] But, it's also important to remember that Occupy did not start out as a movement aimed at one particular policy change—no targeted demands were made from the initial gatherings at Zuccotti Park. Rather, the movement was committed to non-hierarchical "horizontalism," that was, according to Milkman, Luce, and Lewis, "self-consciously politically pre-figurative," allowing it to attract "supporters with a wide array of specific concerns," to propel "inequality into the mainstream of US political debate, changing the national conversation."[31] Occupy planted a rhizome and the 99 percent did indeed change the national discussion, recasting the narrative of political and economic self-interest, and sprouting resistance and action through rhizomatic networks.[32] Many Americans have connected dots between Occupy and "Fight for $15," the minimum wage campaign that *did* improve material conditions for workers in New York and California, and to Black Lives Matter, and to the Chicago teachers' strike of 2012, strikes that burst out again among teachers in 2018. On the political spectrum, one can also locate the ascendancy of democratic socialist Bernie Sanders, on one end, and President Donald Trump on the other, to the rhizome of the 99 percent, because, as Euel Elliot explains, for "both groups, the founding principles of Republican government and representative democracy no longer work. The system, in their view, is broken."[33]

But what, ultimately, can, should, an English professor, let alone a Shakespearean, do with all of this? After all, in the popular imagination, and for better *and* for worse, we are living, breathing representatives of the "political and cultural elites" under fire from both the right and the left. What one should do depends, in part, upon where one falls along the hierarchical chain of income, power, and prestige. Those in the 99 percent of the profession must, first and foremost, continue to explore pedagogies grounded in the realities of our students' lives, and in our institutional lives, doing our best to mitigate the inequities of higher education by equipping our students with the intellectual agility that might actually translate to some real social mobility in an increasingly complex world. And as most of the essays in this collection show, Shakespeare is for many reasons a rich site for doing this. Also at the local and state levels, the 99 percent must disrupt the prevailing public sentiment that we—and our institutions—are just like the 1 percent of the professoriate and their institutions. We are not, and we must make this clear to the public and its representatives, no matter how uncomfortable it makes us with our peers, students, and communities. But we must also advocate for a more honest appraisal of our profession, and, as in Occupy, aim for a more horizontal structure. This means interrogating the academy's prestige economy, which, on one hand, lays claim to political "action" in its critical practices, while on the other hand, confers prestige based upon one's distance from the "labor" of the classroom, where, ironically, real political empowerment resides. It is a prestige economy that legitimates itself by claims of merit, but since they are grounded in ideology, not evidence, such claims suggest a fictive legitimacy. This is where the 1 percent may choose to play a part, to become partners with the 99 percent in striving for broader representation in our professional organizations, on editorial boards, and in grant-making agencies. Indeed, because the 1 percent wields most of what power is left in the academic enterprise, perhaps the 1 percent too should take on the work ascribed above to the 99 percent, so that we reconfigure our enterprise to be 100 percent committed to collective resistance to the inequities of higher education and hence in society.

Notes

1. The origin of the phrase "the 99%" is difficult to pinpoint. In an October 2011 interview with Adam Weinstein for *Mother Jones*, the creators of the Tumblr identify a flyer circulated at the Second General Assembly meeting of Occupy Wall Street, influenced by the work of anthropologist David Graeber. See Adam Weinstein, "'We Are the 99 Percent' Creators Revealed," *Mother Jones*, October 7, 2011: https://www.motherjones.com/politics/2011/10/we-are-the-99-percent-creators/. Accessed May 29, 2018. But others tie it to economist Joseph E. Stiglitz' article published in May 2011 by *Vanity Fair*, "Of the 1%, By the 1% For the 1%." See *Vanity Fair*, May 2011: https://www.vanityfair.com/news/2011/05/top-one-percent-201105. Accessed May 29, 2018.
2. *We Are the 99 Percent*, Tumblr, September 30, 2011: http://wearethe99percent.tumblr.com/post/10848127790/i-am-the-99-occupywallstorg. Accessed May 29, 2018.
3. Denise Albanese, "Identification, Alienation, and 'Hating the Renaissance'," 20, 21.
4. Ethan Earle, *A Brief History of Occupy Wall Street* (New York: Rosa Luxemburg Stiftung, 2012): http://www.rosalux-nyc.org/wp-content/files_mf/earle_history_occupy.pdf. Accessed May 29, 2018. Further, Theda Skopcal thinks "Occupy's biggest accomplishment is the 1% phrase," because it has "become an important way to talk about income inequality in public." Skopcal is quoted in Megan Leonhardt, "The Lasting Effects of Occupy Wall Street, Five Years Later," *Money*, September 16, 2016: http://time.com/money/4495707/occupy-wall-street-anniversary-effects/. Accessed May 27, 2018.
5. Stanley Aronowitz, "The Winter of Our Discontent," *Situations* 4, no. 2 (2012): 37.
6. Albanese, "Identification," 21.
7. Diane Cheng, Debbie Cochrane, and Veronica Gonzalez, *Student Debt and the Class of 2016* (Washington, DC: The Institute for College Access and Success, 2017): https://ticas.org/sites/default/files/pub_files/classof2016.pdf. Accessed May 30, 2018.

8. Ezra Klein, "Who Are the 99 Percent?," *The Washington Post,* October 4, 2011: https://www.washingtonpost.com/blogs/ezra-klein/post/who-are-the-99-percent/2011/08/25/gIQAt87jKL_blog.html?utm_term=.d4c4b55be290. Accessed May 30, 2018.
9. See Andrew Piper and Chad Mellon, "How the Academic Elite Reproduces Itself," *The Chronicle Review,* October 8, 2017: B7.
10. Ruth Milkman, Stephanie Luce, and Penny Lewis, *Changing the Subject: A Bottom-Up Account of Occupy Wall Street in New York City* (New York: The Murphy Institute, 2013), 4.
11. Jeffrey R. Di Leo, *Corporate Humanities in Higher Education: Moving Beyond the Neoliberal Academy* (New York: Palgrave Macmillan, 2013), x, xi.
12. Ibid., xii.
13. Walter Benn Michaels, "Dude, Where's My Job?" *PMLA* 127, no. 4 (2012): 1007. Michaels endorses John Marsh's argument in *Class Dismissed* that a more realistic path toward equity might be a union card, not another degree (1008–1009).
14. For Foucault, see Michel Foucalt, "What is an Author?," in *Language, Counter-Memory and Practice*, ed. Donald F. Bouchard, trans. Bouchard and Sherry Simon (Ithaca: Cornell University Press, 1977), 132. For Garber's use of Foucault, see Marjorie Garber, *Shakespeare and Modern Culture* (New York: Anchor, 2008), xxii. For Wilbers and Duit, see Jen Wilbers and Renders Duit, "Post-Festum and Heuristic Analogies," in *Metaphor and Analogy in Science Education*, ed. Peter J. Aubusson, Allan G. Harrison, and Stephen M. Ritchie (Dordrecht: Springer, 2006), 40.
15. Daniel Vitkus, "How the One Percent Came to Rule the World: Shakespeare, Long-Term Historical Narrative, and the Origins of Capitalism," this volume.
16. Joseph North, *Literary Criticism: A Concise Political History* (Cambridge: Harvard University Press, 2017), 211.
17. Marisa Cull, "Place and Privilege in Shakespeare Scholarship and Pedagogy," 211, 214.
18. Guillory, following Roger Chartier, calls such cultural anticipation something else—the distance between "subjective aspirations and objective chances." See his "Preprofessionalism: What Graduate Students Want," *Profession* (1996): 96. But we think "cultural anticipation" suggests in addition the social construction of those subjective aspirations by the graduate school and its professors.
19. Sharon O'Dair, "Who Did Kill Shakespeare?," 239.
20. Denise Albanese, "Identification," 20, 26–27.
21. Doug Eskew, "Shakespeare, Alienation, and the Working-Class Student," 39–40.
22. Elizabeth Hutcheon, "Literature and Cultural Capital in Early Modern and Contemporary Pedagogy," 117.

23. Matthew Stewart, "The 9.9 Percent Is the New American Aristocracy," *The Atlantic*, June 2018: https://www.theatlantic.com/magazine/archive/2018/06/the-birth-of-a-new-american-aristocracy/559130/. Accessed June 1, 2018.
24. Katharine Boutry, "Creativity Studies and Shakespeare at the Urban Community College," 123.
25. Rochelle Smith, "Poverty and Privilege: Shakespeare in the Mountains," 144, 154, 156.
26. Eskew, "Alienation," 40.
27. Daniel Vitkus, "Capitalism," 161, 178.
28. Fayaz Kabani, "Hal's Class Performance and Francis's Service Learning: *1 Henry IV* 2.4 as Parable of Contemporary Higher Education," 183.
29. Sharon O'Dair, "Who Did Kill Shakespeare?," 238.
30. Christopher Ingraham, "The Richest 1 Percent Now Owns More of the Country's Wealth Than at Any Time in the past 50 Years," *The Washington Post,* December 6, 2017: https://www.washingtonpost.com/news/wonk/wp/2017/12/06/the-richest-1-percent-now-owns-more-of-the-countrys-wealth-than-at-any-time-in-the-past-50-years/?noredirect=on&utm_term=.8d564ab9966b. Accessed May 18, 2018.
31. Milkman, Luce, and Lewis, "Changing," 4.
32. We are thinking of the rhizome here as an example of Gilles Deleuze and Felix Guattari's political configuration of a "multiplicity" that resists the intractability of a "One." See Gilles Deleuze and Felix Guattari, *A Thousand Plateaus: Capitalism and Schizophrenia*, trans. Brian Massumi, Minneapolis: University of Minnesota Press, 1987, 8.
33. Euel Elliott, "How Occupy Wall Street Led to the Rise of Donald Trump" *Fortune,* March 2016: http://fortune.com/2016/03/23/occupy-wall-street-donald-trump-rise/. Accessed June 21, 2018.

Identification, Alienation, and 'Hating the Renaissance'

Denise Albanese

I

In this essay, my aim is to think through the fate of "political Shakespeare," as critical practice and particularly as pedagogical one, with an eye to reposing the question of Shakespeare's supposed eliteness. It's a way of calling out my own faulty assumptions from earlier in my academic and pedagogical career, and for being responsive to what my students at George Mason University have taught me not to teach past. Hence part of my title, which enshrines the reproach of a smart—if reactionary—student who'd told me in frustration that I'd taught him to hate the thing he'd loved, in an uncanny echo of Caliban's retort to Prospero about having learned to curse. But perhaps it is also a way to posit the return of delegitimated forms of readings—"naive" reading, if you will—as a potential resource for thinking through the demands of the political at the current conjuncture.

That Shakespeare belongs to the cultural equivalent of the 1 percent is a claim that, as I've argued, has outlived its truth and hence its utility.[1] Yet it persists as spectral discourse, most perniciously as a residual disposition informing the academic habitus in counterproductive ways.

D. Albanese (✉)
George Mason University, Fairfax, VA, USA

S. O'Dair and T. Francisco (eds.), *Shakespeare and the 99%*,
https://doi.org/10.1007/978-3-030-03883-0_2

Ultimately, I ask whether Shakespeare's significance to those non-elites—which is in many ways a semaphore for the significance of the humanities in general under neoliberal regimes, and particularly in an era of virulent, bargain-basement populism typified by the current political conjuncture—suffers from the professional classroom labors of those whose politics otherwise put them in sympathy with the culturally dispossessed, some of whom nevertheless possess an interest, often hard-won, in Shakespeare.

Since this is an analysis that cannot but be inflected by changing circumstances, I argue that the moment in which I'm writing must be disarticulated from the one that saw the emergence of ideological criticism of Shakespeare in the 1980s. Of course, those earlier insights demand our continuing respect, even if they have been obscured by subsequent shifts and drifts in the critical trajectory of Shakespeare studies. But I also aim to think critically about the present day—specifically, the unexamined disjuncture between a leftist interpretive practice that is the durable legacy of political criticism, and the investments of those students taking English in non-elite universities. For students attending such institutions, "high" literacy is often hard-won; as I argue, they are not necessarily well-served by our insisting on disenchanting the literary object in the service of raising their political consciousness via a practice that once had utility for the professorial class. Since we must always historicize, we must account for the difference in this conjuncture and the one that gave rise to what counts as political criticism.

Hence the necessity to confront the challenge of the title of this volume, *Shakespeare and the 99%*, from the disciplined and disciplinary perspective of the literary critic I was trained to be and of the cultural studies scholar I have struggled to become. If the literary critic in me has always embraced the metaphorical resources of topicality, the latter avatar would insist that the stark distribution of economic resources revealed by those iniquitous percentages (1 and 99), which became the rallying cry of the Occupy movement beginning in New York in September 2011 and spreading globally, be understood in its material historicity. Questions of the criminally unjust distribution of wealth should not be transformed to questions of the cultural—of, for instance, unequal access to or veneration of Shakespeare—without a pause for reflection. That more materialist part of me begs the literary scholar to remember that entry to cultural goods such as Shakespeare never was a principal rallying cry among protestors and fellow travelers for whom the harsh realities of economic immiseration were instead the focus of dissent. To put it simply and as befits the current conjuncture, the stakes of Occupy's struggle were sharper, more elemental, more concerned with dispossession from the very means to live, to survive under the ruthless regime of the biopolitical, rather than whether one possessed the cultural accouterments of a "good" (i.e., bourgeois) life.

But if Shakespeare's is not the first image that comes to mind as representative of the Occupy movement, the economic transformations that *were* the principal point of attack cannot but have left their mark directly and indirectly on publicly funded educational institutions within which Shakespeare plays a large role. As has been well attested to, student debt—the one form of debt that can never be discharged by declaring personal bankruptcy—has ballooned, and research has shown that such debt is accrued differentially, along not just classed but racialized lines. Although the principal culprits are for-profit colleges, debt has also risen markedly among those attending public institutions of higher education.[2] Many states have all but withdrawn fiscal support for their university systems even as the pressures to keep costs down have turned many a campus into a bad parody of corporate enterprise, with all of the punishments but none of the incentives of the market whose facile rationality legislatures and administrators rush to mime.[3] The current national fetishization of STEM, whose disciplines are undergirded by sponsored research, cannot be disarticulated from recent pressures for all kinds of university programs to bring in their own sources of funding: the redistribution of college resources typical of the past often falls by the wayside when it comes to the mendicant humanities, even if they—we—*do* have Shakespeare as our poster boy. My own campus, for instance, is too close to a wholly owned subsidiary of the Koch Foundation, which has been funding "free enterprise" at George Mason long before most of the public had ever heard the brothers' names. And these right-wing entities beckon seductively toward the humanities and, indeed, all other areas of non-economic study: thanks to the largesse of the Kochs and others, and in the name of so-called "humane studies," they offer to fund students willing to (mis)identify the feints of an untrammeled capitalist market as the clarion call of freedom, whose sound, they aver, is to be found in the study of literature and the "classical liberal tradition" as well as in the work of deregulation.[4] Shakespeare is at best an alibi for these structural transformations, the one name administrators honor even as they set about underfunding his local habitation along with other humanities disciplines and modes of thought that do not meet the test of the free market—and, more scandalously, do not wish to.

An institution like George Mason, which became a university only in the 1970s, has never been anything but neoliberal: never, that is, has it been possessed of inertial practices and traditions that could serve as a counterweight to the endless pressure to "innovate" and adapt to circumstances whose rapid motility leaves us faculty continually stunned. Nor has it ever been possessed of a sufficient endowment to insulate it from the fiscal shocks and legislative withdrawal of funding from higher education that have taken place in Virginia in advance of its becoming the national norm. It is within the ambit of such an institution that the following analysis of academic practices has to be placed in order to mark the temporal—and ideological, and material—disjuncture between a critical then and a pedagogical now. Attending to that manifold disjuncture reveals a collision between how some students enter into a literary space, and how they are trained by people like me to change course. My musings derive from two anecdotes, one peculiar to my classroom and the other less so—a version of the latter has probably taken place innumerable times, but gains its motive force from the fact that the exchange I am documenting occurred on the list serve of the Marxist Literary Group, a group to which I belong and among whose members there is an avowed link between the analysis of literature and cultural forms on the one hand, and critique of capitalism on the other.

My way into defining a political criticism appropriate for the present is to start with the supposed "problem" of students' identifying with characters. I want to sketch a kinship between academics' reflexive dismissal of such moves and the critical problem of alienation as articulated in the Western Marxist tradition, a key term for analyses of both labor and aesthetics. Such reactions stand in for the myriad naïve—that is, unprofessional—responses our students have while reading. While they are not identical with pleasure, these responses constitute a felt reaction to the text and its effects, a kind of first-level aesthetics, serving as the antithesis to what I'll call alienated reading: reading at some remove from the text and its affective valences, and assuming a critical analytical stance as part of a schooled encounter. The resources for the current conjuncture provided by those felt reactions should not be readily dismissed, even when they cannot also be uncritically embraced. At the moment, affect is the lever for atavistic political positions, and also for a profound despair at the recrudescence of those positions and for the material practices of power that engender them. I want to think through the retrograde yet audacious possibility that our students may be part of something worth our attention: that their identifying with Shakespeare's characters, or—to speak more broadly, their choosing not to be merely suspicious of textual practice but to feel in the face of the text—might help reframe abeyant conversations about emotions and literature last seen as the dusty province of a bygone liberalism. Not, I hasten to say, because reading "right" guarantees empathy, for instance, still less that empathy in and of itself is a guarantor of social justice. Rather, it is because the familiar responses of students, so long delegitimated and deprived of value by academics wedded to the practice of rational-political demystification, give us a concrete place to engage with one element in the broader-scale affective conditions that govern the present.

I advance such a claim with caution and no small degree of self-reproach. The temperature of left critique in the academy has been rather persistently cool, and the fear of being uncool, in every sense of that word, is real. As Peter Sloterdijk observed some time ago, cynical reason has become our dominant mode of rationality, and it is a rationality that vows not ever to be caught out by vulgar sentiments like sincerity.[5] Yet the politics of the left need to be impassioned as well as critical; moreover, it is urgent we engage with the ontological priority of feeling over thought in the present, and to give that feeling its critically attentive due, when it comes both to local pedagogical forms and more diffuse and abstract national formations. Given what is at stake in the current conjuncture, it is possible nothing else will serve us so well.

II

An earlier moment in academic practice found politically inflected criticism to constitute an invigorating resource for the transformation of consciousness. Such criticism was influenced by the complex engagements to be found in Western Marxism with the "superstructural"—the cultural—elements in the lived totality, and its ambit was both sociological and textual. Insofar as the canon was recognized as an ancillary instrument to domination—of barbarity as much as of civilization, in the words of Walter Benjamin—it became a widely accepted move to identify radical political practice with non-intuitive reading strategies connected to discerning ideological constructs first and foremost as a function of language. To read against the grain, to stand as suspicious of the text and its designs on us, to refuse to embrace a realist fantasy of unschooled pleasure: to do all of these was to reject the ideological a priori that constituted the political unconscious when it came to literary acts, particularly public dispensations around an author as privileged as Shakespeare inevitably remains. In order to dispense with the class-coded appreciation of literature and its aesthetic effects, criticism had to change to critique.

Marxist textual criticism in the United States followed Fredric Jameson's interest in the political significance of genre: hence among other instances the interest in dramatic form on the part of scholars such as Jean Howard. However, when it came to the study of Shakespeare it was British scholars and critics, some but not all of whom were identified as cultural materialists, who pursued analysis via a politicization of subjectivity as a function of language.[6] One influential text for this turn was Rosalind Coward and John Ellis' *Language and Materialism.*[7]

Under particular scrutiny was any formation that addressed characters as "real," and as quasi-beings with whom readers and spectators would and should identify. Consider Catherine Belsey's 1986 *The Subject of Tragedy*, a study that made good on the Althusserian–Lacanian model of subjectivity that Belsey usefully explicated in her 1980 handbook *Critical Practice* and related to the work of Coward and Ellis.[8] In her subsequent analysis of Renaissance tragedy, Belsey set aside New Critical premises about the unity or integrity of text or character, which she had subjected to keen scrutiny in the earlier guide. Rather, through a series of case studies she stressed the incoherence of literary characters, the moments of incommensurability, non-sense, and contradiction that in previous critical modalities were rationalized, brought into harmony with one another according to naturalized dicta about naturalistic continuity of theatrical personhood. Just as ideology cemented over the contradictions in lived experience, the better to nullify the potential for critical reflection, so too did literary naturalism, and many of the critical modalities that accompanied it, cement the textual traces to be found in Shakespeare and his contemporaries into a felicitously New Critical whole.

Such moves as Belsey enjoined were important and productive, even urgent in their time. Among their virtues is the fact that they continued the influential political legacy of Brechtian alienation-effects begun earlier in the century.[9] As is well-known, Bertholt Brecht critiqued as bourgeois the aesthetics naturalized by theater audiences at a performance, an aesthetics that saw characters as real, and, tellingly, as the occasion for an uncanny inhabitation by the actors who performed them. Hence his scorn for the spectatorial rapture that praises an actor for *becoming* Lear, for making a character seem to step off the stage and into real life, and vice versa—for an actor to surrender his being to the part. Under equal scrutiny fell the informing belief that literary drama was meant to be a vehicle for reproducing the illusion of realism. For Brecht, it was a short step from that illusion to ideology as such, since in both cases the seamlessness of the inhabited world encouraged complacence about its exploitative social relations. In contradistinction, Brecht encouraged the development of an anti-naturalistic dramatic form that demanded critical distance from its audience in order to comprehend its operations, and that depended on fragmentation and disruption of any naturalist dispensation from the high aesthetic as a corollary to developing a critical and resistant—not to say revolutionary—consciousness. That drama would refuse a ready synthesis between art and life, that it would not traffic in naturalistic illusion, was embodied by the importance of the alienation-effect to Brecht's dramatic practice.

Much like his friends and interlocutors in the Frankfurt School—Ernst Bloch and Walter Benjamin in particular, although even Theodor Adorno's nihilistic melancholy was the obverse of hope—Brecht could not but imagine that "high" art would play a role in the advancement of social justice in the struggle against capitalist exploitation. If I may be forgiven for the moment for telescoping the subtle and strong distinctions among their positions in the service of a larger point about their writing: whether it be avant-garde or the legacy of the past, art was, unlike mass culture, meant to be anything but instrumental. It was meant neither to serve a form of mindless pleasure (however blissfully experienced), nor the standardized commodity of the market, the products of the culture industry that were both decried and yet examined for the possibility that their technical means, when redoubled as aesthetic effects, could be used to different political ends.

That counterpoising of mass culture with high art—with the sense that the outcome of the struggle for priority between them could yet be in doubt—is yet another marker of the historicity of such critical modes: it too is a historicity that is *not ours*. Nor is our moment the academically heady aftermath of 1968 and the Althusser-inflected conflation of political struggle with the regime of the signifier that resulted in the writing of Coward and Ellis, Belsey, and others. As already noted, ours is a time of more elemental struggle, of the more visceral immiseration of populations made vulnerable through the myriad markers of inequality newly on the radar of virulently reactionary forces.

Even so, it is important to note that the turn to ideology-critique generated new reading strategies that forced us to think about the connections between high literacy and other formations of power. But the turn could be vexed in pedagogical practice for those of us whose students, often immigrant or non-white, did not possess such literacy as an ancillary to inherited class privilege, but rather acquired it through hard-won investments in literature as a site of positive value, and experienced textual enjoyment as the fruit of hard work in learning and feeling, experiencing, the pleasures of reading. In other words, there has often been a disjuncture between our historical investments and class positions as academics on the one hand, and on the other the needs, investments, and class positions of students—many of whom are or have been new to education and to the study of literature. Such a disjuncture puts pressure on where, precisely, left political praxis might be found. Or at least, it should have.

III

In the intervening years, literary discourse around Shakespeare has moved on from that high moment of ideology-critique, which burgeoned in the 1980s and 1990s. Indeed, with some significant exceptions in general the field has moved away from the myriad forms of politically inflected criticism that seemed to proliferate even around race and gender. Even so, it is still all-but-automatic for many faculty—whether professors of Shakespeare or not—to equate progressive or avowedly left politics with resistant reading characterized by the hermeneutics of suspicion. Hence the illustrative importance of my anecdotes.

I begin with the moment from my own classroom history first. I was teaching a course on Shakespeare and early modern culture to English honors students. My own intellectual and political commitment to ideology-critique, characteristic of my formation first by New Historicism and then by Cultural Materialism, led me to stress the contradictions in texts, particularly within characters that were but textual traces of language-borne ideology rather than "real people." It also tended to be suspicious of the text's designs on its readers, especially when it came to Shakespeare's particular proclivity for ending his texts with a vision of harmony I trained them to see as both forced and enforced: consider, for instance, *Titus Andronicus*'s forcible knitting-together of Goth and

Roman, or *Measure for Measure's* procrustean marriage beds, to which all, whether sexual hypocrite and coercive seducer, disease-ridden punk, or veritable virgin, must hie themselves. My students were mostly supple, biddable, intent to master the moves to which I was introducing them, though far from the practiced skeptics I've encountered in more elite institutions, to whom deconstructive moves and second-order readings informed by a highly developed capacity to demystify were interpretive defaults. That distance matters for the terms of this essay: indeed, it is worth noting that my onetime students were a mixed bag, ethnically, racially, and even ideologically. If anything beyond their interest in academic success in general and Shakespeare in particular united them, it was the fact that their relatively high standards of literacy were far from second-nature, far, that is, from the legacy of the class, race, or ethnic group into which they had been born.

Things went well enough, as I had hoped they would; good work was done, and solid, sometimes brilliant, papers tendered. At the end of the semester, however, that one student told me he thought the class had trained him in "how to hate the English Renaissance." At the time, I read that remark as the resistance of someone who'd bet on the wrong horse, who had already shown himself somewhat hostile to feminism and other forms of political criticism, since they occluded his privileged form of aesthetic response. I refuse to surrender that embedded insight, since it is true to the affective register of the class, and since resistance to feminism strikes me now as it did then: in and of itself, as something that cannot be valorized. It goes without stating, however, that the remark has gnawed at me intermittently, the student's political limitations notwithstanding. My own failure to think dialectically at the time became, in the student's utterance, the return of the repressed: I had assumed the historical obviousness of Shakespeare's value (and that of the English Renaissance itself) with perhaps too much confidence, and attended too little to the difference between my temporality, as subject who'd attained bourgeois literacy, and theirs, in its historically tardy pursuit.

The second anecdote concerns the MLG listserve to which I referred earlier. Someone wrote in, lamenting, as many an academic has done with another, that students were finding characters too real, that they were too interested in identifying with them rather than in understanding the literary artifact in all its mystified yet undeniable political complexity. (Although the motivating email did not concern Shakespeare, the point is it may well have done.) The response was universally sympathetic—and univocal: it was explicitly as part of a political project that students should be trained to understand that texts are ideological artifacts. Continued student identification imaged a widespread complicity with realist mystifications that were the place where the fictive does its subterranean work in sustaining the governing ideologies of capitalism.

As a condition of this analysis, I want to make clear that professional pedagogical practice is not and need not be identical with lay reading habits, and it is not my purpose here to suggest they should be. There is no need for us to give our authority away when the forces of a brutally economic logic strive to do that work for us. Nor do I wish to suggest something like the wisdom of the crowds, or in this case the putative masses, be embraced: it is important to critique the sometimes-uncritical fetishization of taste "from below" just because it carries the purported stamp of authenticity. In other words, my argument does not mean the simple reversal of cultural vectors: finding value in the popular, simply because it *is* popular, is a familiar dead end, in, and for, the rigorous study of cultural objects, whether they be pop culture or Shakespeare. Popular tastes, including a distaste for Shakespeare, are no less learned for having been acquired alongside of, and in reaction-formation to, the formal instruction of the classroom. As Paul Willis demonstrated with respect to white masculinity and the British educational system in *Learning to Labour*, working-class resistance to schoolroom discipline, and to schoolroom knowledge as a site of aspiration, should not be valorized for its own sake.[10] Rather, his ethnographic study is a confirmation of Althusser's argument that schools are ideological apparatuses, functioning to guarantee that the reproduction of the relations of production—among other things, the social reproduction of class—are chosen "freely," in that they appear to the recalcitrant student as an unencumbered choice not to embrace what the schools would value, all in the name of something approximating class authenticity that actually betrays the thing it seeks to serve. Such a double bind around so-called "popular resistance" to education, and the Culture it perpetuates, thwarts the development of transformative consciousness that might truly place Shakespeare among the common goods of a national culture, a public accommodation that might be seized for a counter-hegemonic message.

More broadly, sentimental abstractions that offer to stand in for "the people" have an equally vexed history as proxies for more properly materialist understandings of historical blocs of the oppressed—who these days tend not to take high culture in general, or Shakespeare in particular, as an important ground of resistance, if ever they did. The descriptive phrase that guides this collection, the "99 percent," emerges not out of a relationship to Shakespeare or his corollaries but to a historically proximate, rampant, and precisely economic inequality that in this millennium has exploded into visibility. The politics of the Occupy movement have been the politics of time and space—of an enforced leisure due to the absence of meaningful work or else to the theft of time from the demands of work; for the taking-over of public and quasi-public space over a longer period than has tended to be the case with marches and demonstrations.

Yes, "naïve" reading can make me uneasy too, even if it is where many of us started and the space to which we covertly return when we read at leisure and for pleasure—a guilty pleasure, if you will. Even so, the issue I want to alight upon concerns the dilemma each situation limns, which brings overtly political criticism into a sometimes-jarring juxtaposition with students whose moment of coming to literature at the university level cannot duplicate the moment of those who have been teaching it to them. This temporal disjuncture is important, since it marks the difference between a time when Shakespeare could still be proposed as a form of cultural capital, and concomitantly as a site of ideological domination, and the present moment, when such struggles over meaning seem, well, luxurious and even quaint, precisely for the reasons I outlined earlier in this essay.

I hasten to note that it would be considered so within any academic dispensation in English, not merely one claiming the left as its ground. Professionalized reading practices are, by definition, not the reactions of unschooled readers, which is a fact and a corollary of that professionalization, rather than the necessary object of either lamentation or scorn. To regret that we do not read as "regular" readers do is to deny the value of our insights—perhaps an inevitable if depressive move when the humanities themselves do not meet the draconian test of market value, but one that ought not to be undertaken without a sense of what powers, resources, and claims to expertise we give away when we cut the ground out from under ourselves.

As this line of discussion suggests, I am less interested in critiquing academics for being what they are—possessors of a cultural capital whose fungibility as a form of prestige has long been on the wane in a world where financial exchange value dominates brutally—than in drawing attention to the sense that no political value could ever be found in critiquing one's learned instincts, in apprehending them dialectically at every turn. What struck me in the second interchange to which I allude was the certainty that the politics of the class struggle were best served by instructing students in literary techniques and strategies that were, to put it precisely yet ironically, *alienating*. The fruits of students' own reading were taken away from them: even if we academics did not extract a strictly material profit from their dispossession, we occluded their own activity, or, rather, directed it in ways we had preordained as more profitable. On some level, of course, all of teaching is aimed at directing students toward a destination we have prescribed in advance. Here, however, what was lost was any sense of the value of dialectical criticism, of a counterbalance between critique on the one hand, and the pleasure and recognition—the sense of ownership—the students felt on the other.

The critical practices I've been putting at some distance formed me as an intellectual, and I've no wish to deny their considerable interpretive leverage. Moreover, they reinforce that depth model of the literary that is more and more being opposed to "surface reading," which has seemed to constitute a retreat from the political altogether insofar as the study of literature is concerned.[11] Yet those critical practices are also symptomatic—that is, they are reminders of the double valence the term "alienation" assumes, particularly in Marxist discourse. There, it principally refers, not to the radical aesthetics of Brecht, but to the privation of labor power from the laborer, and its subsumption by the owners of the means of production. As Marx formulated it, under capitalism humans do not own our labor power or the fruits of that labor, which is rather possessed by those entities and institutions in whose employ we are. For all that Marx was theorizing the material dispossession of what we make, in tasks expressly dedicated to the maintenance of everyday life, his model of alienation nevertheless can be extended precisely to those reading strategies that aim to provoke oppositional consciousness, but might, if deployed without finesse—and I think of myself here—lead to our students' "hating the English Renaissance."

IV

The move I'm making depends on thinking of reading as "work," certainly, which is far from a distant notion for any critic. Not only is interpretation precisely, unambiguously, *our* paid labor, but we claim that right-to-work for the objects of our reading, through such locutions as "the work of the text," and through attention to textual effects on us. Indeed, by following Barthes some time ago in the movement from "work to text," we have, often without quite reflecting on it, chosen to dismiss the labor of the author—Shakespeare's *work*, for instance—from the scene of writing.[12] But the move I'm making also depends on recognizing the extent to which the students whom I teach at my endlessly innovating university are often first-generation students who have precisely *worked hard* to get to where they are and who have invested in the primacy of Shakespeare, and the importance of literature, despite countervailing trends in American life that have argued with ever-greater insistence that education is, and should be, jobs training, and the humanities a kind of ornament without profit. The hidden presumption is that higher education must serve as jobs training for some, and only for some: those who have come to higher education belatedly, those for whom the notion of a liberal arts degree is presumed to have little motive force because of the pressing absence of familial wealth—increasingly, the only species of safety net our political discourse countenances.

Such exclusions, like the underfunding of the humanities in too many state universities and an increasing number of elite institutions, reveal the supersession of the canon as domination by other, ancillary means. John Guillory, following Bourdieu, influentially argued in *Cultural Capital* that the literary canon was the premier instrument for the maintenance and promulgation of the bourgeois idiolect, an idiolect whose social power went hand-in-hand with economic power.[13] However, in the nearly quarter of a century since Guillory's study was published, that idiolect has itself ceased to be the sign of distinction, even as those who yet possess it are often dismissed as specially pleading elites, given an increasingly virulent discourse serving newly dominant forms of racialized capital while cynically making equally racialized "populist" noises. When first-generation students—Asian, African American, Arab American, Latinex, or for that matter white—ascend to this level of literacy in the twenty-first century in an institution like mine, it is with little hope that high literacy will serve as a lever to bourgeois privilege, even an inchoate hope. Rather, the competence they seek to demonstrate reveals a more generalized yet still obsolescent faith that "excellence" will still find some kind of place in the reward system of postcollegiate life. Their labors, they might well imagine, are not to be in vain. But nor are they to be without the pleasure of encountering a text that is *other* by virtue of language and distance in time, and making it their own.

In a direct sense, students like the ones to whom I've alluded labor over the Shakespearean text and own that labor by finding—or, better, inventing—themselves through the process of identifying with characters. Reading, as I think more of us experience than profess, can with skill and everyday practice engender an apparently spontaneous orientation toward a character, in which the possibilities of the self find themselves afterward enlarged yet the relation is made to seem "natural." Students who've become adept at such maneuvers earlier in their educational history then enter a university literature classroom where that labor is taken from them—where they are trained to be alienated from the text that has heretofore rewarded them, and that has apparently betrayed them into a naïve because emotional encounter with itself. That such alienating maneuvers are offered by left-oriented faculty in the name of a politicized demystification lends them a pungent irony: the ends obscure the violence of the means. And they beg the question of what might be next, or better.

V

Certainly, drawing on the resources of affect, of restoring feeling to the critical conversation, seems productive in a way it has not been for some time. Of course, the appeal of affect theory as a method for textual practice has a great deal to do with the matter of currency: emergent academic trends can exert pressure across a range of interpretive registers simply because of their novelty, because academic models constitute a niche market, and academics wishing to stand out as innovative in a hopelessly crowded job market are not immune to the commodity fetishism of shiny new ideas. Or refunctioned, older, or generationally delegitimated ones. The critical conversation on "the body" as it took place among Foucauldian and feminist scholars has mutated into the question of what it feels like to have a body; phenomenological positions have also re-emerged and been re-energized, meeting with a discourse that has rediscovered the historical anchoring of aesthetic sensation in the body rather than in a measured distance from both embodied and economic necessity.[14]

Yet it would be wrong simply to read the affective as merely the latest in a series of academic trends. All such trends (if, indeed, that is even the appropriate word, academic markets notwithstanding) have a complex and dialectical relationship to the moment of their emergence—they reveal themselves, that is, to have a historically congruent and potentially critical relationship to their initial enunciative context. If, as I have already mentioned, we abide at a moment when political culture has called forth a primitive, reactionary, gendered, racialized collection of emotional responses that undermines even the very phantasm of a rational public sphere and that puts increasing numbers of people at physical risk, it is politically imperative to take such responses as the object of study. More subtly, the state whose agenda is to conjure and then counter the specter of terrorism has now turned threat into an ineluctable affective fact, precisely when the threat is conditional and speculative, as Brian Massumi has argued.[15] That most citizens of the United States who live in comparative comfort and safety nevertheless feel themselves under siege is a historical and, yes, affective fact with complex ramifications for the study of cultural forms like literature—which has, until relatively recently, been the bearer of sentiment rather than the occasion of a pure intellection, notwithstanding its abstracted conversations about "the body."

I find it provocative to consider my students' desire to feel in the face of their reading, and I wish I could break through to some form of uncomplicated validation even as I know the cautions to be launched against one-sidedness. Pragmatically, of course, it is easy enough to work with their sentiments—which also concern resistance and boredom as well as more likable forms of engagement. I can and do, for instance, ask them to think about which characters they identify with and which are not offered to them for such taking-in—why the priggish Cordelia, for instance, who by her very contentment with the fact of being traded from father to husband honors the traffic in women, and not the put-upon Goneril and Regan, who in sucking up to their father at his command recognize the banal and coercive necessity of courtly flattery? Of course, *Lear* as it unfolds puts the two sisters beyond the pale of empathy, but that is beside the point: doing so makes it the easier to take (rather reactionary) sides from the very first, given the pressure of the fairy tale's rule of three and the structural superiority it gives to the youngest.

Yet these pedagogical moves offer little overt political purchase beyond their interpretive context. And the ready passage from reading and empathy—even "corrected" empathy—to some glimpse of a better world has already been tried and found wanting as an end in itself. In a provocative study, Paul Bloom has argued that spontaneous empathy, including that engendered by the study of literature, has no necessary political valence.[16] At the 2018 MLA session devoted to his book, he noted rather mordantly that his literary critic friends were not necessarily better people than his friends who were in the sciences. Empathy may arrive by more than one path, and English professors may be as disagreeable as anyone else; even so, his remark is a witty caution against falling into delegitimated liberal bromides simply because the profession has rediscovered feeling as an object of interest. Feelings scale up with difficulty beyond the immediate, and even the most sincere forms of empathy are not inconsistent with a largely rhetorical concern about a just and livable future.

As it turns out, I cannot answer in the comprehensive terms in which I posed the question at the start of this essay, for all that the social totality I've invoked is very much to the point. Leaving aside the evidence this cannot but provide of my limitations as a critic, the impasse suggests that the function of the affective is itself emergent—that is, it redoubles the structures of feeling that have themselves defined the study of the affective as latent, labile. Some of the most provocative work on affect bypasses the analytical ambit of individual subjectivity, and hence puts at some remove the resuscitation of liberal pieties about only connecting. Instead, it images feeling as a kind of intersubjective contagion in the body politic, and so demands we think about the relationship between this historically instantiated modeling of embodied responses and more conventional and individuated literary reactions of love, hate, identification, and disidentification among our students, which mean something different at every moment of their articulation. The relationship to be thought about is likely neither strictly oppositional not strictly commutative: to put it another way, the national subject of affect—whether the atavistically raging crowd, the panic-stricken horde, or the uneasy, disquieted collective—is not the Other of our students in all their valuable specificity; nor is it co-extensive with them. Rather, all the modes of being affected I've listed, and the many more that I have not had time or wit to imagine, must be understood as mere threads in a network of affiliation whose final historical form is yet to be made wholly present to analysis.

But I will keep trying. Crafting such networked connections at a moment of latency is, as with all work worth doing, fraught with possibilities of error. However, it also offers the possibility that attending to feeling in all its proximate manifestations will provide new resources for political-critical practice—ones that, with luck, engage with students in the specific characters of their felt responses as readers who've worked with what they've worked to read, while acknowledging the historical specificity of their capacity as subjects to feel those responses in the current regime, where economic disparity grows by governmental fiat and a formerly abeyant resentment is deflected onto improper and vulnerable objects. And it would also recognize the fact of our joint temporality, of the institutional nexus that binds us together—and of the forms of the political whose emergence we may, with luck and grace and with an occasional assist from Shakespeare, help to make together.

Notes

1. Denise Albanese, *Extramural Shakespeare* (New York: Palgrave Macmillan, 2010).
2. Tressie Macmillan Cottom, *Lower Ed: The Troubling Rise of For-Profit Colleges in the New Economy* (New York: The New Press, 2017); Kayva Vaghul and Marshall Steinbaum, "How the Student Debt Crisis Affects African Americans and Latinos" (Washington, DC: Washington Center for Equitable Growth, 2016): http://equitablegrowth.org/research-analysis/how-the-student-debt-crisis-affects-african-americans-and-latinos/. Accessed May 20, 2018.
3. So much has been discussed widely by scholars of critical university studies; see, for instance, Bill Readings, *The University in Ruins* (Cambridge: Harvard University Press, 1997); Christopher Newfield, *Unmaking the Public University: The Forty-Year Assault on the Middle Class* (Cambridge: Harvard University Press, 2011).
4. See the Institute for Humane Studies at George Mason University, part of the Schar School for Government and Policy, which defines itself as a place whose vision is that academia "**becomes** a place where classical liberal ideas are regularly taught, discussed, challenged, and developed, and where free speech, intellectual diversity, and open inquiry flourish" (emphasis added); see https://theihs.org/who-we-are/#sthash.QoaDl9A9.dpbs. Accessed May 27, 2018. Later on the page the "classical liberal tradition" is defined in terms of "limited government [and] economic freedom" as well as questions of personal liberty. IHS offers to fund any graduate student who seeks to "advance and explore the ideas of freedom as an academic": https://theihs.org/undergraduates/funding-graduate-school/#sthash.MCpHshbg.dpbs. Accessed May 27, 2018. IHS is partly funded by the Koch Foundation as well as other right-leaning libertarian sources; see https://en.wikipedia.org/wiki/Institute_for_Humane_Studies.

5. Peter Sloterdijk, *A Critique of Cynical Reason*, trans. Michael Eldred (Minneapolis: University of Minnesota Press, 1988).
6. Jonathan Dollimore and Alan Sinfield, eds., *Political Shakespeare: New Essays in Cultural Materialism* (Ithaca: Cornell University Press, 1985); John Drakakis, ed., *Alternative Shakespeares* (London: Methuen, 1985).
7. Rosalind Coward and John Ellis, *Language and Materialism: Developments in Semiology and the Theory of the Subject* (London: Routledge and Kegan Paul, 1977).
8. Catherine Belsey, *Critical Practice* (London: Routledge, 1980); *The Subject of Tragedy: Identity and Difference in Renaissance Drama* (London: Routledge 1985).
9. Bertolt Brecht, "Alienation-Effects in Chinese Acting," in Bertotlt Brecht, *Brecht on Theatre: The Development of an Aesthetic* (13th ed.), eds. Steve Giles, Marc Silberman, and Tom Kuhn, trans. John Willett (New York: Hill and Wang, 1992), 91–99.
10. Paul Willis, *Learning to Labour: How Working Class Kids Get Working Class Jobs* (New York: Columbia University Press, 1981).
11. Stephen Best and Sharon Marcus, "Surface Reading: An Introduction," *Representations* 108, no. 1 (2009): 1–21.
12. Roland Barthes, "From Work to Text," in Roland Barthes, *The Rustle of Language*, trans. Richard Howard (New York: Hill and Wang, 1986), 56–64.
13. John Guillory, *Cultural Capital: The Problem of Literary Canon Formation* (Chicago: University of Chicago Press, 1993).
14. Sara Ahmed, *The Cultural Politics of Emotion*, 2nd ed. (London: Routledge, 2014); Lauren Berlant, *Cruel Optimism* (Durham: Duke University Press, 2011).
15. Brian Massumi, "The Future Birth of the Affective Fact: The Ontology of Threat," in *The Affect Theory Reader*, eds. Melisa Gregg and Gregory J. Seigworth (Durham: Duke University Press, 2010), 52–70.
16. Paul Bloom, *Against Empathy: The Case for Rational Compassion* (New York: Ecco, 2016).

Shakespeare, Alienation, and the Working-Class Student

Doug Eskew

Sometimes at an academic conference, I'll mention that I work in Colorado. People usually respond with something like, "Oh, I love Colorado!" or "Colorado is so beautiful!" I agree with both of those sentiments—and I always tell them I agree; I tell them how fortunate I am to live and work here. Here's what I don't tell them: I don't work in the part of Colorado they are thinking about, the Colorado of pine forests, ski resorts, and brewery tours. I work in southern Colorado, in the city of Pueblo, on the dry southeastern plains, culturally, geographically, economically isolated from the wealthier parts of the state. It's dry down here. And poor. And decidedly unwhite. Pueblo is not Boulder, with its Buddhist university and Google campus. It's not Denver, with its housing crunch and ramen shops. It's not even Colorado Springs, with its military bases and megachurches. If you are looking for white people and mountains, don't look to Pueblo. Pueblo will disappoint you.

If you travel to the affluent, northern parts of the state, you'll most likely never meet a person from Pueblo. A sizable number of Puebloans have never left the southern part of the state, have never traveled northward at all. Northward to the elite culture of Denver, Boulder, and Fort Collins.

D. Eskew (✉)
Colorado State University, Pueblo, CO, USA

S. O'Dair and T. Francisco (eds.), *Shakespeare and the 99%*,
https://doi.org/10.1007/978-3-030-03883-0_3

Northward to rub shoulders with the rich and famous in Aspen and Vail and Telluride. Even when Puebloans travel to those places, they often keep to themselves where they're from, for they know their kind aren't exactly welcome. As Eric Schlosser points out, "Snobs up north" call Pueblo "the asshole of Colorado."[1] On a recent episode of the *Pod Save America* podcast, which was recorded live in Denver, an audience member named Gina volunteered to play an on-air quiz. One of the hosts, Jon Lovett, asked her, "Are you from Denver?" Gina replied, "I'm originally from Colorado but not from Denver." "You are equivocating," Lovett said, not understanding why she wouldn't just say where in Colorado she originates. When she finally said that she is from Pueblo, Lovett asked, "What's the defensiveness for?" Gina said, "It's a thing here. Trust me, it's a thing."[2] When two famous, middle-class Denverites, Trey Parker and Matt Stone, portrayed Pueblo on their TV show *South Park*, they displayed its difference by having Puebloans speak only Spanish and by making its police force Mexican Federales. When people say, "Colorado is beautiful," they are almost never talking about the arid, southeastern plains, with its scrawny sagebrush and plentiful tumbleweeds. They are not speaking of Pueblo, which was once known for its steel mill and strong union but is now known for its cheap, black-tar heroin and its disastrously high per-capita murder rate. When Pueblo made it into *The New York Times* recently, the article was titled, "A Surge of Violence in a City of Gangs."[3]

Despite a bias that prefers aspen groves to sagebrush, moose to coyotes, and affluent white people to working-class people of color, Pueblo is beautiful—remarkably beautiful, with its big sky and sunny days unobscured by mountains or forests, its landscape of plateaus and desert buttes, mesas, and broad basins. The people are beautiful, too. To this day, most families in Pueblo trace their lineage to the late nineteenth or early twentieth centuries, when the enormous steel mill and nearby mining camps drew thousands of immigrants, mostly from Italy, Mexico, and eastern Europe. Puebloans still tend to identify with one of these groups. They say, "I'm Italian," "I'm Mexican," or "I'm Bojon." These immigrants came to Pueblo for hard work then and their families remain now despite a lack of good-paying jobs. These Puebloan forebears survived or were murdered in the Ludlow Massacre of 1914, and they worked in the enormous steel mill until the steel market crash of 1982. These forebears came as outsiders and they stayed in the South, isolated, worked in the mines and the mills, and made a home there. Their descendants, these beautiful, strong Puebloans, developed a culture that outsiders have largely never heard of. For the "snobs up north," there is no reason to think of them at all. When they do think of it, they often have racist or classist thoughts: Pueblo is Mexico or it's an asshole.

At the same time that the whole of the community is alienated from the rest of the state, these working-class students of Pueblo often come to the university classroom pedagogically alienated—alienated from the educator who stands before them, alienated in that they are uninterested in what they are supposed to be learning. Interestingly, pedagogical alienation is a kind of alienation that does not separate southern Colorado students from those in the north. It's something they share—a double negative that bridges the gap of the other alienations. Pedagogical alienation is on the rise throughout the United States, widespread among all kinds of differing demographics. As Jonathan Martin puts it, "Qualitative studies, journalistic investigations, and faculty observations of college life depict many, if not most, American undergraduates as intellectually disengaged, [and] instrumentally oriented toward their studies."[4] Martin additionally notes that among working-class students, this alienation is worse: "instrumentalism and passivity… as well as overt forms of student resistance are more prevalent and severe in predominantly working-class classrooms."[5] We are used to this: when the affluent suffer a debilitating cultural trend, the non-affluent suffer it worse.

Already in this essay, I have spoken of alienation in several different ways. And while these varying forms have much in common, they are not the same and should not be conflated. While cultural forms are intertwined with economic forms, for instance, the cultural is not the economic. The geographical is not the educational. And none of these forms of alienation is the same as the pedagogical. Nevertheless, in much of the literature on trends in teaching, these varying kinds of alienation are seen as precisely that: variations on the same real and basic thing. Alienation is alienation is alienation.[6] While I admit to the power and utility of such an essentializing move, my desire in this essay is to speak of a constitutively different kind of alienation—an alienation that often gets lumped among other alienations and gets treated like the others as something that needs to be cured or fixed. My suggestion will be that this other kind of alienation—an alienation from an academic subject for which the student can only feel estrangement, can only be seen as alien to their lives—if this kind of alienation presents a culture shock to students at the same time that it provides the intellectual methods of coming to terms with that shock, then this alienation is, can, and should be a good thing for the intellectual lives of working-class students.

This beneficial kind of alienation is clearly visible in classrooms where Shakespeare is taught. The text itself, the Shakespearean text, is one of the most alienating that American students will encounter. Rarely do we ask students to read such an old text and ask them to learn a good deal about its context—the day-to-day minutia of life in Elizabethan and Jacobean England, its politics, foreign policies, ideological paradigms and contradictions, its specific histories and England's place in the European Renaissance. We even often ask our students to consider the fallout of this Age of Shakespeare, what Shakespeare, his reputation, and his reputed context mean to latter times such as ours. A lot of the time (perhaps even "usually"), a student's honest answer to this question of what Shakespeare means to people today is that Shakespeare doesn't mean much at all. Shakespeare is a requirement in school—that's it. Students recognize that we tend to ask them to dig deeply into Shakespeare's life and times for no other reason than to wrap their minds around the Shakespearean text. What is unclear to many students is why the Shakespearean text is worth all of that effort. Shakespeare was, after all, no eminent person, even in his own day. Yes, he would eventually buy his way into being called a gentleman and he did perform before Queen Elizabeth and her successor, King James. But any number of men had very similar successes; scores of men and women have had similar success in the intervening four hundred years. In many, many ways, the only notable thing about Shakespeare is that teachers continue to tell their students that he is notable.

The unquestioned reverence for Shakespeare is everywhere in the culture. As unquestioned, this reverence is a perfect example of ideology: an idea that seems to have its own agency, a thought that seems to do the thinking on its own. People revere Shakespeare for no better reason than that people revere Shakespeare. Last year, when students at the English Department at the University of Pennsylvania removed a framed portrait of Shakespeare from its building and replaced it with a portrait of Audre Lorde, a bit of an uproar among the public ensued. The uproar wasn't so much about who replaced Shakespeare (although some conservative media outlets pointed out that Lorde was "black," "gay," and "feminist"), but that Shakespeare (Shakespeare!) had been replaced. At elite universities, this kind of reverence for Shakespeare has been out of fashion for decades, perhaps especially among Shakespeareans themselves. Students in Boulder or Fort Collins do not hear their professors echoing Jonson's claim that Shakespeare "was not of an age, but for all time."

No longer are students in those institutions fed the lie that Shakespeare was a writer whose plays and poems transcend time, transcend economic and social norms, whose words speak unencumbered to the human soul. Still, when I arrived in Pueblo a decade ago, having earned a PhD from an elite public university, I was shocked at the bardolatry there. My newly retired predecessor had taught from that tradition; many of my colleagues expected I would continue that tradition. At my very first function as a professor, a meeting of the arts and humanities college, I was asked to introduce myself. I stood, announced my name and told my new colleagues that I studied rhetorical theory and early modern literature. After the meeting, one soon-to-retire English professor, an otherwise sage and delightful human being, stopped me, and accusingly repeated my term: "early modern," he harrumphed. I did not interpret his tone as a threat. I interpreted it as disappointment. "Oh, you're one of *those*," he seemed to be saying. Not many months into my work at the university, one student told me of a "rumor" among the student body that seemed to confirm the kind of a Shakespearean I was. "They say you're a Shakespeare teacher who doesn't like Shakespeare. Is that true?" he asked.

It's unfortunate, but I've had to answer this question too many times to count, from both students and faculty at my university to, on one occasion, a fellow professor at a meeting of the Shakespeare Association of America. Of course, I "like" Shakespeare; I even revere him. But my lack of rapturous adulation remains a disappointment to many. Colleagues, for instance, have thought that I should develop a general education course on Shakespeare, one that would enable the average student at our below-average university to commune with the ineffable spirit of "the bard." These colleagues wish I were like the professor, played by Sally Kellerman, in the 1986 film, *Back to School*, who walks to a lectern on the first day of class and captivates the classroom simply by reading a literary text. In the case of this particular film, even Rodney Dangerfield cannot resist the mystical spirit of the literary text; he finds himself in a trancelike state, at his feet shouting, "Yes! Yes!" along with Molly Bloom. That's the kind of thing that recruits and retains students, my colleagues seem to be thinking.

My colleagues are probably right. If I could perform that role, drop my skepticism, drop academic rigor, and teach the appreciation of the bard, many students would be happy. If I could model a kind of worshipful posture, rather than a critical one, my students would be much more comfortable. But I model intellectual curiosity and scholarly inquiry instead of unquestioned devotion and literary ecstasy. I model these scholarly activities (and the values that inform them) because these are values that can benefit our communities. This is the work, the scholarly work, that brought me into the academy. Before I had discovered scholarly work, I was a broken, high-school dropout who, at eighteen years old, had only read a single book cover-to-cover—that book was a hagiography of Jim Morrison called *No One Here Gets Out Alive.* Jim Morrison, who was no intellectual, was probably the closest thing to an intellectual I had ever encountered. And a worshipful attitude toward him was particularly comfortable for me because in my working-class surroundings, we may have had no models of intellectual inquiry, but we did have abundant models of devotion and worship. We had abundant models of ecstatic religious devotion and the ways in which charismatic leadership can amplify that ecstasy. To my thinking, I can bring more to my students' education by modeling intellectual inquiry than I can by modeling the performing, authoritative professor who, armed with the cultural authority of the Shakespearean text, elicits swooning among students. That kind of literary experience is not what I brought to Pueblo, Colorado.

It makes sense that in a culturally alienated landscape, you might find the remnants of bardolatry, because the transcendent Shakespeare doesn't ask critical questions about where Pueblo fits into the larger map of cultural and economic progress. I am not saying that the people of Pueblo aren't critical or that they do not know their outsider status in socioeconomic terms. There is a healthy progressive community in Pueblo and throughout southern Colorado. But those who recognize the extent of the problems and the status of their isolated and working-class community, those people are far from a majority. Case in point: in the most recent presidential election, the voters in this Democratic stronghold of Pueblo county cast more ballots for the Republican candidate than the Democratic one for the first time since 1972. The last time they voted for a Republican, they voted for Nixon; forty-five years later, they voted for Trump.[7]

The transcendent and uncritical Shakespeare is perfect for topsy-turvy times like these, when working-class Democrats vote for demagogic Republicans. The transcendent Shakespeare does not ask uncomfortable questions about authority and economics. The transcendent Shakespeare is not just for all time; he's for all kinds of people. He's for Republicans and Democrats, the bourgeois and the proletariat, the elite and the working class; he supports Obama and he supports

Trump. The transcendent Shakespeare is the same for the high school dropout, for the first-generation college student, and for the student who comes from a long line of educated elite. The transcendent Shakespeare asks no questions about the relationship between those who are educated at the regional comprehensive university, those who are educated at the community college, and those who barely make it out of high school. Transcendent Shakespeare doesn't see difference between the people of Boulder and the people of Pueblo, between the people of the arid, sagebrush shrublands down south, and the foothill and subalpine communities up north. The transcendent Shakespeare is not a critical Shakespeare.

The irony about this transcendent Shakespeare is that as much as he's all around us, he's not everywhere; he's not actually transcendent. More and more, he's found in the most isolated of places: the random elite classroom, the no-name community college, and, until somewhat recently, the Colorado State University, Pueblo. Like Nietzsche's God, he's dead because people increasingly do not believe in him, yet he remains alive because pockets of belief remain in places like working-class universities. People in these places are taught to believe that Shakespeare was and is for all time, despite the fact that, here we are, living among one of these "all times," and we can clearly see that he does not speak to us because he is simply no longer being heard. If there is any doubt that most people nowadays have no idea what his words mean, take even the most famous lines from one of Shakespeare's plays, take a dozen lines from one of Hamlet's soliloquies or an exchange between Romeo and Juliet, take a well-known sonnet—"Let me not to the marriage of true minds" or "Shall I compare thee to a summer's day?"—take these lines to your mom or dad, to your best friend, to your high school math teacher, to your wife, husband, lover—take those lines and ask any of them if they understand the words.

I am a professor of Shakespeare, but I do not come from educated people. And even now that I am, nominally, one of the educated elite, the people in my life, the people I care about, and in whose presence I spend most of my time, these people do not comprehend Shakespeare's words. Even though students in my Shakespeare class tend to be students majoring in English literature, my students rarely understand Shakespeare's words. I am surrounded by people who cannot fathom the Shakespearean text and the only reason I know what is going on there, why I can fathom the Shakespearean text, is that I dedicated much of my life to an elite education centered around that text. By contrast, if the people in your life understand Shakespeare, they have been taught to understand a kind of English that most other speakers of English cannot understand. If you are surrounded by people like this, you are an elite in ways I can barely comprehend. The people I come from are not like that; my students are not like that.

In places where bardolatry is still taught, a kind of ideological violence is visited upon the students. They are taught that Shakespeare speaks to the human soul at the same time that Shakespeare's transcendent words make no sense to them. For students in this position, to believe that Shakespeare speaks to the human soul is to acknowledge that either they are not human or they do not have a soul. The terrible reality is that for those of us who teach working-class students, in order for our students to comprehend the early modern text at all, we must tell them, in modern English, what is going on. I remember well my first college course in Shakespeare. Our sole textbook was the then "standard" edition of the plays and poems: the door-stopping *Riverside Shakespeare*. Each onion-skinned page had two columns of tiny text and at the bottom of each page were footnotes of such a scholarly nature that they were as opaque as the early modern text they were supposed to illuminate. Because I was a dutiful student, I read every word of each of the assigned plays. These words, even though they were supposed to be in English, read to me as if they were in a foreign language. When I made it to class, and the professor lectured on each play: that's where I discovered the plot and learned the "meaning" of it all. And even though I knew I couldn't really read what I was reading, I continued to read it and pretended to understand it. I bought into the fetishization of the written word and of Shakespeare to the extent that I faked my comprehension. I bought into that mythology that any truly literarily minded student should be able to sit down, read a literary text, and commune with it on some kind of deep, human level. Yet there I was, day after day, sitting down with the almost-sacred text of *The Riverside Shakespeare*, and I didn't get it at all.

Like many students from working-class backgrounds, I would end up dropping out of college. (I made a go of it three separate times, at three different universities until I finally got through.) I don't know precisely how much of this faking I did played a part in my inability to finish, but I can't believe that the mythologies and fetishes helped any. When I came to Pueblo, I was encouraged to teach in that same tradition that had at one time alienated me. I couldn't do that, of course. What I could do, however, was demystify, as much as possible, the nature of the Shakespearean text and our various relationships to it. The last thing I want is for students to imagine their education in terms of fetish and dissembling. The last thing students need is an intellectual model who believes that Shakespeare can speak to their mysterious "souls" even though his words make no sense to them at all. The last thing I want is for my students to pretend that they "get it," all the while wondering what it means that Shakespeare does not speak to them—this godlike genius who speaks to all human beings. For my own students, who are predominately not just working class but also largely members of the Latinx, African American, and LGBTQ communities, it is particularly useful to teach Shakespeare outside of a paradigm that makes him an exemplary, white patriarch.

This anxious pretense reminds me of attending a Southern Baptist church as a child. Each and every service concluded with an "alter call," when the minister would ask members of the congregation to bow their heads, close their eyes, and meditate on the possibility that they had never really been "born again." Even though most of the people there had been "saved"—they had prayed for forgiveness and had been immersed in baptismal waters—the minister would ask everyone if their salvation had been real. A typical alter call was accompanied by an organ playing at low volume, playing a song such as "Softly and Tenderly," with somewhat terrifying lyrics like, "Time is now fleeting, the moments are passing / Passing from you and from me / Shadows are gathering, deathbeds are coming / Coming for you and for me." With the music slowly playing, the minister would speak into a microphone with a hushed voice:

> Brothers and sisters, now that everyone's heads are bowed and their eyes are closed, I want you to ask yourself a question: if you died today, are you sure you would find yourself in eternal glory? in the arms of a loving lord? in the sweet embrace of Jesus and the presence of the almighty Father? If you died today, would the Son of God greet you in heaven, saying, "Well done, good and faithful servant," or would Satan, smiling, spread his wings and greet you among the sulfurous fire of Hell itself, where you would endure never-ending agony and the absence of the almighty?

Week after week, service after service, we were asked to be certain about our intentions in the past, asked if we really meant it when we asked God for forgiveness. We needed to be certain, absolutely certain, for the consequence of not really being born again was eternal damnation in Hell. You may not be able to imagine how uncertain one can be of past intentions unless you've been asked to judge those intentions within the glare of an eternal outcome. Growing up and going to church, to be free of anxiety meant that I needed to be certain, but week after week, I couldn't be certain. A lot of evangelical protestants of that time recognize this anxiety, the unrelenting doubt that results from interrogating the past, a past that is impossible to work with.

Scholars of early modern culture will recognize this kind of protestant anxiety. And whereas some have theorized the benefits of it—Alan Sinfield, for instance, imagines that "Envisioning one's fate in the hands of the Reformation god of incomprehensible love and arbitrary damnation must have been a great provoker of self-consciousness"—I doubt that any one of us might wish to use this kind of anxiety as a feature of our pedagogy.[8] All of this talk of Shakespeare speaking to the human soul, however, leads precisely to this place where students sit, anxiously questioning the state of their being. Like the parishioner of fundamentalist religious faith who sits frozen in a state of existential dread and self-loathing, many students, perhaps especially working-class students, sit in the Shakespeare classroom. As the professor describes the connection of Shakespeare's words and the human soul, the student thinks, "How can I be fully human if Shakespeare does not speak to me?" Or perhaps the student thinks, "This is total bullshit" and drops the class or changes their major. Unlike the parishioner, the student does not have to sit there and take the unthinking and demeaning mythology of Shakespeare's connection to the human soul.

Like many English departments these days, the one in Pueblo has seen a drop in its number of majors. Faculty here are doing whatever they can to attract and retain students. To this end, some teachers look for aspects of alienating texts that students can "relate" to—it's a kind of justification, both for themselves and to their students, that there's a good reason why we spend so much time studying literature. The justification game, however, is a double-edged sword, as Stephen Booth has taught us. In teachers' desperation to justify the study of Shakespeare, they end up lying to students, telling them things about the text that they "do not [them]selves believe to be true."[9] When teachers tell students that *Hamlet* speaks their lives, for instance, students, on some level, know this not at all the case. In order to get a grade, however, students pretend that *Hamlet* instructs their lives either because they hope it to be true or because they are playing along with yet another lie that authorities tell them. Booth points out that this lying and pretending is "intellectually lethal," for it results in an "educational system" that "train[s] just the sort of leaders that have been leading" the United States: "ones who equate truth with what they wish were true."[10] I was recently speaking with a colleague about Booth's argument and here is this person's defensive rejoinder: "Booth is speaking from his experience at an elite institution, where they train the 'leaders' of the country. We train leaders of southern Colorado and Pueblo, not of the world." I agree that we do not train the leaders of the United States (Dana Perino, George W. Bush's White House Press Secretary, is probably the closest any of our students has gotten to being a national "leader"). Still, I refuse to believe that we should accept our second-rate status. We certainly should not make lying to our students a centerpiece of our pedagogy and claim that we teach this way because our students are working class.

We have an ethical problem when the pedagogy for working-class students includes lying to them and the pedagogy for students at elite institutions does not. Likewise, we have an ethical problem when universities who serve large numbers of socioeconomically underserved students use an outmoded, second-hand critical tradition. Shakespeare studies have progressed in the past few decades and, at elite institutions, we can assume that students are taught from the latest advances in the field. Booth does not address this difference between the Shakespeare taught at elite institutions and the Shakespeare taught at places like "Podunk U" (a term I recently heard a Denverite describe Colorado State, Pueblo). I do not fault Booth in this; it's an honest limitation of his argument. The difference that Booth does address is between the high school Shakespeare and the university Shakespeare. Even though he uses the pronoun "we" throughout his essay, he faults high school teachers for the "benign lie" more directly than he does teachers in universities, complementing that they have greater power over "the intellectual life of the country."[11] For Booth, the problem begins in high school where it is deeply entrenched in the social and intellectual lives of our children. If students are primarily disserved by a high-school pedagogy based on a lie, which can be, to a certain extent, ameliorated by a university pedagogy based on first-rate scholarship, how much worse are students served when the Shakespeare of "Podunk U" replicates the lies of the high school? In this case, working-class students are doubly disserved; the doubling of the lies at the secondary and university levels deal them a blow that is doubly "intellectually lethal."

In many ways, the most beneficial pedagogies have their basis not just in an honest presentation of how the Shakespearean text does or does not relate to the people and times four hundred years in the future, but just as importantly, they present that text with a good deal of its alienating features intact. Booth's lethal lies are, in large measure, ways to smooth over alienating features of the early modern text. To be sure, student texts attempt to smooth over features of original texts that would just create confusion in students: spelling and punctuation are modernized; footnotes provide definitions of words and helpful context; and so on. But students, especially those who have been underserved in their educations, can still get lost in the incomprehensible English of Shakespeare, even when the text has been edited and modernized. Still, getting lost can benefit students, especially the working-class students, just as long as we, the professors, embrace the confusion that makes a student feel lost, just as long as we let them know they will get lost, prepare them for getting lost, and help them navigate the alien terrain once they are there. We should help the student "make sense" of the text, teaching them points in the plot, allusions, context, definitions of words. But we should allow, we should highlight, aspects of the text that do not make sense to them. Making the texts of Shakespeare easily accessible for working-class, isolated students in Pueblo would mean that we take a text that is different from their day-to-day environment, that is ideologically different, and, in a multitude of ways, we make that text ideologically similar. Confronting dissimilarity, by contrast, especially ideological dissimilarity, is one of the hallmarks of humanist education. When we make things easier for working-class students, we reduce the quality of their education.

Forty years ago, in *The Future of Humanities*, Walter Kaufmann argued that this introduction of the shockingly dissimilar is one of the chief values of humanistic education. But in order to introduce the dissimilar ideology, the humanities professor cannot take the easy road, cannot lecture students on some kind of magical connection between a four-hundred-year-old play and their life and times in southern Colorado. Kaufmann imagined that humanities professors need to teach their students to read better. "Reading is the core of the humanities," Kaufmann argued and furthermore claimed that "most students never learn to read well."[12] Kaufmann described four kinds of reading: exegetical, dogmatic, agnostic, dialectical—only the last of these did he believe was intellectually helpful. The first kind of unhelpful reading, "exegetical," is the kind that many professors of Shakespeare teach their students. When a person reads exegetically, they endow a "text with authority, then read [their] own ideas into it"; in return, the reader gets the ideas back, unchanged, with the exception that their ideas are now "endowed with authority."[13] The second kind of reading, "dogmatic," occurs when the reader comes to a text believing it to be opposed to their own notions of authoritative truth, and, as a consequence, they never see the text as anything more than objectionable. A person who reads dogmatically "refuses to see what is distinctive in the text and could not just as well be found at home."[14] The third kind of reading, "agnostic," occurs when the reader doesn't much care about authority or truth at all but still finds a way to avoid dissimilarity. To read agnostically is to pay attention to something small—a detail, a section, grammar, etymology—so as to avoid encountering anything that doesn't accord with one's own ideology. "The author is spirited away" by such detailed focus, Kaufmann says of reading agnostically, and "the encounter with a challenging You is avoided."[15]

Each in their own way, all of these three ways of reading allow the reader to avoid an encounter with what is dissimilar, what is alienating in the text. Reading in these ways is thus like the worst kind of tourism, where the traveler sees the unfamiliar culture or country only through the window of a bus and through guided walks in tourist districts and visits to their sanitized restaurants. Anything objectionable or offensive (and, often, most interesting) remains behind the physical buffer of the travel industry. With exegetical, dogmatic, and agnostic reading, ideas that are challenging or different remain behind an ideological buffer.

Kaufmann calls his fourth kind of reading "dialectical." The point of reading in this way is to facilitate an encounter with a "challenging You" and the "culture shock" this kind of encounter predicts:

> Far from trying to avoid culture shock, dialectical readers look for it. They enlist the aid of the text in an effort to examine their own life, faith, and values.... The dialectical reader seeks vantage points outside the various consensuses by which he has been conditioned. The text is to help him to liberate himself. The text is an aid to autoemancipation.[16]

In order for a text to provide this kind of shock, that text must be challenging, difficult, different, even objectionable. Alienated from each other, the text and the reader form a relationship of antithetical pairs. For Kaufmann, this is an entirely Hegelian encounter, for "feeling offended or shocked," readers articulate their own ideologically familiar position and do so specifically against the position held by the alienating text. On some level, readers recognize the difference, the existential debt, their own position owes this "challenging You" of the alienating text. In this dialectical encounter, this back-and-forth between opposing positions, an *aufheben* is achieved when "the reader's previous point of view is transcended and his level of consciousness raised."[17] Kaufmann claims that this kind of consciousness-raising can be achieved by other means: travel, art, theater—and this is where students in Pueblo come in. Students in Pueblo have little access to travel or these other elite arts. Yes, of course, they have a local museum and local theater, but nothing of the quality and quantity that an elite student has access to, nothing that, I imagine, would satisfy Kaufmann. Their travel is either entirely localized, or the kind of affordable and sanitized travel offered by the tourism industry. What they do have access to is texts, which, if their professors resist the temptation to make less alienating, can provide this best kind of education, the kind of education that more and more only affluent students enjoy.

When we teach a text such as the Shakespearean one in the student's own terms, when we seek to make the text more accommodating, we dilute its educational power. One example of this kind of dilution can be found in the ways we teach *Richard II*, especially with regard to its homoerotic elements. When student editions of the play discuss king Richard's relationship to his favorites in terms of sexuality, they tend to use the word "homosexuality." But as specialists recognize, homosexuality, as we understand the term, did not exist for Shakespeare or his time. Indeed, the term itself, "homosexual," did not exist until the late nineteenth century. In Shakespeare's time, there was no concept of a personal identification based on the gender of one's sexual partners; there was no discrete term for a person who preferred having sex with others whose genitals looked, more or less, like their own. When homoerotic activities were spoken of, such references were usually embedded in seditious behavior of some kind. Otherwise, as Jonathan Goldberg puts it, "the Renaissance does not distinguish two forms of sexuality as if they were totally distinct."[18] In other words, during Shakespeare's time, to think of sexuality in terms of heteronormativity made no sense.

But when students consult their edition of *Richard II*, editors tend to speak of the pre-modern sexuality as if it were modern sexuality, with all of its assumptions about identity, morality, and even DNA. When Bolingbroke accuses Bushy and Green of disrupting "the possession of a royal bed" and "stain[ing] the beauty of a fair queen's cheeks" with their "sinful hours" and "foul wrongs",[19] students might assume that the "sin" here is homosexuality. Standard editions of the play do not help matters, most of which simply echo modern assumption by calling the relationships between Richard and his favorites "homosexual" and offering no alternative explanation of early modern sexual ideologies. Some editors go further. Charles Forker, for instance, claims rather defensively that the "implication of homosexual attachments between Richard and his flatterers… has no historical validity," as if "historical validity" is something Shakespeare seems interested in. Moreover, Forker claims that Shakespeare did not intend any sort of homoeroticism, because such an idea "disturbingly contradicts the impression of devoted fidelity between the king and his consort."[20] I would be disturbed if Shakespeare had drawn relationships between these characters in ways that lacked complexity, lacked of contradiction. David Bevington, in another example, calls Bolingbroke's words, "homophobic slurs."[21] And while the phrase gestures toward a defense of homosexuality against its modern detractors, the phrase nevertheless introduces both homosexuality and homophobia into a world where they did not exist. By translating early modern sexuality into modern terms, editors modernize the text down to level of specific, single words, and in doing so they make it easier to digest.

When we teach students to recognize the historically accurate conceptions of sexuality, we are not only being scholarly; we are requiring them to encounter a dissimilarity that is probably uncomfortable, and perhaps even shocking. Such an encounter asks students to define their own understanding of same-sex desire and to reconcile their own commonsense understandings with the ideological constructions many centuries in the past. As it concerns commonsense understandings, my students in Pueblo tend to hold what often counts for as "progressive" views on sexual preference: a "gay gene" or some other situation in which people are born with a predetermined sexual preference. In the words of Lady Gaga, homosexuals are "born this way." In the ideological economy of Pueblo, this "progressive" view is in fact progressive because it stands opposed to a religiously conservative view in which people make conscious choices about sexual partners and those choices account for intentional transgressions against the "natural" order and the will of God. But what might happen to such a progressive view when it encounters different ideological constructions of homoerotic desire, constructions that escape the ideological binary of mainstream American thought? One possibility would be that the progressive idea of a "gay gene" would be revealed to be terribly fundamentalist in its own right.

Of course, if Shakespeare and the people of his time lived their lives outside of these dispositions our students assume to be natural and inescapable, and if our students, through a kind of literary culture shock, are made to treat those dissimilarities seriously and not avoid Kaufmann's "challenging You," some of their least-challenged assumptions may undergo a beneficial transformation. I can hardly imagine a better lesson in critical thinking, especially for students who are geographically bound, and thus ideologically bound, to the alienated place of Pueblo, Colorado—a lesson that shows that even the dearest and most fundamental ideas of a culture are themselves bound by time and place. Those fundamental ideas provide assumptions on the level of vocabulary, misinforming students of what constitutes, in the case of Bolingbroke's indictment of Richard's favorites, "sinful hours" and "foul wrongs." Of course, it only makes sense for a modern, American reader to assume that the "sin" and the "foul" would be gay sex, but the better-informed reading (the one that can create a culture shock) reveals that for Shakespeare's time, the "sin" and the "foul" was keeping Richard from his queen, irrespective of homoerotic activities. On the campus of a university whose students are largely working class, one hears an incessant refrain that our teaching should bring the subject to the student. My argument has been that we cannot help our students encounter these challenging Yous if we cannot see the difference between alienations that have a harmful effect and an alienation that has a beneficial effect. Sometimes we need to bring the student to the subject—a subject whose alienating features remain intact. Without these features, students cannot benefit from the culture shock that a four-hundred year-old text can have on a student who may never have the opportunity to experience culture shock in any other way.

None of my perspectives in this essay are an easy sell—not to working-class Puebloans, not to elites in northern Colorado, not to the good people who teach the underserved in Pueblo and in places like Pueblo. For the working class and the elites, my claims strike at an ethos that each group imagines both distinctive and good. As Pierre Bourdieu taught us, while such virtues arise unmotivated out of the conditions within which social groups develop, members are encouraged to "love the inevitable" and to embrace an ethos that these conditions, these inevitabilities, restrict and produce.[22] It is perfectly understandable then that the people of Pueblo might not be happy to hear that their pride in being more "real" than the citizens of Denver, or being closer to an uncorrupted and natural way of life than even the hippies in Boulder, not only keeps them isolated but keeps them deprived of the benefits of elite culture. It is understandable, as well, that elites might not warm to the suggestion that they benefit from class differences in which working-class leanness functions to particularize their elite abundance. That is to say, the deprivations of one community are constitutively related to the advantages of others. Even though my message may not be entirely welcome, that is my job as a scholar and a critic: to give utterance to uncomfortable positions so that we might do something about the second-class nature of our students' education.

Those of us who serve underserved demographics but who have elite educations of our own navigate a complicated social terrain. We were trained to be scholars at elite institutions, trained to give ourselves over to the life of the mind and to produce writing that aims for nothing more than limited scholarly argumentation. Once we received our elite degrees, however, in order to find jobs, we moved to whatever university would have us; we ended up working and living in places that chose us, not where we wished to live. My own case was different: it wasn't just happenstance that brought me to Pueblo, Colorado. The class markers that I will never be able to mask or shake—my diction, my crooked teeth, my complete lack of subtlety and inability to spell correctly—presented me as someone who would be at home among working-class students. The class markers were correct: I *get* my students in ways that escape many of my colleagues. When students visit my office, they see two framed diplomas, one is for a PhD from the University of Texas at Austin, the other is for a GED from the Texas Education Agency. I want them to see that you can begin from humble origins and, even without a high-school degree, receive the highest degree available from an elite institution.

For some new faculty in Pueblo, leaving behind the ethos of a research institution is a relief: they never really accepted the values of an active profession in the humanities. Like a prisoner who is "gay for the stay," they "put on" those values until they got their PhDs, and once they settled into their tenure-track job beyond the research university, they focus on teaching the classes and doing service and administrative work. Not me. As much as I am devoted to these students who have backgrounds and hardships much like my own, when I was earning my PhD, I fully bought into the ethos of the professorial class. I learned to "love the inevitable," as Bourdieu has put it—and I still love it, even though I know I have no choice in the matter. People like me stand astride two worlds, the working class and the elite, and we are not comfortable in either. To many of our colleagues at research universities, we are not particularly scholarly. Despite the fact that we have active intellectual lives, we rarely produce monographs and our work is not often recognized. To many of our colleagues at non-elite universities, our commitment to scholarly pursuits stands in a direct and harmful relation to our commitment to our students. As a chancellor of the Colorado State University system commented in 2014, scholarly commitment at my university is "an unproductive burden on students."[23]

This outside–insider perspective of mine is, I believe, beneficial to my students. They too are in a liminal position: at once a member of their working-class community and receiving what counts, for many of them, an elite education. Kaufmann's dialectical reading should enable them to navigate these polarities, synthesizing them so that they are not, in the end, polarities at all. When students have learned how to navigate alienating texts and cultures they should, moreover, be in a position to recognize their own dialectical relation to elite cultures from Boulder, Colorado to Cambridge, Massachusetts. I often hear a dictate that professors at institutions like Colorado State, Pueblo should "meet students where they are" in order to engage them in one or another academic subject. If we wish that they learn as much as possible in our classes, if we wish that they receive the best education possible, our goal should not simply be to "meet" them or "relate" to them or even "inspire" them in the model of evangelical Christianity. We should alienate them as well.

Acknowledgements For assistance in the writing of the essay, the author would like to thank Don Geiss, Rodney Herring, and the editors of this collection.

Notes

1. Eric Schlosser, *Fast Food Nation: The Dark Side of the All-American Meal* (Boston and New York: Houghton Mifflin and Harcourt, 2001), 91.
2. Jon Favreau, Dan Pfeiffer, Jon Lovett, and Tommy Vietor, "A Government Eclipse," *Pod Save America (podcast)*, February 9, 2018: https://crooked.com/podcast/government-eclipse-livedenver/.
3. Julie Turkewitz, "A Surge of Violence in a City of Gangs," *The New York Times*, April 8, 2016.

4. Jonathan Martin, "Freire vs. Marx: The Tension Between Liberating Pedagogy and Student Alienation," *Discourse of Sociological Practice* 6, no. 2 (2004): 34.
5. Ibid., 34.
6. In the lead essay in the collection, *Critical Pedagogy: Where are We Now?* Joe L. Kincheloe describes the need for critical pedagogy to provide "alternatives to the alienation of the individual." Kincheloe begins with an unsurprising definition of alienation ("individuals in contemporary society experience social reality mainly as a world of consumerism and not as the possibility of human relations") but then goes on to describe alienation from information, alienation from institutions, and "a form of 'second-degree alienation,' a state that is unconscious of the existence of alienation" (37).
7. Mark Z. Barabak, "Voters in This Democratic Part of Colorado Backed Trump. After 100 Days, They Have No Regrets," *Los Angeles Times,* April 27, 2017. Accessed December 14, 2018: http://fw.to/oouxFNH.
8. Alan Sinfield, *Faultlines: Cultural Materialism and the Politics of Dissident Reading* (Berkeley: University of California Press, 1992), 160.
9. Stephen Booth, "The Function of Criticism at the Present Time and All Others," *Shakespeare Quarterly* 41, no. 2 (1990): 266.
10. Ibid., 268. Booth might have something interesting to say about the leadership of the country now, over a quarter of a century after his essay was first published.
11. Ibid., 265–266.
12. Walter Kauffmann, *The Future of Humanities: Teaching Art, Religion, Philosophy, Literature, and History* (New Brunswick: Transaction Publishers, 1995), 47.
13. Ibid., 48.
14. Ibid., 57.
15. Ibid., 58.
16. Ibid., 61.
17. Ibid., 63.
18. Jonathan Goldberg, *Sodometries: Renaissance Texts, Modern Sexualities* (Stanford: Stanford University Press, 1992), 22.
19. William Shakespeare, *King Richard II*, ed. Charles R. Forker (New York: Bloomsbury, 2002), 3.1.13, 9, 14–15.
20. Charles Forker, ed., *King Richard II* (London: Bloomsbury, 2002), 310.
21. David Bevington, *The Complete Works of Shakespeare*, 5th ed. (New York: Longman, 2003), 743.
22. Pierre Bourdieu, *Outline of a Theory of Practice*, trans. Richard Nice (Cambridge: Cambridge University Press, 1977), 77.

23. Jonathan Rees, “Higher Education Is Not Available à la Carte,” *More or Less Bunk* (blog). Accessed December 14, 2018: https://moreorless-bunk.wordpress.com/2014/02/24/higher-education-is-not-available-a-la-carte.

The Whip Hand: Elite Class Formation in Ascham's *The Schoolmaster*, Shakespeare's *Love's Labour's Lost*, and the Present Academy

Daniel Bender

Class Lines: Do Not Cross

In his Preface to *The Schoolmaster*, Ascham explains that the Queen's advisors have just received alarming news. The whip hand of an Eton schoolmaster has created an outcome averse to kind-hearted humanists: "I have strange news brought me, saith Master Secretary, this morning that diverse scholars of Eton be run away from the school for fear of beating."[1] The "diverse" schoolboys who escaped from Eton receive official sympathy, but they had engaged in cross-class antics, alarming enough to reach the ears of Elizabeth's chief councilor, Robert Cecil, "this morning." Although training to be future elites in Tudor England's monarchic-republic, Latin school boys had turned their backs on Eton and fled into the extramural world of Tudor commoners. It is more than a little likely that they found themselves amidst the laboring classes—a yeoman here, a tanner there, a few day laborers further down the road. Food and shelter would have to come from a charitable

D. Bender (✉)
Pace University, Pleasantville, NY, USA

S. O'Dair and T. Francisco (eds.), *Shakespeare and the 99%*,
https://doi.org/10.1007/978-3-030-03883-0_4

commoner. This cross-class association triggered a recurrent nightmare among Tudor elites that the doctrine of the social orders was intended to dispel.[2] Would the boys feel some sympathy for, or worse, form some affiliation with, sweaty but amiable commoners? Would a cross-class *entente* weaken their loyalty to Latin-speaking peers and the Eton High Master himself? Ascham does not address the class implications of Latin schoolboys mixing with commoners, but the "strange news" delivered first thing in the morning suggests that the sociological implications of the escape from Eton were too disturbing for dinner-time discussion. As Aristotle explained in *The Politics*, "a state in which many poor men will be excluded from office is full of enemies."[3]

This essay will describe two educational systems separated chronologically by four centuries but connected by a matching ideology. Tudor Latin schools did not advertise their allegiance to elite class formation, nor did they acknowledge the institutional power relations of the kind allegorically encoded in the act of a schoolmaster whipping a subordinate. On the contrary, the Tudor Latin school operated under the banner of benign goals: instilling moral virtues, teaching the devices of public oratory, welcoming the fresh air of open debate. Elite commitment to class polarization could be made discursively invisible by filling readers' minds with blandly universalist statements about the virtues of humans as a species. Despite the historical cleavage of four centuries, I will argue, the current academy prefers to proceed as if social class division is not reproduced by academic institutions, despite convincing descriptions of the current academy's class bias delineated by Sharon O'Dair and others.[4] Of course, academic humanists, regardless of their critical allegiance, are not called by the early modern title of schoolmasters. As I argue in this essay, however, the early modern master-apprentice relation is encoded in student-professor relations of the twenty-first-century academy. It is not that Shakespeare studies or other fields of humanist study give special place to Caesar or Cicero or the Greco-Roman empires of antiquity. No journals or books that I know of give pride of place to an oligarchic or elite culture. On the contrary gender and racial equality and the ethics of diversity reflect an orientation very different from early modern England. What connects the early modern past to the present is the absence of concern for class inequality where "class"—a vexed and unwelcome term—describes a broad differentiation between administrative/expert status and rank-and-file labor. While the terms just offered can be quickly challenged, I offer a concrete specification of rank-and-file: college students who are required to take courses in literature, including the famous Bard, and who are dependent on the expert knowledge of professors if they are to claim any competence in literary study. The current academy exercises the whip hand of intellectual dominance through this ethic of expertise. Just as Navarre and his scholars will discover things "hid and barred" from common sense[5]—a task that rank-and-file folks like Costard and Jaquenetta could not attempt, given their illiteracy—so college students are said to lack the hermeneutic tools to explore the work of art. Empty bowls of hermeneutic protocol, students are in need of a training that will allow them to become astute readers. This structurally defined inadequacy reanimates the schoolmaster-servile student relation.[6]

If this indictment of the current academy seems harsh, I offer as compensation a proposal that may rescue Shakespeare studies from its perceived difficulty among college students. College students were never included in the fabled public sphere theorized by Jürgen Habermas, but his theorization has received a much-needed populist upgrade in Michael Warner's *Publics and Counterpublics*. Warner argues that a public sphere can be created by an act of collective volition and vocalization. A group decides that it has the right to organize and voice its concerns and thus materializes as a counterpublic in the eyes of existing publics.[7] To put the proposal in simpler terms: students might embrace literary study if the work of art could be opened to their life experiences, and then fuel the drive toward a publicity that is typically denied by literary study. One example of a sub-altern public created *sui generis* and specifically by students will illustrate students' desire to become a working counterpublic. On February 14, 2018, Parkland High students lived through a mass shooting with fatalities and multiple injuries. Within a week, these high school students had organized rallies and demonstrations; they also became lobbyists, making their way en masse to offices of the Florida State Legislature. Warner's theorization of sub-altern publics received nearly instantaneous validation. While my proposal admittedly pushes back against the master-inflected persona of the academic specialist, it represents one possible remedy to the class divide that separates elite academy from the class of sub-altern known as college students, who typically graduate and take jobs that have little use for elite cultural capital, including Shakespeare.

It may not be comforting to Shakespeareans to read an essay that calls for a reconstructed Shakespearean pedagogy. I can prime that receptivity if I make an effective case that the academy—from Ascham to Shakespeare to the current twenty-first-century incarnation—suffers from not seeing "the dangers of academic specialization."[8] The danger is that the drastic difference in status—the learned professor, the inexperienced student—allegorizes what is essentially a form of class domination. To understand the cause of this active-passive relation encoded in the current academy, we need to look to formative influences from the past. Ascham's *The Schoolmaster* is the clearest illustration of humanist education committed to elite class formation. His handling of the Eton runaways demonstrates, however, why social class is best avoided as a subject: Ascham prefers to obscure the power relations being modeled by the Tudor Latin school. He does this by sounding the all-inclusive ideology of Christianity. Ascham explains that the good master will "monish" the student "gently" so that the schoolboy will go forward in "both love and hope of learning" (20). In a culture that designated masters as figures of absolute authority, however, power-sharing and collective decision-making are out of the question. Pierre Bourdieu and Jean-Claude Passeron's famously paranoid study of education as reproduction of class division held that schools, seeking a good reputation in the public sphere, disguise their social reproductive functioning: "The most hidden and most specific function of the educational system" consists in "masking…the structures of class relations."[9] Ascham's dinner-table condemnation of whipping suggests his allegiance to a classless state of charity towards all. The idea is obscured, however, when *The Schoolmaster* identifies elite behavior as the ticket to economic and social privilege. By hiding the drastic differences in status encoded in "master-student," Ascham illustrates Bourdieu and Passeron's assertion that educational systems mask power relations.

Ascham's favorite classical authors, Cicero and Caesar, were arch-representatives of class hegemony and triumphalist policies in general. For Cicero, a defender of large-holding land owners and a detractor of plebian assemblies, eloquence could be a weapon to keep plebeians from crossing the line marked *equites* or elite political class. Cicero greeted legislation that favored land restoration to dispossessed farmers with outrage; he became the sworn enemy of the elites known as *populares* who supported land restoration.[10] Ascham's other favored author, Caesar, epitomizes the glamor of the military-political ruling class. As a commander of legions, Caesar feeds humanist fascination with command over others, with others in this case being compliant Roman legions, which wheel and heel at his command. But this fascination with command, the pleasure of the master, is kept implicit, something for the discerning reader to decipher. Masking relations of force celebrated in Caesar, Ascham waxes poetic about Caesar's limpid prose style!

Readers who make their way into the depths of the text, however, discover a different curriculum, a rhetorically-mediated method of domination where castigating idioms—scorn, mocks, censure, expressions of contempt—are part of the working symbolic capital of the Latin school graduate. A preliminary example will suggest how this hidden curriculum in elite ethos works. Underperformers are "small fruit" that will "fall and rot" while other students will be "fair blossoms" of eloquence and civic efficacy (26). Ascham uses the elite class of Latin schoolboys to separate high and low performers. In so doing, he is modeling an allegory of cross-class separation and subordination. Commoners who protested official policy—as they did in the cataclysmic class war of 1549 known as Kett's Rebellion—were at first controlled by rhetorical means. Accusations of ingratitude, shaming epithets, moral contempt—all the idioms of castigation—were the first defense of Norfolk-area Lords in dispersing the large and growing assembly of armed commoners.[11] None of the published writings that followed England's class war worried about castigating and humiliating commoners. On the contrary, talking down to agitated commoners was an accepted means of restoring order so that elites could resume their rule and commoners their labors. In *Love's Labour's Lost*, four aristocratic males and four royal women model strikingly similar class-dominant behavior. And like his predecessor Ascham, Shakespeare masks the potentially offensive portrayal of class privilege. In the mythos of spring, the young aristocrats will take up self-renewal and self-improvement, while the locals who perform in a Pageant and will be taunted, try to recover their dignity. This dramaturgic resolution led to C. L. Barber's influential description of the comedy as "festive." Jaquenetta, Costard, and the locals who perform for the royals are simply omitted in Barber's account. In the closing celebratory Songs, laborers appear in a lyric palimpsest where, disembodied and voiceless, they carry logs, transport milk, and stir kitchen kettles.[12] Translating *Love's Labour's Lost*'s class dynamic to the current academy, I would argue that the contemporary version of Tom, Dick, and Joan are college students in literature classrooms.

If I turn from Ascham's dominance-modeling curriculum in the 1560s to public education in America now, I find dominant-submissive functions operating at full tilt. In his high school days, my son Tom was bright and energetic, except after a long, depressing day of school. "It's one mandatory class after another and constant tests on subjects you've never chosen, and it goes on and on. It's a nightmare, Dad. Can you do something about?" I sat still, a teacher-statue, and said very little. Some years later, hungry for reading outside of early modern studies and its methodology wars, I came across a documentary that forecasts mega-slums as the largest demographic development in the world. Mike Davis's *Planet of Slums* describes a tragic version of Marx's oppressed proletariat: one class has homes and beds and drinks clean water; another class sleeps in shipping containers and drinks contaminated water. My thoughts returned to my son Tom, whose education had been clearly stunted by a curriculum that mandated what subjects he would take; the power that underwrote the high school curriculum was held closely by the Connecticut Department of Education. Tom had no say in determining what subjects counted as worthy of study or in determining how to study them or indicate his understanding of them. Davis' description of urban wastelands presents a far more tragic condition, but the problem of evacuated agency is the same. The slum-dweller may work very hard but her labor is contingent and marginal; the slum economy does not permit the accumulation of capital that would lift the laborer from after-market trader to small producer. Neither the slum dweller nor the depressed high schooler possess agency reckoned as the capacity to improve their conditions according to their own lights and labor. As a literature professor, trained in archival research and textual interpretation, I had my own agency problem: I was unpracticed in the social protocols of advocacy. What was I supposed to do about my son's educational despair? Or the emergence of mega-slums that are the hidden by-products of capitalist success?[13]

Ruminating on class difference before teaching my class on *Hamlet*, and wondering what to make of Shakespeare's dramaturgic commitment to Danish elites inhabiting a castle, I heard breaking news about Elsinore-like corruption in the state of New York, where I teach. In the wake of reported corruption in high-places in the New York legislature, Governor Andrew Cuomo had invoked the Moreland Act, which authorized investigation of legislators and, possibly, scrutiny of their business contacts and supplementary income. Thinking at once to provide academic study of *Hamlet* and to create a writing opportunity where my students would enter a public sphere foreclosed by pure academic method, I asked my students to do something about official corruption. Faster than you can say working for the 99 percent—or Hamlet, Claudius, and

Gertrude—my students wrote letters to ethics commissioners and state legislators that formulated anti-corruption measures and methods more effective than the current ones. Low-capitalized college students were proposing policy; highly-capitalized political elites were expected to listen. My Shakespeare class had traded sociopolitical places!

I describe this literature-initiated civic activism and my students' quickened responses to suggest that the standing paradigm of Shakespeare studies—teacher as expert, student as novitiate—is superannuated. In *The Limits of Critique*, Rita Felski writes that literature faces "a legitimation crisis." Specifically, a "sadly depleted language of value" leaves students unmoved by literary experience, leading Felski to wonder, "Why should they care?"[14] Felski's perception that students are for the most part alienated from literature study is clearly right. The work of art does not invite *their* initiative or *their* goal-setting; on the contrary, the academic study of the chosen text calls for the discipline of self-subordination. For what Felski does not address is the problem of specialized methodology and expertise. Students are expected to forsake their own interests and their own voices, in order to learn the interpretive protocols of the master-exegete. It matters little, therefore, whether students in a Shakespeare classroom are inducted into one school of literary analysis or another. Though Felski finds fault with the historicist model that purportedly is driven by the need to "expose hidden truths…that others fail to see," her alternative only substitutes one master-apprentice model for another.[15] Both methods require submission to readings legitimated by institutional approval, thereby marginalizing student agency and any public presence that might follow from an active engagement with the material issues of the text. The Marxist historian Georg Lukács observed that the laboring classes often suffer "supine fatalism" when faced with the intransigence of their employers; a similar fatalism may be read into student enrollment in mandatory, "breadth-requirement" literature classes.[16] Elitism in the current humanist academy is no historical accident.

A quick survey of Tudor Latin school scholarship adumbrates the current academy's identification with elite social roles. T. W. Baldwin's mid-twentieth century study, *Shakespeare's Small Latine and Lesse Greek*, greeted the Latin school curriculum as the rediscovered treasure of antiquity's elite.[17] Rebecca Bushnell's *Culture of Teaching: Early Modern Humanism in Theory and Practice* gives warm consideration to humanists as gardeners who nurture adolescent males in the benign soil of language arts.[18] Lynn Enterline's *Shakespeare's Schoolroom: Rhetoric, Discipline, and Emotion* is alert to dominant-subordinate relations in terms of gender, but Enterline interprets whipping along original party lines; a master who whipped a misbehaving student was "inculcating obedience" and helping the boy's psychosocial development as a "self-censoring subject."[19] Freyja Cox-Jensen's *Reading the Roman Republic in Early Modern England* at least mentions class bias and polarization in passing. Tudor education produced a "political class to serve the crown," but this insight is buried under the historiographic orthodoxy that Tudor Latin schools were about the "acquisition of virtue."[20] In *The Bonds of Love*, Jessica Benjamin makes the case that social relations are always entangled in power relations, an insight that helps to evaluate historiographies of Tudor education. In giving elite education credit for producing efficacious agents of the Tudor polity while leaving the Tudor underclass out of its historiography, scholars of the Tudor school unwittingly reproduce the master-servant dynamic that is perhaps the most chilling psychoanalytic finding in *The Bonds of Love*: "… my desire and agency can find no outlet, except in the form of obedience."[21] Whether we look at the early modern academy as represented by Ascham or at Shakespeare's hypothetical academe or at the current academy, we find the same result regarding public effect: If the humanist academy is engaged in territorial head-butting and writes in an arcane, highly specialized language, what civic value is possibly being provided? I have already quoted Bourdieu and Passeron's insight that academic institutions function as sorting systems of social class; they "confer on the privileged the supreme privilege of not seeing themselves as privileged."[22] For our students—almost all of them, anyway—worried by a deteriorating globe and growing economic uncertainties about jobs, the seductive power of ascending to a privileged class is less than plausible. If a literature curriculum added a civic component, whereby students are invited to mobilize as a counterpublic, Felski's findings of despair and Benjamin's diagnosis of demoralization might be lifted.

In his review of Joseph North's *Literary History: A Concise Political History*, Bruce Robbins flirts with pedagogic innovation of this kind. Might the humanist academy concern itself with advocacy or at least interest in the life world of the 99 percent? Robbins shakes the dust from what is a militant model of civic activism, one that humanities scholars find frightening: "However you feel about activism, there is no imaginable dispensation under which literature departments would train students in leafleting or organizing demonstrations."[23] Granted, scholars are not street fighters. But activism need not follow this one extreme mode. As Daniel Vitkus also argues in this volume, a pedagogy of transhistorical engagement—corruption in Elsinore matched to corruption in the New York State Legislature—represents a restrained, discursively-mediated path to public agency among the least agential beings in our educational system. Robbins is not the only one thinking of literature breaking out into a public sphere of influence. North himself imagines at one point in his book an "interventionist" critical approach, powered by "collective" efforts.[24] How would literary criticism be interventionist? No practical plans follow from the activist overture. Both Robbins and North articulate a language of civic engagement, but neither makes the big leap: planning extramural applications for intramural literary study. Roger Ascham's *The Schoolmaster* can help us to understand why.

Castigating Commoners: Royal Precedents to *The Schoolmaster*

As a student at Cambridge University, Ascham knew that a popular uprising, the so-called Pilgrimage of Grace, had been suppressed by Crown soldiers and by the rhetorical weapon of invective. Henry VIII's "Answer to the Rebels in Lincolnshire" is perhaps the most lurid model of the genre. With its pose of direct address, as if a King were conversationally present, the "Answer" is a communicational assault that threatens to materialize into a military one. "We and our nobles," he tells the commoners mobilized in the cause of defending the old religion, "neither can nor will suffer this injury at your hands unrevenged." Henry denies that the commoners in Lincolnshire have the right to deliberate about matters of church policy and state intervention. "How presumptuous then are you, the rude commons of one shire" and "most brute and beastly" to "find fault with your Prince."[25] Once copied and read aloud, Henry's tongue-lashing could find force-multipliers in the form of Sheriffs and Mayors who could read aloud his Majesty's humiliation of commoners, perhaps at different times of the day. The "Answer to the Rebels" may represent the first wave of elite invective as a tool of mass control. As Jean Howard and Paul Strohm have argued, the tolerance for politically active commoners declined steadily as the Tudor century progressed.[26]

Ascham did not have royal prerogative to bash commoners into scared silence. As royal tutor he nevertheless needed to equip Latin schoolboys with the rhetorical tools for cross-class disciplinary dress-downs. Ascham also knew that speech animated by cross-class disciplinary motives of putting down or abashing a hostile audience had been the high-status skill set of his more approachable peers. In the 1550s, a decade before *The Schoolmaster*, Ascham had worked as Latin secretary to Richard Morrison, renowned for having penned *A Remedy for Sedition*, an official rebuke of commoners for lacking "True and Loyal Obeisance." Like his mentor, Morrison lays into the protesters' inflated sense of political significance and lack of deference as shameful deficiencies in their character. He explains, for example, that the commoners only protest ecclesiastical changes because they had "an abundancy of idleness" and lacked "honest crafts."[27] Thus the value of castigation or rhetorical abuse as a tool of cross-class management was confirmed by an illustrious humanist turned government agent.

Another of Ascham's colleagues, Cambridge scholar John Cheke, wrote a similar diatribe against commoners in the aftermath of Kett's Rebellion (1549). In that Rebellion, commoners had been scared and angered by enclosure of wastes and collectively held land. In this expansionist proto-capitalism that saw sheep herding as lucrative and farm leases as paltry, commoners faced predatory rent increases or "fines," which, quickly or in time, forced families out—and sheep pastures in.[28] Despite writing a petition that itemized twenty-nine requests for economic regulation and intervention against land-enclosing Lords, they were told to disperse. Refusing, they ended up occupying England's second largest city, Norwich, and soon after, suffered losses of up to three thousand people in open-field combat against the English cavalry. Cheke's contemptuous retrospection of these events, *The Hurt of Sedition*,[29] provided Ascham with a fresh mentoring in law-and-order rhetoric. As humanist defender of good order and godly obedience, Cheke seeks to humiliate, not conciliate. The East Anglian working class and small landholders who rebelled were "clowns" and "boyes." Once again, castigation is the chosen weapon to regulate the English lower classes.

The invectives of Henry VIII, Richard Morrison, and John Cheke would be familiar to a humanist scholar asked to be royal tutor to Princess Elizabeth. Although I have argued that class formation is usually kept invisible, masked by a generic language of virtue or eloquence that is supposedly classless, this does not mean that elites keep in check a penchant for castigating the English laboring class. Ascham, for example, tells his noble or would-be noble readers that it is not wise to accept the "common order in common schools" where rules of good Latin usage are "hardly learned" (13, 15). Or he identifies poetry as a pleasure reserved for those of powerful intellect and thus generically different from commoners and their appetite for carnal pleasures. The "worthy poets of Athens and Rome" were eager to "satisfy the judgment" of "one learned man" rather than please "the humor of a rude multitude"; this attitude, of course, is shared by Prince Hamlet. Even the Roman playwright Terence, a perennial favorite in the Tudor Latin school curriculum, is chastised for his moral laxity and crudity. Terence was a slave in a patrician Roman home, but eventually became a *liberti* (freed slave) and then, most troubling of all for a man like Ascham, taught himself the art of complex dramaturgy that rivaled his learned peers. It is nearly predictable that Ascham cannot control his anger at a class-trespasser and African immigrant Terentius Afer. Though Terence was prized for the satirical depiction of Roman sons seeking to evade controlling Roman fathers, Ascham regards him as a lascivious entertainer who depicts "the body of a naked person from the navel down" (143).

But the open antagonism toward non-elite groups is occasional; what I've presented is a distillation of cross-class contempt that does not represent Ascham's primary mode of writing about class. As I've suggested, Ascham prefers a safer, masked strategy to instill elite class identification. Rather than repeatedly castigate commoners, he divides a hypothetical class of all elite schoolboys into goats and sheep, low-performing and high-performing members of the Tudor humanist community. After describing a student who is only beginning to study Latin, Ascham then unleashes a serialized set of criticisms of the hapless schoolboy, who sinks to the bottom of his "class":

> Tully would have used such as word, not this; Tully would have placed this word here, not there, would have used this case, this number, this person, this degree, this gender; he would have used this mood, this tense, this tense, this simple rather than this compound, this adverb here. (15)

The premise that students should reproduce Cicero in antique original Latin is bizarre. It runs against humanist precepts that translation should honor present and past linguistic forms. Quintilian, the much-admired Roman theorist, studied by Tudor scholars, recommended that an original text be given an updated linguistic translation since there is "nothing harder" than to "produce an exact likeness."[30] A far more influential humanist in Ascham's time was Eramus, whose satire *Ciceronianus* mocked Ciceronian purists, precisely for the practice that Ascham seems to support: the exact reproduction of the long-deceased Roman orator. One cannot communicate to Christians in post-imperial Europe, Eramus explains, if one is expected to reproduce anachronistic speech, including eulogies to Jupiter Maximus and vestal virgins.[31] Why then does Ascham make a serial critique of the student for failing to produce pure Cicero?

The answer is that Ascham is working on the hidden curriculum of the Latin schools. As a model of the master, he needs to present a living picture of a powerful, domineering, authoritative male, a future oligarch or Tudor administrator. If I translate Ascham's serialized criticisms of a Tudor schoolboy into psychological modeling of social dominance and superiority it might read as follows: "Considering how many errors you have made, you need to double your efforts to please me." While the apparent context for Ascham's tongue-lashing involves a schoolmasterly concern for proper language usage, that context is merely expedient. Ascham needs some context, any context, in which to display the elite capacity for social control. The same feeling of a pretext rather than a context applies to Ascham's rant against young gentlemen of England: "It is your shame," Ascham explains, that "one maid should go beyond you all" in "… in excellency of learning" (66). Ascham does not mention that Princess Elizabeth had the benefit of tutors available day and night, so of course her language skills would likely exceed those of others. But unequal rates of leisure for study and translation are not the point; Ascham's "It is your shame" passage displays the dominance-generating power of blame, a tactic he repeats throughout the text: "The fault is in yourselves, ye noblemen's sons, and therefore ye deserve the greater blame that commonly the meaner men's children come to be the wisest counselors and greatest doers in the weighty affairs of the realm" (40). As Bourdieu and Passeron explained, a schoolmaster is a reproducible image, something that Latin schoolboys can reproduce by imitation. For this reason, teachers "constitute the most finished products of the system of reproduction."[32]

Ascham is so drawn to the ethos of social dominance that he gives his greatest allegiance not to the English Commonwealth but to the ancient Roman Empire. Roman mothers and fathers were "the best breeders and bringers up of the worthiest men" (60). Unsurprisingly, Ascham's curriculum places those two icons of sociopolitical dominance, Cicero and Caesar, at the top of its list. Also unsurprisingly, one source of Cicero's political power and moral greatness was his scorn for the popular assemblies: "Therefore, to say no more of this Greece, which has long been overthrown and crushed through the folly of its own counsels, that ancient country, which once flourished with riches, and power, and glory, fell owing to that one evil, the immoderate liberty and licentiousness of the popular assemblies."[33] Ascham is also excited by Caesar's *The Gallic Wars.* In an action-packed narrative of conquest after conquest, Caesar's text glorifies both elite command and the advantages of strict obedience.[34] The legions of the Roman army obliterate individual subjectivity for the sake of group fusion, an image that the eager-to-please Ascham could easily update in English class relations as imperial monarch revered by obedient commoners.

The ethos of dominance and its mediated forms of raillery, rebuke, and reviling does not stop with *The Schoolmaster*. Shakespeare will theatricalize as Christmas entertainment an academy where elites seek "fame" at first through academic study. Failing to become famous scholars, they decide to become socialized and realistic at the behest of four female royals. The "attainder of eternal shame" (1.1.162) that they experience through much of the comedy should be understood as educational and traditional. The young men learn to be elites through interclass experiences of shame and mockery. Once acculturated, they then engage in shaming and mockery across class boundaries by silencing commoners in their effort to perform the Pageant of the Nine Worthies. To track the migration of humanist-sponsored class antagonism from educational text to Shakespeare's court comedy, we need to revisit the so-called regeneration of Shakespeare's errant schoolboys in *Love's Labour's Lost.*

Love's Labour's Lost: Fear of a Plebeian Sphere

Costard is a local clown and occasional carrier of letters between elite men and women. When he enters the same sociopolitical space as the royals, he is allowed to speak. This is not, however, an instance of cross-class affability. For Costard's role in the plot carries on the Henrician attribution of animality; the "brute and beastly" Costard brags of sexual opportunism with Jaquenetta. "She will serve my turn" (1.1.291). True to Henry's scathing vision of commoners as lacking self-control, Costard is depicted as a law-breaker who deserves the lash of judicial correction. As he is led off stage, Costard treats his civic violation flippantly, expressing a recidivist hope that "affliction will smile again" (1.1.305). In a single scene, the courtly audience has learned the lesson of lower-class irresponsibility that Ascham had pushed on his elite readers: Lower-class men and women tend to focus on the navel downward. For that reason, they are inept participants in a public sphere where questions of education and cultural value are being debated.

Admittedly, Shakespeare blurs the boundaries of aristocratic and lower-class recklessness by having both lower-class and aristocrats deemed incompetent or bumbling in their approach to civic matters. Will Navarre scam the ladies of France out of the loan repayment that is the reason for their royal visit? No, he is held to account and delinquent payment made. Will the royal misogynists who housed the women in tents in the field apologize for their lack of hospitality? Since they don't, the women bring out the elite weaponry of merry mockery and witty epithet. The public shame inflicted by "tongues of mocking wenches" (5.2.256) parallels the punishment meted out to Costard. But there's a big difference. Costard was only punished once—and he returns to the stage with his jocularity intact. But for the aristocrats, shaming and the tongue-lashing are experienced regularly, much like the routines of a classroom. Far from presenting verbal aggression as an aberration, it is given the status of a hearty competition among peers: "…and praise we may afford / To any lady that subdues a lord" (4.1.1011). This regimen of interpersonal subduing is passed off as wicked good fun and elite high spiritness, but it a form of sociological training. Once the lords are acculturated to shaming and castigating, they unleash cross-class mockery.

The climax of class hostility in the play occurs in the "Pageant of the Nine Worthies" (5.2). As a humanist schoolmaster, Holofernes uses the classical legacy of the antique world and its heroic elites as material for an inspirational show. The familiar theory of imitation and emulation applies: By seeing powerful men bringing fame and prosperity to their nations, the courtly spectators will be inspired to similar deeds. Under the official rubric of courtly humanist entertainment, however, a threatening social dynamic is at work. Commoners are performing in a theatrically-created public sphere! The Pageant is, in effect, a conduit for lower-class participation in theatrical realities that are normally reserved for elites, a situation that cannot be allowed to stand. What happens is a cross-class beat-down.

Armado had claimed imaginative affiliation with Caesar ("I came, I saw, I conquered"); in the Pageant, he tries to impersonate the Greek warrior Hector. Activating the historically available idioms for silencing commoners, Berowne calls for a lemon to mask the smell of an unbathed actor; Longueville, showing aristocratic solidarity, calls for cloves to mask Armado's alleged body odor. Nathaniel, a curate who thus holds some influence in his local sphere—a village or town, which is outside of royal purview—is also humiliated when he attempts to speak in the aristocratic public sphere: As Alexander the Great, he was the world's commander, but Boyet refers to Nathaniel as offending his nose and Berowne shames Nathaniel further by saying that his conquering might is his body odor. The most sustained castigation, in the Ascham-manner of serialized criticism, is reserved for Holofernes. He is mocked seventeen times during his attempt to enact the famous general Judas Maccabaeus, so that the village schoolmaster and his sub-elite social position is made clear and the threatening entrance into elite culture (even though theatrical) is ended. Though Holofernes speaks Latin, his face is like "an old Roman coin, half seen" (5.2.606). And the maker of the Court Pageant, Holofernes, is further subdued by being told that his autonomous identity as humanist schoolmaster is determined by his superiors: "We have given thee faces" (5.2.614). The fact that Holofernes stumbles when exiting the stage adds a sharp reminder of his exile from the elite public sphere. Humiliated and mumbling a rebuke, which the elites ignore, he will not speak again. Finally, Jaquenetta is usually ignored in analysis of the Pageant scene, her absence from academic criticism adding a final undermining note to readings that see the Pageant as an extension of Christmas revelry. Described as pregnant and as having no assured partner, she is an image of animality. She embodies Tudor elite culture's standing charge that commoners, unable to regulate their behavior, need to be regulated. This depiction of the laboring class represents something more damaging than the "scoff power" that Lynn Magnusson attributes to the men's relentless disruptions of the "Pageant."[35]

The Future of Criticism: Creating a Counterpublic in the Literature Class

In *Love's Labour's Lost*, a theatrically-constituted working class is forced off the public stage so that their voices will not be heard. The present state of professional criticism is structured similarly, whereby expert professors ask students to reproduce methods of literary analysis, and thus provide intellectual labor that enriches the professorate. A new hybrid criticism, half exegesis and half civic intervention in the extramural world, would give students agency and a counterpublic identity, akin to one improvised by Parkland High students. Students allowed to cross the class divide structured in the elite academy would enter the public sphere.

The current literary academy, in scattered but nevertheless consistent iterations, recognizes its reduced status in college curriculae and indeed in higher education. We all know about falling numbers of majors, and I have already cited Felski's finding that college students seem not to care about *Beowulf* or Baudelaire. But this assessment of academic humanism's decline assumes that the problem is with a specific methodology. If literary criticism offers an alternative methodology, as Felski does, then presumably students will *want* to study Shakespeare or *Beowulf* or Baudelaire. Yet the alienation from academic humanism seems to go deeper: students understand that literature belongs to an expert or master class, attuned to literary traditions and with much time on the archival clock. Students are, by circumstance, necessarily and always dependent and incomplete versions of their expert elders: students in colleges and universities achieve a temporary but keen insight from the texts prized by the academy, but students remain, at best, reproducers of adult or master knowledge. In turn, students lose identity as agents of their own interests.

Nevertheless, there are hints that this master-student model is a problem specific to literary criticism. In his review of North, referred to above, Bruce Robbins observes that scholarship "gets off on interpreting the world." The language of erotic satisfaction seems to hint at a withdrawal, or possibly regret. The material world, in its whirling and tumultuous condition, leaves academic humanists cold. Humanist scholarship, Robbins writes, "can't be bothered to do anything non-scholarly to change it."[36] North expresses a similar anxiety about academic humanism's lack of interest in civic application. North hopes that we "imagine" a "new paradigm" for "active cultural intervention."[37] Felski, Robbins, and North share a common awareness that literary criticism is in need of disciplinary reconstruction. Like other colleagues, they recognize the insularity of our labors and the speciousness of our claims not to be.

While there are many paths to such reconstruction, a recent book that speaks to Robbins's interest in "changing the world" and North's interest in "intervention" is Doris Sommer's *The World of Art in the World: Civic Engagement and Public Humanities.*[38] Sommer argues that the work of art can be animated by re-enactments of conflict and meaning in the public eye. She then describes various public performances that move the work of art from its exegetical frame into the world of performance art. My own proposal for reconstructed literary study focuses on two areas for reform: Shakespeare's historical remoteness and the desirability of inviting students to form a counterpublic identity. These reforms can be achieved when students are given pedagogic space and permission to translate the Shakespearean text into civic contexts that most concern them. The goal is, as I mentioned above, a hybrid criticism, half exegesis and half civic intervention in the extramural world, a civic-oriented Shakespearean pedagogy.

Consider the problematic effects of mandatory curriculae, whether post-secondary or secondary, the kind that left my son Tom demoralized and depressed during high school. Here *Love's Labour's Lost* offers educational hope, in its oddly progressive insistence on what may be called pracademic learning. In his Prometheus Fire speech, Berowne argues that motivation to learn is fueled by uncertainties and unknowns, encountered in real-time social situations: "And where we are our learning likewise is" (4.3.320). Berowne's argument holds the seed of an alternative pedagogy for our times: "where we are our learning likewise is" argues inherently against mandatory curriculae, which, as one educational historian has argued, are masked strategies to instill "deference, docility, and support for capitalist institutions."[39] Recognizing the demotivating effect of mandatory learning, Sarah Fine has recently made a plea for "intellectual playfulness" in the high school curriculum—a proposal that would grant students some choice in their educational experience.[40]

In my own Shakespeare class, I invited students to write analytically on *Love's Labour's Lost* and its peculiar resolution. What should we make of the young royals' promised reformation? Will one year of introspection and self-discipline produce more socially responsive suitors, attentive to the immediacy of social experience ("Where we are")? But I also invited students to make the transhistorical and civic turn toward advocacy and reform. We had studied the financial ineptitude of Navarre and his cohort. The Princess, with her delegation, explains that the King of France had repaid a loan to Navarre's father; Navarre, having no record of such transactions, exemplifies a financially challenged adolescent, dependent on the financial expertise of elders. My writing prompt for civic outreach invited students to devise a high school course in financial literacy for Navarre's parallel demographic of high-schoolers, a group notably inexperienced in credit-card use and unfamiliar with such terms as principal, compound interest, default, and accelerated repayment. We had also studied Jaquenetta's troubling personal circumstance. Working-class and illiterate, Jaquenetta in Act 5 is discovered to be pregnant, with no reliable partner. Jaquenetta dramatizes the present-day problem of unplanned teen pregnancies. But rather than just claim the relevance of Jaquenetta to their lives, I invited students to take initiative in the cause of curriculum development—a pedagogical move that would give to my students the reformist powers reserved to the royal ladies. Specifically, I asked students to design a course that identifies the personal pressures and sociological indicators that result in an unplanned pregnancy.

Consider North's desire for "active interventions" in strategic terms. How might a professor facilitate such interventions in a Shakespeare classroom? In *As You Like It*, Duke Senior's praise of nature as a regenerative force in human relations—"books in brooks," "sermons in stones," and "good in everything"—has always delighted my students. The speech and its pastoral assumptions are ripe for presentist and activist work, given student familiarity with narratives of ecological degeneration. Most students recognize the implications of global warming and climate change, even if the most alarming effects have yet to register. An approach that interrogates pastoral conventions—especially as embodied in the Duke's glittering pastoralism—is fairly standard pedagogy. An unusual but agency-enhancing pedagogical move would ask students whether the social restoration that follows from communion with nature is possible today and to follow up that question with invitations to address environmental degradation: anti-fracking, alternatives to fossil fuel, the reduction of industrial meat production. In moving from analysis of *As You Like It* to advocacy for the environment, students gain the psychological boost of self-efficacy, a sense of determinative agency that the expert-amateur model, rooted in the whip hand of long ago, cannot offer.

In concluding this essay, I return to *Hamlet*, and the happy circumstance I described earlier, when I was teaching the play at the very moment official corruption was unearthed in New York state. My students were very familiar with the corruption of Elsinore, but they thought carefully and on their own when facing the question of official corruption in state politics. I explained that the Moreland Commission on Public Corruption investigated reports of kickbacks to New York state legislators; I added the galling detail that the Commission was shut down when the attorney general asked for legal clearance to examine the bank records of the state legislators. Realizing that something was rotten in the state of New York—and that their professor supports their voices as a legitimate counterpublic—my students became energized, motivated to have their voices heard. They wrote elected representatives with strategies to increase transparency, improve surveillance, and monitor intramural investigations where—echoes of Elsinore—one set of elites incestuously monitors another. Like the Parkland High students who formed an instantaneous counterpublic, my students took up the study of Shakespeare as the precursor text for the larger text of their life-world outside the walls of academe. If we design a humanist pedagogy where students engage in advocacy and activism guided by literary study, we may present a humanist academy congenial to their development and sustained labors. Relevance, it turns out, isn't personal. It is social.

Notes

1. References to Ascham's text are from *The Schoolmaster*, ed. Lawrence Ryan (Ithaca: Cornell University Press, 1967). The discussion of the Eton runaways begins on page 3 of Ascham's text proper. Subsequent references are to this edition and are cited parenthetically.
2. Tudor political theorist Thomas Smythe made the case for degrees or "orders" within society using the argument that societal harmony, like cosmic harmony, depends on including those capable of policy-formulation and excluding the vast uneducated populace, who lack the analytic and reasoning skills to debate public matters. For Smythe's exclusion of "men which doe not rule," see L. Alston, ed., *De Republica Anglorum: A Discourse on the Commonwealth of England* (Cambridge University Press, 1906), 46ff.
3. Aristotle, *Politics*, Book 3, The Internet Classics Archive, edited by Daniel C. Stevenson. Web Atomics, 1994–2000: http://classics.mit.edu/Aristotle/politics.3.three.html. Accessed June 24, 2018.
4. See Sharon O'Dair, *Class, Critics and Shakespeare: Bottom Lines on The Culture Wars* (Ann Arbor: University of Michigan Press, 2000), 8–9. O'Dair describes the MLA's objection to recognizing working-class literature on the grounds that social class was defined too enigmatically to be listed as an MLA sub-field. See also Walter Michaels, *The Trouble with Diversity: How We Learned to Love Identity and Ignore Inequality*

(Metropolitan Books, 2006); and Christopher Fitter, *Shakespeare and the Politics of Commoners: Digesting the New Social History* (Oxford: Oxford University Press, 2017).

5. William Shakespeare, *Love's Labour's Lost*, ed. G. R. Hibbard (Oxford, 1990), 1.1.57. Subsequent references are to this edition and cited parenthetically.
6. The metaphor of students as empty before being filled with expert knowledge is inspired by Paolo Friere, *Pedagogy of the Oppressed*, 30th anniversary ed, trans. Myra Bergman Ramos (New York: Continuum Press, 2005), 76: "It follows logically from the banking notion of consciousness that the educator's role is to regulate the way the world 'enters into' the student. The teacher's task is to 'fill' the students by making deposits of information… And since people 'receive' the world as passive entities, education should make them more passive still and adapt them to the world."
7. Michael Warner, *Publics and Counterpublics* (Cambridge: Massachusetts Institute of Technology Press, 2002), 65–82.
8. Joseph North, *Literary Criticism: A Concise Political History* (Cambridge: Harvard University Press, 2017), 95.
9. Pierre Bourdieu and Jean-Claude Passeron, *Reproduction in Education, Society and Culture*, trans. Richard Nice (London: Sage Publications, 1977), 208.
10. See Robert Morstein-Marx, *Mass Oratory and Political Power in the Late Roman Republic* (Cambridge: Cambridge University Press, 2004). For Cicero's pretense of favoring land restoration, followed by specious reasons to reject land reform as a plot to defraud the people, see 194–196.
11. For elite class attempts to quell the rebellion by social dominance, including cajolery, warning, and shaming, see Jane Whittle, "Lords and Tenants in Kett's Rebellion," *Past and Present* 27 no. 1 (2010): 38–42.
12. C. L. Barber, Shakespeare's *Festive Comedy: A Study of Dramatic Form and Its Relation To Social Custom* (Princeton: Princeton University Press, 1959). See, for example, the Songs as evoking what Barber calls a feeling for "community and season" (128). No mention is made of the presentational divide, where laborers struggle to survive the winter, while the amorous dalliances of Spring recall the amorous playing of the elites.
13. See Mike Davis, *Planet of Slums* (New York: Verso, 2006).
14. Rita Felski, *The Limits of Critique* (Chicago: University of Chicago Press, 2015), 5.
15. Ibid., 1.
16. The phrase "supine fatalism" appears in Georg Lukács, *History and Class Consciousness: Studies in Marxist Dialectics*, trans. Rodney Livingstone (Cambridge: Massachusetts Institute of Technology Press, 1971), 196.
17. T. W. Baldwin, *William Shakespeare's Small Latine and Less Greeke* (Urbana: University of Illinois Press, 1944).

18. Rebecca W. Bushnell, *A Culture of Teaching: Early Modern Humanism in Theory and Practice* (Ithaca: Cornell University Press, 1996).
19. Lynn Enterline, *Shakespeare's Schoolroom: Rhetoric, Discipline, Emotion* (Philadelphia: University of Pennsylvania, 2012), 44.
20. Freyja Cox-Jensen, *Reading the Roman Republic in Early Modern England* (Leiden: Brill, 2012), 31.
21. Jessica Benjamin, *The Bonds of Love: Psychoanalysis, Feminism, and the Problem of Domination* (New York: Pantheon Books, 1988), 53.
22. Bourdieu and Passeron, *Reproduction*, 208.
23. Bruce Robbins, "Discipline and Parse: The Politics of Close Readings," rev. of *Literary Criticism: A Concise Political History*, by Joseph North *Los Angeles Review of Books*, May 14, 2017: https://lareviewofbooks.org/article/discipline-and-parse-the-politics-of-close-reading/#!.
24. North, *Political History*, 172.
25. Quoted in *Humanist Scholarship and Public Order: Two Tracts Against the Pilgrimage of Grace by Sir Richard Morison with Historical Annotations and Related Contemporary Documents*, ed. David Berkowitz (Washington, DC: Folger Shakespeare Library, 1984), p. 107.
26. Jean E. Howard and Paul Strohm, "The Imaginary Commons," *Journal of Medieval and Early Modern Studies* 37, no. 3 (2007): 549–577.
27. "A remedy for sedition vvherin are conteyned many thynges, concernyng the true and loyall obeysance, that comme[n]s owe vnto their prince and soueraygne lorde the Kynge," quoted in Berkowitz, *Two Tracts*, 128.
28. For discussion of specific grievances, see Daniel Bender, "Native Pastoral in the English Renaissance: The 1549 Petition and Kett's Rebellion," in *Conversational Exchanges in Early Modern England*, ed. Kristen Abbott Bennett (Newcastle upon Tyne: Cambridge Scholars Publishing, 2015), 1–18; James Holstun, "Utopia Pre-empted: Kett's Rebellion, Commoning, and the Hysterical Sublime," *Historical Materialism* 16, no. 3 (2008): 3–53.
29. Sir John Cheke, *The true subject to the rebel, or, The hurt of sedition, how grievous it is to a common-wealth written by Sir John Cheke ... ; whereunto is newly added by way of preface a briefe discourse of those times, as they may relate to the present, with the authors life.* I use the text by Henry Craik, ed., *English Prose* (New York: The Macmillan Company, 1916); Bartleby.com, 2010: www.bartleby.com/209. Accessed June 27, 2018.
30. Quintilian, *Institutes of Oratory*, trans. H. E. Butler (Cambridge: Harvard University Press 1969), 10.19.1.
31. Erasmus, *Ciceronianus.* Quoted in Izora Scott, *Controversies, over the Imitation of Cicero in the Renaissance* (Davis, CA: Hermogoras Press, 1991), 62–63.
32. Bourdieu and Passeron, *Reproduction*, 198.

33. Cicero, *Defense of Lucius Flaccus.* University of Chicago: Perseus Projects Texts, 2018: https://perseus.uchicago.edu/perseus-cgi/Flac14.16. Accessed June 24, 2018.
34. Although *The Gallic Wars* focuses on military campaigning and unfolding events, it do look to the sociology of power, admiring Caesar's unquestioned dominance, as, for example, in the contented observation "Quod iussi sunt faciuent" (They do what they are ordered to do). Julius Caesar, *The Gallic Wars* in The Internet Classics Archive, ed. Daniel C. Stevenson (Web Atomics, 1994–2000): http://classics.mit.edu/Caesar/gallic.6.6.html. Accessed June 24, 2018.
35. Lynne Magnusson, "Scoff Power in *Love's Labour's Lost* and the Inns of Court: Language in Context," *Shakespeare Survey* 57 (2004): 203ff.
36. Robbins, "Discipline and Parse."
37. North, *Political History*, 209.
38. *Doris Sommer, The World of Art in the World: Civic Engagement and Public Humanities* (Durham: Duke University Press, 2013).
39. Jamie Brownlee, "Elite Power and Educational Reform: An Historiographical Analysis of Canada and the United States," *Paedogogica Historica: International Journal of the History of Education* 49, no. 2 (2012): 2.
40. Sarah Fine, "A Slow Revolution: Toward a Theory of Intellectual Playfulness in High School Classrooms," *Harvard Educational Review* 84, no. 1 (April 2014): 1–23. Intellectual playfulness is part of the essay's title, but variations on greater latitude in student's participation are present throughout.

'Instruct Her What She Has to Do': Education, Social Mobility, and Success

Mara I. Amster

Stipulate that education brings with it the possibility, although not the guarantee, of social advancement and mobility. Shakespeare's dramas explore this possibility when characters engage in the process of education in small and large ways—instruction in pragmatic approaches, lessons in moral behavior—and then achieve political, social, or economic improvement. Even when they do not—Othello's absorption of Iago's lessons in identifying an adulterous wife seems a prime example—the impulse toward self-betterment and self-advancement through some sort of educative program remains consistent. When it does succeed, as is the case with *As You Like It*'s Orlando whose lessons in wooing result in his becoming heir to Duke Senior, the potential for upward movement is vast. What, though, does a successful education look like for Shakespeare's women? What types of mobility can it bring them? What role does gender play in defining both "successful" and "education"? And perhaps most relevant to the concerns of this collection, can these questions be applied to our current educational institutions if issues of gender are supplemented with those of class?

M. I. Amster (✉)
Randolph College, Lynchburg, VA, USA

S. O'Dair and T. Francisco (eds.), *Shakespeare and the 99%*,
https://doi.org/10.1007/978-3-030-03883-0_5

If the canon is crowded with moments of male education, it is similarly marked with examples of female education. Their programs of study are unseen, but Portia's knowledge of the law (*The Merchant of Venice*), Helena's knowledge of medicine (*All's Well That Ends Well*), and Marina's knowledge of rhetoric (*Pericles*)—a trio of knowledges divided across the trivium and quadrivium of the liberal arts—indicate sustained intellectual engagement resulting in social advancement and romantic advantage for all three women. Outside of Shakespeare's drama there were, of course, women who benefitted from humanism's belief in female education. A classical education, one emphasizing the disciplines of the liberal arts and stressing the art of rhetoric, was intended to strengthen the "pupil's moral fiber and fitness to be an active member of a social elite" and was, at times, available to female students, especially if they were of the nobility or gentry.[1] Noted humanist educators believed women could be educated, even if such ideas were often buried within longer musings on the importance of female chastity as the central aspect of female education. In a chapter devoted to the "learning" of "young maidens" in his tract *Positions*, Richard Mulcaster writes, "We see yong *maidens* be taught to read and write, and can do both with praise"; in Chapter 4 of Juan Luis Vives' *Instruction of a Christian Woman*, titled "Of the Lernyng of Maides," he gestures toward the books "she shalbe taught to rede" and the biblical translations she "shall learne to write."[2] Thomas Elyot's *Defence of Good Women* provides a bit more specificity as it includes not only a dialogue in which one speaker, Candidus, argues for the importance of educating women but also showcases an exemplar of such education, Queen Zenobia.

Nevertheless, for all the interest in educating daughters of the elite in the published works of Vives, Elyot, and Roger Ascham in *The Schoolmaster*, as well as in the writings of Thomas More, among others, the education girls were afforded, in practical terms, differed significantly from that experienced by their brothers. If the purpose of a humanist education was to prepare men for the rigors of public life, where did it leave women whose lives were never intended to be public? If fifteenth-century educator Lauro Quirini is correct and the truly educated individual is "schooled in the art of discourse, and in the study of right debating," what does that mean for women whose voices were not supposed to be heard?[3] What exactly were these women being educated for?

Lisa Jardine notes that, for the humanists, educating a woman is an "end in itself … it is not viewed as a training for anything." However, the fact that little public employment could be found for the educated woman does not mean her training was neither practical nor professional. Michel Montaigne, in his chapter "Of Pedantisme," writes that when it was demanded of Agesilaus what children "should learne," he answered, "*What they should doe being men.*" Alter this statement to consider female education as preparation for "what they should doe being women," and it can be argued she was trained for something: to become a wife, mother, and domestic manager. As Mulcaster writes in his chapter on female education, "a yong maiden" is to be "trained in respect of marriage, obedience to her head."[4]

For women, education and the social mobility intended to accompany it depends on grounding oneself in a specific sexual and gendered position. Karen Newman's term "erotic education" might be used to encompass the ways in which the woman is educated.[5] This education instructs her to become a sexual being—a wife and a mother—prepared and content to remain under the care and guidance of a man, preferably her husband. As such, the role one's husband plays in this education—and, especially, how its eventual success is judged—cannot be ignored.

In at least two cases, Shakespeare speaks directly to questions of what women are being educated for and how the rationale and benefits for this education are predicated on their sex: the educations of Katherina in *The Taming of the Shrew* and Katherine in *Henry V*.[6] In both cases, the educative program is a success: both women emerge at the end of their respective plays in socially advanced positions as properly domesticated English wives or wives-to-be. Both educations are also erotic since, for Petruchio and Henry, masculine authority and dominance become, respectively, linked with "erotic restraint" or spoken of in "erotic terms."[7] At the same time, however, each play, while supporting the notion of education for a gender-specific future, questions how the real measure of success is judged and who ultimately gains the greatest advantage.

Proper linguistic deployment is central to the success awaiting Katherina and Katherine. Renaissance-conduct literature long connected desirable female behavior with relative silence. Richard Brathwait, in his *English Gentlewoman*, argues "to enter into much discourse or familiarity with strangers, argues lightnesse or indiscretion"; Barnabe Rich, in *My Ladies Looking Glasse*, defines a "bad" woman as one who "is full of words, shee is loude and babbling." Utter silence would seem to be the answer according to Vives: "If thou talke littel in company, folke thynke thou canste but littell good; if thou speake muche, they reken the lyght … if thou speake counyngly, thou shalt be called a shrewe." But Vives' own words indicate that not speaking at all is not the solution to this apparent problem, especially if one is a woman whose role necessitated her presence in public. Baldessar Castiglione suggests a middle ground: a full ban on speech should give way to an acknowledgment that acceptable speech should be matched to its appropriate circumstances. A woman should speak "with agreeable and comely conversation suited to the time and place."[8] Think here of *Pericles*' Marina who uses her rhetorical skills to retain her chastity, convert the men of Mytilene, and still succeed in providing income for the brothel.

It is important to note here that learning how to deploy language with balance and grace is not a skill specifically geared to female students; the humanist impulse was to educate students in tempering those passions that threatened the accepted social structures and in cultivating a "rationality submissive to authority"; self-regulation and self-discipline were key. What is specific to women, though, is just how vexed controlling those passions and regulating one's self might have been since any type of female speech was seen as potentially dangerous. Humanist Leonardo Bruni most emphatically sets forth the boundaries of female education with regard to speech: "rhetoric in all its forms—public discussion, forensic argument, logical fence, and the like—lies absolutely outside the province of woman." George Puttenham, in his chapter "Of Ornament," writes a woman's "chief virtue is shamefastness … a natural fear to be noted … so as when they hear or see anything tending that way, they commonly blush." How does an educated woman speak when simply opening her mouth is an act flouting expectations about female silence?[9] Because figuring out how, where, and when to speak is of such concern, it is no surprise both *The Taming of the Shrew* and *Henry V* emphasize this particular type of learning.

* * *

Classed and gendered education takes center stage in *The* both *Taming of the Shrew* as soon as Lucentio and Tranio enter in act 1, when the former speaks of his desire to "haply institute / A course of learning"[10]; it appears even earlier if the performance retains the Induction scenes. Lucentio's plan to become a student morphs into a desire to teach when he spies Bianca. She quickly becomes subjected to a formalized type of education, marked by the presence of tutors in "music, instruments, and poetry" (1.1.93) and instruction in Greek and Latin. Baptista's own desire to satisfy his daughter's education in the subjects with which she "taketh most delight" (1.1.92) is echoed by Bianca's own joy that she will be able to "learn my lessons as I please myself" (3.1.20). Bianca's forthright comment, spoken with a confidence gained arguably from access to texts prioritizing female agency and eroticism like Ovid's *Heroides* or *Metamorphoses*—the two texts Lucentio uses to disguise his true intentions—demonstrates that this foray into a more traditional humanist curriculum may have its drawbacks.[11] Not only does Bianca assert herself during her lessons, this assertiveness extends to her life as a married woman, as act 5 reveals, when she refuses to come when Lucentio calls and fails to speak as he wishes. If Bianca's "silence flouts" (2.1.29) her sister, prompting Katherina to seek revenge, it silences her husband: Lucentio does not speak for another twenty-five lines after Biondello brings news of Bianca's refusal.

Bianca's selective silence is mirrored by Katherina's talk just as Bianca's role as student is refracted through the lens of Katherina's. This is a play, of course, whose very title calls attention to the role of female speech and, specifically, the ways in which the unruly female tongue must be brought into submission for a comic ending to occur. Katherina's misuse of language is the primary marker of her shrewishness; her other negative qualities—her inability to defer respectfully to the men, her displays of physical violence—stem from this initial failure to moderate and modulate where, when, and how she should speak. For Katherina to become an acceptable member of Paduan society, to transform from a "wild Kate" (2.1.277) to a "household Kate" (2.1.278), she must learn to control her tongue and adhere to Castiglione's guidance for use: to combine a "vivacity of spirit" with a "certain pleasing affability," both marked by "serene and modest manners."[12]

Petruchio, unlike Bianca's suitors, is well aware that a different aspect of the humanist educative program needs to be emphasized to achieve this desired goal. His own ease with classical texts and his opinions about what Katherina should wear style him in the mode of a humanist scholar and demonstrate his comfort with its philosophies. Whereas Bianca's suitors, disguised as tutors, woo her under the pretense of education, Petruchio educates Katherina while ostensibly engaging in the act of courtship.[13] Ostensibly, since there is no need to woo, while Baptista tells Petruchio that he will need to obtain "her love" (2.1.129), that does not happen. The match is affirmed over Katherina's protests. The couple's first scene of courtship, preceded by Baptista's advice that Hortensio return to his lessons with Bianca because "she's apt to learn" (2.1.165), highlight the start of Katherina's education as well.

A letter from Erasmus notes "a wife will respect a husband more whom she recognizes also as her teacher" and, while it is questionable whether Katherina displays respect for Petruchio, his dual role is well established. The pattern Petruchio sets in their initial meeting—he will contradict everything she says, manipulate her language so she no longer recognizes what she has said, and interpret her words to others such that they become unintelligible to her—is repeated in the following scenes where the two are together. This dynamic is at work when he tells Baptista that the two have decided her public behavior will be the opposite of her private behavior and again when he throws meat he says is burnt on the floor despite her contention that it is "well" (4.1.169). These strategies, highlighted by some performances as a form of domestic abuse, circulate around a linguistic pedagogy that relies on the humanist principles of preparing women to be wives. Part of becoming a good English wife is learning to "submit [one]self and be obedient" to one's husband, to be "convinced" she is "not her husband's equal."[14] For Katherina, this means accepting Petruchio's language as her own. It may even be said she is learning a new language: his.

Stephen Greenblatt has written that learning another language "is to acknowledge the existence of other people and to acquire the ability to function … in another social world." So much of what we see in Petruchio's "taming school" are lessons forcing Katherina to acknowledge how others see her by placing her in the role of observer. She watches Petruchio berate his servants, behaving in a manner akin to hers in earlier scenes, and hears how these interactions sound. As Bruni wrote in a letter, "For if a woman throws her arms around while speaking, or if she increases the volume of her speech with greater forcefulness, she will appear threateningly insane and requiring restraint."[15] Physical restraint is never used in the play—a move marking this shrew-taming tale as different from its sources—but Katherina is able to see how her language looks and sounds and, the play implies, these visions encourage her to accept a new set of speech patterns. Katherina demonstrates most emphatically her acceptance of Petruchio's words as her own in their moon-sun debate: "And be it the moon, or sun, or what you please; / And if you please to call it a rush-candle /

Henceforth I vow it shall be so for me" (4.5.13–15). Critics have argued her language here contains varying degrees of irony and subversiveness, indicating she does not accept this philosophy of linguistic submission[16]; however, her outward devotion to it—she agrees, just a few lines later, to call Vincentio a "young budding virgin" (4.5.37)—mark the moment where Petruchio's educative program finds its first major success. It is, however, during the play's final act that Shakespeare reveals just what educating a woman to be a wife means for her husband.

* * *

Educating Katherina to be a wife means domesticating her, making her fit for, and fit into, the domestic realm. While Baptista notes he has a daughter "call'd Katherina" (2.1.44), Petruchio ignores her father's words, and her own—she continues to insist "[t]hey call me Katherine that do talk of me" (2.1.184)—and renames her Kate. Petruchio calls her Kate over sixty times, returning to "Katherine" only in act 5 after she has been suitably altered. His renaming of her, his establishment of a new language to display and reflect her new identity, is echoed in *Henry V* as Henry calls his Katherine Kate thirty-one times even as one of Shakespeare's source materials, Holinshed's *Chronicles*, continually identifies her by her full name.[17] Anglicizing these women's names is not the only thing these prospective grooms have in common; just as Petruchio undertakes a plan to make Katherina "conformable," Henry does as well. Henry's work, though, is achieved through Katherine's own lessons in self-schooling.

While Katherina's education is undertaken by the man poised to be her husband and is greeted by her less-than-enthusiastic response, Katherine's, on the other hand, is unprompted by any family member or advisor. Whether the English lesson occurs as a sign of willingness or coercion is unclear, but the text, providing no sign of or word from Katherine until act 3, scene 4, implies she undertakes the endeavor on her own terms.[18] The Chorus explains she has been offered by her father, along with some "unprofitable dukedoms" (3 Chorus 31), to Henry and, while Henry is underwhelmed, Katherine seems aware that her own linguistic skills need to be sharpened since a dynastic marriage is inevitable. She tells her lady-in-waiting Alice she must learn to speak English: "*il faut que j'aprenne a parler*" (3.4.405).

With the help of Alice, she learns the English names for a number of body parts and initiates her own English lessons. Any concern that Katherine or Alice oversteps by taking on the masculine role of teacher is lessened by two facts: there are no men present and the women are dealing with translation, a branch of learning open to women since it positions Katherine in the role of conduit rather than authority figure. This lesson is intriguing, though, since the body parts being translated are not those usually associated with this type of foreign language instruction: the eyes, the nose, and the mouth.[19] These are, after all, the orifices through which we experience the world: sight, smell, and taste. Katherine begins with her hand—a body part used to understand one's physical context—but she quickly moves to body parts that heighten her role as spectacle, intended to be viewed or touched by others. Katherine's choice of which body parts to translate and her mispronunciations of the English versions cause her to engage in a series of bawdy puns she readily acknowledges as "*mauvis, corruptible, gros et impudique*" (3.4.53–54). That she knows these words are not ones she would speak in front of gentlemen tells us her knowledge of English must be greater than she admits.

The inclusion of this language, in particular Katherine's repetition of "le count" (3.4.51, 52, 55, 59), emphasizes that this seemingly innocent private moment, designed perhaps to contrast with the war's public horror, follows immediately on the heels of Henry's speech at the gates of Harfleur. It is hard not to connect Henry's rhetoric of the violent sexual conquest of France—"What is't to me, when you yourselves are cause, / If your pure maidens fall into the hand / Of hot and forcing violations?" (3.3.19–21)—with Katherine's sexualized lesson. As such, Katherine's pedagogic endeavor to teach herself her new country's language takes on additional, and less comic, overtones. The scene has been interpreted as a moment where Katherine is "schooled" in the ways female bodies become objects of sexual exchange and as one where English expansionist goals are "worked out on" Katherine's body.[20] The violence the women of Harfleur are spared has been transferred onto the French princess's body as she endures her own linguistic lesson.

At the same time, however, the fact that it is Katherine's sexualized female body under scrutiny during her lesson draws attention to one of the primary reasons why women were supposed to be educated: to become good mothers. This is, it might be argued, a doubled form of sex education: the sexual body as object of study and sexual intercourse as the desired outcome. Education prepared the aristocratic woman for the work of reproduction and child rearing, her main contribution to her community.[21] If it was the mother's job to inculcate her children with the attributes of good breeding, of which proper speech was an important aspect, then it was necessary she herself be trained through a strong humanist curriculum. Erasmus writes that "the duty of a mother" is to "fashion ... [her child's] no less tender mind with good education." English speech becomes "fused conceptually" with the "material practices of the house": Katherine's private lesson connects her to the larger domestic space she will inhabit in her new role.[22] In addition to joining together two kingdoms through her marriage, she is to provide legitimate male heirs for the English throne; she will, Henry feels certain, "prove a good soldier-breeder" (5.2.206). He is wrong about this as the Epilogue confirms: the infant "Henry the Sixth ... / ... / made his England bleed" (5 Epilogue 9–12). Strangely, the play fails to gesture toward Katherine's eventual success, as it were, in internalizing this particular lesson, omitting any reference to her future role as grandmother to Henry VII.

* * *

If Katherina has chosen by act 4 to accept Petruchio's language as her own and if Katherine's English lesson in act 3 has shown that she is prepared to become an English queen, there would seem to be no need for either play to include their final act. That is to say, both women have proved to be successful pupils, embracing the language of men. Yet, both plays include scenes conveying seemingly extraneous information. Why does Katherina need to set her hand under Petruchio's foot in view of family and friends? Why does Henry, already promised his French bride, need to engage in an extended scene of courtship? It is in these final scenes that the fundamental role of female education becomes clear: It is not enough for the women to be educated for their roles as wives, they have to be able to, in the words of Linda Pollock, "permit their husbands to regain supremacy."[23] Female education is not just about domesticating the feminine tongue but, equally or more importantly, it is about bolstering the masculine ego.

Pollock artfully argues that education for women was something of a balancing act: a young woman (of a certain social or economic stature) needed to know how to "combine deference with independent action" to become a wife who could practice "selective ... subordination." The purpose here was to guarantee female behavior enhanced familial reputation. Elyot, who argues in his *Defence of Good Women* for the right of wives to exercise their own judgment, summarizes this conduct by comparing it to a performance of sorts. If a wife cannot do what her husband wishes, "than should she seme rather to give him wise counsaile, than to appere disobedient."[24] What Katherina and Katherine do in these final scenes is akin to Elyot's call for "seeming," engaging in behavior that works to provide Petruchio and Henry, respectively, with what each needs to enhance his own reputation. For Katherina, this means making public Petruchio's successful taming; for Katherine, it means allowing Henry to be seen—and to see himself—as more than a military conqueror.

Katherina's final speech is something of a conundrum: do her words signal that Petruchio has not only tamed her but also broken her or do they indicate the couple have come to an understanding and become a team? Reading Katherina's speech to the women through the lens of successful pedagogy complicates the binary choices of submission or independence usually offered. Using this lens requires a few backward steps. Corinne Abate draws attention to stage directions for act 2, scene 1 in the 1623 First Folio. She notes the original directions have Baptista, Gremio, and Tranio entering before Petruchio begins to say his lines, "For am I he born to tame you" (2.1.276), rather than after he has finished. Abate argues this difference is key to understanding the dynamic between Petruchio and Katherina since the earlier entrance implies Petruchio says these words knowing he has an audience. Nowhere in his private conversation with Katherina does he talk about his desire to alter or tame her; his inclusion of these lines serve as a purposeful performance for the men who are already predisposed to this type of sentiment.[25] If Petruchio has been teaching Katherina about acceptable behavior and, specifically the types of language accompanying that behavior, then this early show of bravado becomes relevant for how Katherina's later public performance is read.

Katherina's education was focused on speech: where to speak, how to speak, and what to speak. When Petruchio charges Katherina to "tell these headstrong women / What duty they owe their lords and husbands" (5.2.130–131), he is doing so on the heels of Lucentio's and Hortensio's failures: their wives have refused to do their bidding. When his wife responds affirmatively to his command, his status among the men immediately rises. "Here is a wonder" (5.2.106), Lucentio notes, thinking, perhaps, that educating Bianca in music and philosophy did not succeed in preparing her for life as a dutiful wife. Not only does Katherina come when called but she launches into a rhetorically complex speech—the longest one in the play—about feminine submission. Indeed, her speech shows not only her transformation from shrew to good wife but also, and more importantly, Petruchio's from successful educator to "governor" and "king" (5.2.138). He emerges as the "winner" (5.2.187) through Katherina's linguistic prowess.[26] No indication is given whether Petruchio is aware of what Katherina is doing—is this a game upon which they have mutually agreed?—but his potential foreknowledge becomes irrelevant as his position is advanced through her education.

Petruchio, as Lynda Boose notes, is one of a number of male comic heroes whose prestige is elevated through the actions of their wives; for example, Bassanio (*The Merchant of Venice*), Orlando (*As You Like It*), and Sebastian (*Twelfth Night*) all rise in economic and social status through marriage.[27] Henry is a different case, though; even before he marries Katherine, he is an English king who has conquered France against overwhelming odds. Yet Shakespeare chooses to close the play with a scene that seems unnecessary: Henry does not need Katherine's approval to marry her. Nevertheless, he continues to ask for it. Unlike the corresponding scene in *The Taming of the Shrew* in which Katherina's public pronouncements serve to boost Petruchio's public standing, *Henry V*'s final scene is a private one, witnessed only by Alice. As such, the larger audience for whom this scene is designed matters. Henry has, throughout the three plays in which he appears, been spectacularly successful at all he has attempted; however, what he has not done is prove himself a lover and, by extension, a man who can solidify his claim to the throne through legitimate heirs. The rituals of chivalric masculinity require Henry to win his lady's heart and Henry attacks this project as he has done all previous challenges: with gusto and energy.[28] Wooing Katherine in such a lengthy manner—the two speak together for almost 200 lines, although Henry's words comprise the conversation's bulk—allows him to demonstrate this otherwise unexplored aspect of his personality.

Katherine greets Henry's insistence that she accept his proposal with continual resistance. Her deflections—"I cannot tell wat is dat" (5.2.177); "I cannot tell" (5.2.195); "I do not know dat" (5.2.211)—are grounded on her inability to understand the English language, in spite of her earlier lesson. As a result, she pushes Henry to shift his strategy to make his own desires clearer, to maneuver around her seeming linguistic deficit in an attempt to secure her consent; she is teaching him how to woo her, almost as if she were following the advice of Richard Brathwait that "the way to winne an husband is not to wooe him, but to be woo'd by him." Alan Sinfield and Jonathan Dollimore argue we never see Henry "trying to win the hearts of the French citizens," but, in this final scene, he is engaged actively in courting one particular French citizen.[29] Indeed, his opening lines to her ask that she "teach a soldier terms / Such as will enter at a lady's ear" (5.2.99–100). Roles are reversed in this courtship as Henry asks Katherine to be the teacher.

She is also mitigating his earlier words at the gates of Harfleur, which appeared to advocate rape as a strategy of war, by allowing him to show a humbler side: "I cannot look greenly, nor gasp out my eloquence, nor I have no cunning in protestations" (5.2.142–144). His claim that he is neither eloquent nor cunning belies what the audience has already witnessed and what they are, indeed, currently experiencing as each of Katherine's short responses is met by a torrent of Henry's words; these statements, however, work to construct a "plain king" (5.2.124), a rhetorically grounded, unornamented speaker. Much in the same way Katherine's decision to learn English on her own makes her an agent rather than an exchangeable object, she is an agent here as well, working to "redeem" Henry's image by allowing him to become a courtly knight, albeit an awkward one.[30] Here he is just a man wooing the woman he wishes to marry rather than a conqueror subduing the enemy.

Both women are treated similarly at the end of each of their plays. A. D. Cousins notes Erasmus, Vives, and More all make use of the Pygmalion myth as they shape educational plans for women who are to be molded and influenced. Much in the same way Pygmalion wakes his lover with a kiss, Shakespeare's men complete their brides' initiations into their new roles with the requisite kiss.[31] Petruchio repeats his earlier demand, "kiss me, Kate" (5.2.180), and Henry tells Katherine she "has witchcraft in [her] lips" (5.2.275–276). Neither play provides a definitive stage direction for whether the kisses are reciprocated or desired. What they do show, however, is that after each kiss, both women never speak again. The successful performance of their educations wins one husband public praise and money and the other a personal sense of chivalric masculinity. As such, female education becomes just that: education in how to become a female.

* * *

Shakespeare's plays are concerned with the types of social mobility education can offer to women—and how, by extension, the success accrued to these newly educated women transfers to their male "teachers." Such an interest may feel quaint to our twenty-first century world. After all, female students have outnumbered their male counterparts on college campuses for over thirty years and university curricula seem unconcerned with teaching women how to be women. This does not mean the power dynamics exhibited in *The Taming of the Shrew* and *Henry V* are absent; rather, it may mean both the players and the terms of the game have changed. Substitute low-income high-achieving (LIHA) students[32] for the women of the drama and consider if the model explored by Shakespeare remains useful. While this cohort of students reap clear benefits from inclusion in institutions of higher learning, the ways in which the elite colleges and universities present their recruitment rationales indicate that neither bettering students' lives nor undertaking an altruistic objective is the primary goal of this admissions project. Something else is at stake.

First, an important caveat: the analogy here is far from perfect. Comparing the educational paths of two fictional characters to the policies and programs set forth by numerous academic institutions to argue a concrete correlation is not the purpose of this exploration. Rather, the argument is intended to consider what might be called the act five connection: the way that public performance—the manner by which the institution presents itself to its audience—can illuminate how ideals of social mobility gained through education get subsumed into larger calls for diversity and inclusion. If female education, for Petruchio and Henry, becomes a vehicle for male aggrandizement, then providing educational opportunities for LIHA students becomes part of the university's persuasive and pervasive marketing campaign.

The desire to recruit greater numbers of LIHA students contains traces of the humanist belief that education contributes, as Jardine notes, to "the pupil's moral fiber and fitness to be an active member of a social elite," both with its emphasis on morality in the form of community service and elitism in the form of economic advancement. The mission statement of Amherst College reads, in part, "Amherst College educates men and women ... so that they may seek, value, and advance knowledge, engage the world around them, and lead principled lives of consequence." Such intentions are in keeping with those posted from other elite colleges; for example, Vassar College speaks of "engaged citizenship" and Sarah Lawrence College says their graduates are "prepared to be engaged citizens and vital contributors in … [the] global society."[33] Reserving this type of preparation solely for those students whose family income meets a certain criteria is a "waste of talent that hurts not just the students but our nation, as we compete with other countries in the global knowledge economy," according to the executive director of the Jack Kent Cooke Foundation.[34] There is a need to broaden the mission since not only will the talent of the individual student be channeled in a positive direction but the greater community—both domestic and international—will benefit.

Movement into the social elite is the other major benefit of such educational outreach. Studies consistently demonstrate access to higher education works to increase economic mobility. An extensive investigation undertaken by *The New York Times* shows that LIHA students who attend elite universities end up in the 75th percentile of the income distribution on average, almost catching up to the already-affluent student in the 80th percentile. John Friedman, associate professor of economics at Brown University, notes, "If you can get poor kids to a really good college, that's a really good pathway to success … College seems to be equalizing opportunities for students."[35] Even if not nearly enough students gain access to the economic mobility that accompanies graduation from an elite college—much has been written about why so few eligible students apply—the numbers bear out the positive effect such schooling has.

Some of the "equalizing" Friedman observes, interestingly, comes not just from being accepted into an elite university but from being educated in the language spoken there. If Katherina and Katherine need to learn how to speak properly to advance socially, so too do the LIHA students need to be acclimated to their new linguistic surroundings. For example, Princeton's Scholars Institute Fellows Program is designed to expose students from "historically underrepresented" backgrounds—first-generation and LIHA students top the list—to the "hidden curriculum of institutions of higher education." One workshop, "How to Speak Prof-o-saurus," playfully explains how professors live in a different habitat and, therefore, must be spoken to in their own "strange language." Student feedback noted the workshop helped to "erase the intimidating stigma associated with professors," but one wonders if a primary goal is, rather, to erase the traces of speech with which the LIHA student enters the university.[36] Learning how to converse with a professor means un-learning one's own language; such a skill would, it seems, be useful to all entering college students, but the assumption here is that financially secure students are already well versed in academic discourse.

Just as Katherina and Katherine benefit from their educations, LIHA students advance: financially, intellectually, and socially. And just as Petruchio and Henry gain from their roles as educators, colleges and universities stand to profit. Apart from the desire to enrich the workforce with newly engaged citizens, there is the wish, voiced by Princeton University president Christopher Eisgruber, to "create urgency" about the American class divide, to create more opportunities that will, in turn, have a transformative effect on the current system. This urgency has been translated, for instance, into Princeton's commitment to economic diversity with a result that 21 percent of its class of 2022 receives Pell Grants, up from only 6.5 percent for the class of 2007.[37]

Is this concerted effort, then, about social philanthropy or economic altruism? The readings of Shakespeare would suggest something else. In much of the writing about the recruitment and enrollment of LIHA students, "diversity" and "inclusion" appear over and over, albeit sometimes couched in other language. While diversity has been traditionally used to refer to race and sex, it now includes the categories of class, gender, sexuality, religion, and geography, among others. Support for diversity is one of the core characteristics of Generation Z—those students born between 1996 and 2010—according to studies seeking to define them as an understandable cohort. Advertising and marketing professionals tout the claim "diversity is the new normal," forming the sensibility of this cohort.[38] It should not be surprising, then, to find colleges and universities highlighting and emphasizing their commitment to diversity in their recruitment materials—think of all those glossy brochures featuring an array of students of color sitting under a tree as their professor gestures wildly—and that economic diversity, in particular, has become more important in their campaigns. Amherst seeks to educate those "of exceptional potential from all backgrounds … whatever their financial need"; Vassar values all its members "including those from underrepresented and marginalized groups"; and Sarah Lawrence graduates "world citizens who are diverse in every definition of the word."[39]

Diversity, while a real phenomenon registered in the kinds of bodies populating a class, is also, according to Tim Pippert, a sociologist at

Augsburg College, "something that's being marketed." And this allows a return to the plays: just who is the audience for that marketing? Access to elite education as affordable is emphasized on university admission pages and is clearly intended for the LIHA student; the first line on Amherst's financial aid page reads, "Your family's financial circumstances will ***never*** affect whether you're admitted or not."[40] More and more of the elite schools are waiving any parental contribution if families earn below a certain income threshold. Nearly all of these schools' websites speak their desire to populate their incoming classes with students who may otherwise believe that financing a college education is out of reach; statistics on how much financial aid they provide feature prominently since one of the largest hurdles colleges needs to overcome is sticker shock of prospective students. Nevertheless, despite the fact that the number of students who qualify for Pell Grants is up almost a third from 2008, the percentage of LIHA students enrolled at elite universities is only up 3 percent—from 12 to 15 percent of their total student body.[41] The promotion of socioeconomic diversity, consistently and prominently displayed, does not necessarily result in real diversity.

At the same time that financial messages seem pointed toward the prospective LIHA student, other messages about diversity appear to target a different audience. Interested students are told diversity "liberate[s] you from the tunnel vision of an ethnocentric and egocentric viewpoint" and allows you "to sharpen your self-knowledge and self-insight."[42] Who, one might wonder, is the "you" whose worldview is being liberated and sharpened? Certainly, students who sit anywhere on the socioeconomic ladder will gain from exposure to different perspectives. It seems fair to say, however, that a LIHA student will not need to be told her class will be populated with those from different socioeconomic backgrounds; nor will she have to be convinced her vision of the world will change upon entering the university. Harvard University president Drew Gilpin Faust problematizes, perhaps unintentionally, this "you" in a video entitled "Why Campus Inclusion Matters." She explains that, for "people who are resistant to change," "the educational element of experiencing diverse individuals," is vital in allowing access to "people who are different from you, people who challenge you, people who expose you to new perspectives on the world."[43] It is hard to see the "you" here as being anyone other than the socioeconomically privileged student for whom sharing a classroom and a dorm with a LIHA student is conveyed not as an unwanted obstacle but rather as another tangible opportunity the college will provide. Diversity here is part of the public sales pitch.

The importance of considering who the audience is and how it shifts resonates in a 2017 controversy at Harvard regarding socioeconomic diversity and the university's outward commitment to it. A student-initiated proposal to institute a summer enrichment bridge program for underrepresented students, following the model of Princeton's Scholars Institute, was rejected by the administration. The student response was rapid and the organizer of the proposal, in an editorial, succinctly summarized what she sees as the primary problem: "You flaunt us in your diversity statistics," Savannah Fritz told the Dean. Another student, Hunter Richards, extended this sentiment: the university used her "identity" as "a prop, a statistic, a cautionary tale."[44] Fritz, Richards, and others argue their presence in marketing materials, charts, and graphs was vital to the university; their actual success, they implied, was not. Sociologist Tim Pippert's research in the relationship between a college's racial diversity and its presentation of it appears to support this belief: his team found the whiter a college was, the more diversity was represented in college brochures. It is the display of diversity—this flaunting, as Fritz wrote—that seems to take precedence. Indeed, the fact that LIHA students graduate at lower rates than their more affluent peers—wealthier students graduate four times more often—supports the argument that it is the enrollment of LIHA students, rather than their retention, that matters more.[45]

Shakespeare's scene 5 moments underscore masculine achievement through the actions of newly educated women. While the methods by which elite colleges and universities promote socioeconomic diversity are far from parallel to what occurs in the drama, it is possible to read their attempts to make public their efforts through this Shakespearean lens, if only to complicate the vision of what success might mean—and for whom it has meaning—for this growing group of about-to-be educated students. If Petruchio and Henry become more manly through the education of the women, the upper-middle class and wealthy students become better people—more sensitive and more open-minded—as a result of the education of the LIHA students.

Notes

1. Joan Gibson, "Educating for Silence: Renaissance Women and Language Arts," *Hypatia* 4, no. 1 (1989): 10; Lisa Jardine, "Cultural Confusion and Shakespeare's Learned Heroines: 'These Are Old Paradoxes,'" *Shakespeare Quarterly* 38, no. 1 (1987): 4.
2. Richard Mulcaster, *Positions* (London, 1581), 166, 168; Juan Luis Vives, *A Very Fruteful and Pleasant Boke Called Instruction of a Christen Woman*, ed. Richard Hyrde (London, 1547), sigs. C4v, D.
3. Lauro Quirini, quoted in Lisa Jardine, "Women Humanists: Education for What?," in *Feminism and Renaissance Studies*, ed. Lorna Hutson (Oxford: Oxford University Press, 1999), 50.
4. Jardine, "Women Humanists," 69; Michel Montaigne, *The Essayes*, trans. John Florio (London: Grant Richards, 1908), 165; and Mulcaster, *Positions*, 174.
5. Karen Newman, *Fashioning Femininity and English Renaissance Drama* (Chicago: The University of Chicago Press, 1991), 103.
6. In order to avoid confusion, I refer to the two women by these names, following the Folio text's use of Katherina.
7. Jean E. Howard and Phyllis Rackin, *Engendering a Nation: A Feminist Account of Shakespeare's English Histories* (London: Routledge, 1997), 194.
8. Richard Brathwait, *The English Gentlewoman, Drawne Out to the Full Body* (London, 1631), 41; Barnabe Rich, *My Ladies Looking Glasse* (London, 1616), sig. F1v; Vives, *A Very Fruteful*, sig. L2; and Baldessar Castiglione, *The Book of the Courtier*, trans. Charles Singleton (New York: Anchor Books, 1959), 207.
9. Dennis Brooks, "'To Show Scorn Her Own Image': The Varieties of Education in *The Taming of the Shrew*," *Rocky Mountain Review of Language and Literature* 48, no. 1 (1994): 7–8; Leonardo Bruni, quoted in J. K. Sowards, "Erasmus and the Education of Women," *The Sixteenth Century Journal* 13, no. 4 (1982): 79; George Puttenham, *The Art of English Poesy: A Critical Edition*, ed. Frank Whigham and Wayne A. Rebhorn (Ithaca: Cornell University Press, 2007), 352; and Jardine, "Cultural Confusion," 4.
10. William Shakespeare, *The Riverside Shakespeare*, ed. G. Blakemore Evans (Boston: Houghton Mifflin Co., 1974), 1.1.8–1.1.9. Hereafter all Shakespearean quotes will be from the *Riverside* and will be given parenthetically.
11. Carole Levin and John Watkins, *Shakespeare's Foreign Worlds: National and Transnational Identities in the Elizabethan Age* (Ithaca: Cornell University Press, 2009), 199–200.

12. Castiglione, *Courtier*, 207.
13. Elizabeth Mazzola, "Schooling Shrews and Grooming Queens in the Tudor Classroom," *Critical Survey* 22, no. 1 (2010): 5; Brooks, "To Show Scorn Her Own Image," 20.
14. Desiderius Erasmus, quoted in Sowards, "Erasmus," 83; Robert Dod and John Cleaver, *A Godly Form of Household Government* (1614), quoted in *Renaissance Woman: A Sourcebook*, ed. Kate Aughterson (London: Routledge, 1995), 80; and William Whately, *A Bride Bush* (1617), quoted in Aughterson, 31.
15. Stephen Greenblatt, *Shakespearean Negotiations: The Circulation of Social Energy in Renaissance England* (Berkeley: University of California Press, 1988), 49; Leonardo Bruni, quoted in Jardine, "Women Humanists," 50.
16. See, for example, Carolyn E. Brown, "Katherine of *The Taming of the Shrew*: 'A Second Grissel,'" *Texas Studies in Literature and Language* 37, no. 3 (1995): 304.
17. Laurie E. Maguire, "'Household Kates': Chez Petruchio, Percy, and Plantagenet," in *Gloriana's Face: Women, Public and Private, in the English Renaissance*, ed. S. P. Cerasano and Marion Wynne-Davies (Detroit: Wayne State University Press, 1992): 131. Puttenham notes that using these diminutive names might indicate a type of derision or contempt (305).
18. Helen Ostovich, "'Teach You Our Princess English?': Equivocal Translation of the French in *Henry V*," in *Gender Rhetorics: Postures of Dominance and Submission in History*, ed. Richard C. Trexler (Binghamton, NY: Medieval and Renaissance Texts & Studies, 1994), 153.
19. Gibson, "Educating for Silence," 20; Katherine Eggert, "Nostalgia and the Not Yet Late Queen: Refusing Female Rule in *Henry V*," *ELH* 61, no. 3 (1994): 532.
20. Laurie Finke, "Knowledge as Bait: Feminism, Voice, and the Pedagogical Unconscious," *College English* 55, no. 1 (1993): 11; Newman, *Fashioning Femininity*, 101.
21. Ruth Mazo Karras, "Women's Labors: Reproduction and Sex Work in Medieval Europe," *Journal of Women's History* 15, no. 4 (2004): 155.
22. Desiderius Erasmus, *The Woman in Childbed*, quoted in Aughterson, 105; Wendy Wall, *Staging Domesticity: Household Work and English Identity in Early Modern Drama* (Cambridge: Cambridge University Press, 2002), 60–61.
23. Linda Pollock, "'Teach Her to Live Under Obedience': The Making of Women in the Upper Ranks of Early Modern England," *Continuity and Change* 4, no. 2 (1989): 246.

24. Ibid., 237; Sir Thomas Elyot, *The Defence of Good Women* (London, 1540), sig. E2.
25. Corinne S. Abate, "Neither a Tamer Nor a Shrew Be: A Defense of Petruchio and Katherine," in *Privacy, Domesticity, and Women in Early Modern England*, ed. Corinne S. Abate (Burlington, VT: Ashgate, 2003), 34.
26. Lynda E. Boose, "*The Taming of the Shrew*, Good Husbandry, and Enclosure," in *Shakespeare Reread: The Texts in New Contexts*, ed. Russ McDonald (Ithaca: Cornell University Press, 1994), 214–215.
27. Ibid., 216–217.
28. David Steinsaltz, "The Politics of French Language in Shakespeare's History Plays," *Studies in English Literature* 42, no. 2 (2002): 329. Thanks to Jason Cohen for reminding me of a similarly long and seemingly unnecessary wooing scene in *Richard III.*
29. Corinne S. Abate, "'Once More Unto the Breech': Katherine's Victory in 'Henry V,'" *Early Theatre* 4 (2001): 73-–80; Brathwait, *The English Gentlewoman*, 106; and Alan Sinfield and Jonathan Dollimore, "History and Ideology, Masculinity and Miscegenation: The Instance of *Henry V*," in *Faultlines: Cultural Materialism and the Politics of Dissident Reading*, ed. Alan Sinfield (Berkeley: University of California Press, 1992), 132.
30. Lance Wilcox, "Katherine of France: Victim and Bride," *Shakespeare Studies* 17 (1985): 66.
31. A. D. Cousins, "Humanism, Female Education, and Myth: Erasmus, Vives, and More's 'To Candidus,'" *Journal of the History of Ideas* 65, no. 2 (2004): 217.
32. I am using the acronym LIHA as advanced by Caroline Hoxby and Christopher Avery in "The Missing 'One-Offs': The Hidden Supply of High Achieving, Low-Income Students," *Brookings Papers on Economic Activity.* (Washington, DC: The Brookings Institute, 2013)https://www.brookings.edu/wp-content/uploads/2016/07/2013a_hoxby.pdf. Accessed June 4, 2017.
33. "Mission of Amherst College," Amherst College: https://www.amherst.edu/amherst-story/facts/mission. Accessed June 4, 2017; "Mission Statement," Vassar College: http://info.vassar.edu/about/vassar/mission.html. Accessed June 4, 2017; and "Mission, Vision & Value," Sarah Lawrence College: https://www.sarahlawrence.edu/about/mission/. Accessed June 4, 2017.
34. Cited by https://www.jkcf.org/our-stories/new-report-calls-for-an-admissions-preference-for-low-income-students/. Amber Styles, "New Reports Calls for an Admissions Preference for Low-Income Students," Lansdowne, VA: Jack Kent Cooke Foundation (2016): http://blog.jkcf.org/welcome-to-the-jack-kent-cooke-foundation-blog/new-report-calls-for-an-admissions-preference-for-low-income-students. Accessed June 5, 2017.

35. "Some Colleges Have More Students from the Top 1 Percent Than the Bottom 60," *The New York Times*, January 18, 2017: https://www.nytimes.com/interactive/2017/01/18/upshot/some-colleges-have-more-students-from-the-top-1-percent-than-the-bottom-60.html. Accessed June 5, 2017; Emily Tate, "Uneven Access, Equal Success," *Inside Higher Ed*, January 19, 2017: https://www.insidehighered.com/news/2017/01/19/rich-students-flock-elite-colleges-study-finds-graduating-college-levels-playing. Accessed June 5, 2017.
36. "Workshops and Events," Scholars Institutes Fellows Program, Princeton University: https://sifp.princeton.edu/sifp-experience/workshops-and-events. Accessed June 4, 2017.
37. David Leonhardt, "Princeton—Yes, Princeton—Takes on the Class Divide," *The New York Times*, May 30, 2017: https://www.nytimes.com/2017/05/30/opinion/princeton-takes-on-class-divide.html. Accessed June 6, 2017. The studies I have read use the percentage of students receiving Pell Grants—government grants awarded to students whose families typically earn less than $40,000 a year—as a way to assess a college's commitment to economic diversity.
38. "Diversity, Engagement, Hip Hop Are Keys to Connecting with Gen Z," *Cision PR News Wire*, May 17, 2017: https://www.prnewswire.com/news-releases/diversity-engagement-hip-hop-are-keys-to-connecting-with-gen-z-revolt-study-says-300459461.html. Accessed June 6, 2017.
39. "Mission of Amherst College"; "Mission Statement," Vassar College; and "Mission, Vision & Value," Sarah Lawrence College: https://www.sarahlawrence.edu/about/mission/.
40. Deena Prichep, "Beware of Those College Brochures That Tout Diversity in Campus Life," *MPR News*, December 29, 2013: https://www.mprnews.org/story/2013/12/30/education/beware-of-those-college-brochures-that-tout-diversity-in-campus-life. Accessed June 4, 2017; "Financial Aid & Costs," Amherst College: https://www.amherst.edu/admission/financial_aid. Accessed June 4, 2017.
41. Jon Marcus and Holly K. Hacker, "The Rich-Poor Divide on America's College Campuses Is Getting Wider, Faster," *The Hechinger Report*, December 17, 2015: http://hechingerreport.org/the-socioeconomic-divide-on-americas-college-campuses-is-getting-wider-fast/. Accessed June 6, 2017.
42. Jeremy S. Hyman and Lynn F. Jacobs, "Why Does Diversity Matter at College Anyway?" *US News and World Report*, August 12, 2009: https://www.usnews.com/education/blogs/professors-guide/2009/08/12/why-does-diversity-matter-at-college-anyway. Accessed June 6, 2017.
43. Drew Gilpin Faust, "Why Campus Inclusion Matters," *The Atlantic*, August 24, 2016: https://www.theatlantic.com/video/index/497252/why-campus-inclusion-matters/. Accessed June 6, 2017.

44. Savannah Fritz, "We Can't Wait Another Year," *The Harvard Crimson*, March 23, 2017: https://www.thecrimson.com/article/2017/3/23/fritz-we-cant-wait/. Accessed June 7, 2017; Hunter Richards, "Burning Bridges," *The Harvard Independent*, April 9, 2017: https://www.harvardindependent.com/2017/04/burning-bridges/. Accessed June 7, 2017.
45. Prichep, "Beware"; Mikahil Zinshteyn, "The Growing College-Degree Wealth Gap," *The Atlantic*, April 25, 2016: https://www.theatlantic.com/education/archive/2016/04/the-growing-wealth-gap-in-who-earns-college-degrees/479688/. Accessed June 4, 2017. The statistics here refer to graduates from all colleges and universities, not just the elite institutions.

Literature and Cultural Capital in Early Modern and Contemporary Pedagogy

Elizabeth Hutcheon

In a moment when contemptuous denunciations seem to require an optimistic and full-throated defense of the liberal arts, this essay is written with a certain amount of ambivalence. It is an answer to the question, why teach Shakespeare? Why, in this day and age, with a college population who largely see the degree as the gateway to the middle class, and who, if they want anything at all more than the credential itself, want practical wisdom that will help them in their jobs as economic development administrators, athletic trainers, and physicians' assistants? Tacitly, and until the last forty years or so, the answer to the question of why we teach Shakespeare was that entry to the middle class required the cultural capital that knowledge of Shakespeare signals, but the coin bearing Shakespeare's image is not worth what it once was. Even if it were, the transmission of cultural capital and the privilege its possession bestows feels like a less than admirable reason for teaching literature.

My answer is that Shakespeare's work is a uniquely powerful site of negotiation and potentiality, at which students can better understand the interaction between cultural capital, class, and power. To those who argue that such work could be done with any cultural text, I suggest that

E. Hutcheon (✉)
Huntingdon College, Montgomery, AL, USA

S. O'Dair and T. Francisco (eds.), *Shakespeare and the 99%*,
https://doi.org/10.1007/978-3-030-03883-0_6

Shakespeare offers educators a unique opportunity precisely because his influence penetrates both elite and popular culture. His prestige as the last man standing from the traditional canon means that higher education administrators and boards of trustees are likely to fight to retain the teaching of Shakespeare after other pillars of the liberal arts have fallen. Furthermore, Shakespeare's work, as I will argue, is suffused with discussions of the possibility of effecting social and political change via the tools bestowed on students by education.

And to those who might argue, as Audre Lorde famously does, that "the master's tools will never dismantle the master's house," I suggest, first, that recent scholarship on Shakespeare has effectively pushed back against such a position. Second, though, and more importantly, I suggest that Shakespeare's own career is an object lesson in the ambivalent benefits of humanist—and by extension, liberal-arts—education. Shakespeare rose from the merchant class to the gentry through the skills he learned during his humanist grammar-school education. From this position he was able to create, in his plays, a lasting critique of the structures of power and privilege that education helped—and helps—to maintain.

That a knowledge of literature is linked to the acquisition of cultural capital is not new. For decades scholars have followed Pierre Bourdieu in asserting that there is "a socially recognized hierarchy of the arts, and within each of them, of genres, schools, or periods, corresponds a social hierarchy of the consumers. This predisposes tastes to function as markers of 'class.'"[1] In other words, familiarity with, or an affinity for, certain kinds of art, or in this case literature, implies a certain degree of social standing. Today, it's unclear whether literature has lost all of its value as a marker of social status, but as English departments are cutting the required courses for their majors, Shakespeare is often the last to go. Shakespeare's resiliency derives at least in part because of a wider perception that Shakespeare is the "most worthy," that students are not "really educated" if not exposed to his work. In 1999 Patrick Brantlinger comically imagined the possible response if his department, at a Midwestern public university, were to cut the Shakespeare requirement:

> "But what will happen," said a young Americanist, "if we exclude Shakespeare and then the parents of our students—or, God forbid, our Board of Trustees—find out about it?" Suddenly, there it was, for all of

> us to see: the nightmarish specter of headlines in the Indianapolis *Star*: PROFESSORS STRIKE SHAKESPEARE FROM REQUIREMENTS. We pictured an inquisition by our Trustees, who in their wisdom might rule that every student be required to take Shakespeare.[2]

Brantlinger's comic vignette only works because Shakespeare is seen to be specifically important and culturally necessary. As evidence, consider that Shakespeare has long been seen not just as a part of what every educated and middle-class person should know but also as fundamental to a universal human nature, as R. W. French observes, not that long ago, in 1976: "a class is composed of human beings, all very much alive in the present; and it is Shakespeare, of all writers, who speaks most directly, most fully, to the essential humanity in all of us."[3] The emphasis on the cultivation of a universal human nature as the goal of education is found in the *Harvard Red Book* of 1945, where, according to Geoffrey Galt Harpham, "The ultimate goal of education…was not the development of abstract intellectual ability and definitely not vocational skills, but 'mastery of life; and since living is an art, wisdom is the indispensable means to this end.'"[4] Shakespeare's status among educators and the public alike is such that even today, in the standards for the Common Core—which have been roundly criticized from a least a couple of ideological and pedagogical positions—Shakespeare is the only author mentioned by name.

The challenge facing teachers and scholars of Shakespeare, then, is this: given Shakespeare's problematic status as a symbol of an uncomfortable way of thinking about the canon, what do we do? Scholars have been trained to resist the rote canonization of "great writers" and Shakespeare as "the greatest writer," and many resist hierarchical notions of culture and power. Furthermore, it is problematic to imagine that colleges are creating "a community of free men," as imagined by the *Harvard Red Book*.[5] Harpham highlights this in his reading of the *Red Book*, where he argues that there "are two quite different goals that are conjoined in the Red Book: personal enrichment and freedom on the one hand, and a coherent, cohesive society on the other."[6] Instead, after Foucault, it is impossible to think of education's fantasy of freedom without its underlying forces of social control. Sharon O'Dair articulates the tension between humanist education and the working class in particular in *Class, Critics, and Shakespeare*. There is, she argues, a problem with the way our institutions of higher education transmit cultural capital:

> [I]n the academy as we know it, the affirmation of a lower-class identity is hardly compatible with the affirmation of an (upper) middle-class identity, which is what higher education affirms. Working-class kids who succeed in the academy or subsequently in the professions are reconstituted and normalized as (upper) middle class. In the academy, working-class identity is not merely not affirmed, but actively erased.[7]

Our current academic discourse exists in a fantasy of inclusion, in which no voices are marginalized, when in fact the stated purpose of higher education is in many ways to enable working-class students to achieve a position in the professional classes, which entails an abandonment of a working-class cultural identity.

This poses a challenge when we think about the questions of working-class mobilization and advocacy; how might the lives of the working class be materially improved? Walter Benn Michaels, like O'Dair, suggests that colleges and universities, especially elite ones, really don't perform the transformative role we have traditionally assigned to them in this process, noting the irrelevance

> of most of the proposed solutions to the systematic exclusion of poor people (it's actually the systematic exclusion of three quarters of the population) from elite universities, which involve … ideas like increased financial aid for students who can't afford the high tuition, support systems for the few poor students who manage to end up there anyway, and, in general, an effort to increase the "cultural capital" of the poor.[8]

For Benn Michaels, enabling a tiny number of working-class students to attend elite institutions perpetuates the idea that poverty is earned, that the educational system is a meritocracy. The working class is something to be escaped or eradicated, certainly in terms of individual identity. None of this, and particularly not the "cultural capital" obtained by those members of the working class who attend elite colleges and universities, helps the material conditions of the majority of the working class.

The question then is, how do scholars and teachers of Shakespeare, especially those who teach primarily working-class students, teach him? Indeed, what is the value of teaching him at all? In this essay I'd like to argue, first, that there is still a practical value that is linked to the acquisition of canonical knowledge, especially for students who do not enjoy the habitus of cultural capital that comes with upper-class status. Second,

I argue that Shakespeare is himself aware of the costs and benefits of cultural capital, which he highlights throughout his corpus. Finally, I hope to invite students to see Shakespeare as a place for working out questions about the use-value of cultural capital. I believe that there are productive ways to describe and teach Shakespeare that can be valuable to students, even if these are not the same reasons that motivate Boards of Trustees to keep Shakespeare in the curriculum.

My conceptual framework here is influenced by the work of Ruby Payne, who argues that cultural capital, or the habitus of the middle class, is one of a variety of resources, including financial, that promote social mobility.[9] The understanding of poverty that Payne's analysis encourages incorporates both a Marxist idea of class, determined primarily by economic factors, and a Weberian idea of status, determined by noneconomic ones such as cultural capital; as O'Dair explains, "Class is associated with production and thus with markets, and status is associated with consumption and thus with cultural groups."[10] In addition, throughout this essay I use the term "cultural capital" to signify two things: on the one hand, I mean what Bourdieu refers to as "embodied cultural capital," such as an upper-class accent or manners so internalized as to constitute a habitus; on the other hand I refer to the version of cultural capital Bourdieu calls "cultural training," the acquisition of the body of knowledge that makes the internalization of a prestigious habitus possible.[11]

The idea that intellectual freedom is accompanied by forms of social control is familiar, and scholars of the Renaissance frequently identify the ways in which sixteenth-century pedagogical programs navigated this paradox. The English grammar-school system, in which Shakespeare was educated, exemplifies the issue. The humanist curriculum adopted by the grammar schools arose hand-in-hand with the need for an educated mercantile class, as ecclesiastical and aristocratic power began to decline. Men educated in the humanist system needed initiative and ingenuity to administer the country, but not so much as to subvert the political system. The two key humanist principles of *imitatio* and *inventio*—that students should be able both to imitate classical forms and to invent their own—clearly mirror this social imperative to both obedience and creativity. In particular, humanist pedagogical practices in the sixteenth century were designed to teach students to be effective *rhetors*, and this rhetorical mastery was achieved through the imitation of classical texts. Both the skills developed in the classroom and the body of knowledge gained in the development of those skills provided boys with cultural capital, in terms of developing an upper-class habitus as well as providing them with a shared body of knowledge. In *The Poetics of Primitive Accumulation*, Richard Halpern argues that the humanist pedagogical system used the strategies of imitation and emulation to produce obedient political subjects. He identifies imitation as "a set of practices that places the subject in an imaginary relation with a governing model."[12] These kinds of "disciplinary practices," Halpern argues, lead to a "regulated production of difference" that allows the humanist pedagogical system to "[extend] its power through the production of *negligible* differences that bind the subject to it without challenging its boundaries."[13] Timothy Hampton makes a similar point in *Writing from History*, claiming that

> [i]n setting forth the deeds of the exemplar the Renaissance text provides the reader with an image of the self, a model of an ideal soul or personality which mediates between the ideal of public virtue and the reader's self-understanding. In this sense, it aids in the process of socialization, of the creation of norms of behavior—procedures crucial to ideological hegemony and to practices of subjectivization.[14]

More recently, scholars like Rebecca Bushnell and Lynn Enterline have pushed back against this Foucauldian approach, reclaiming ground for humanist pedagogy's ability to foster creative thinkers.[15] Bushnell argues that "humanist education, in its formative stages in sixteenth-century England, could generate authoritarianism and resistance simultaneously."[16] Furthermore, as in late-twentieth-century America, sixteenth-century Britain saw a dramatic increase in the number of students enrolled in formal schools. No longer confined to the rich or monastic, education became available to all kinds of children who a century earlier would not have had such access.

Many of the working-class students in college today find themselves in a similar situation. Historically excluded from the world of higher education, these students and their families are often left wondering what the purpose of education is. I want to propose in this paper that teachers of Shakespeare are in a position to help forge a path through these at times incompatible understandings of education, where education can be thought of as providing the opportunity for independence and creativity as well as a form of social control. Throughout his career Shakespeare over and over again interrogates discourses of power and cultural capital and the way in which these discourses meet in the schoolroom. As Enterline and Bushnell suggest, Shakespeare demonstrates two things in his work: the way that knowledge is freeing and fosters creativity as well as the ways in which systems of pedagogy can be used to control thinkers and students. Shakespeare's own life fits into this model as well; as someone who would historically have been excluded from the classroom, he used the sixteenth-century expansion of access to education to improve his social and economic position, but throughout his plays we see characters struggling with the costs of conforming to socially sanctioned models of discourse. I want to suggest to students that they, like Shakespeare, are capable of doing both: it is important to learn to speak in ways that are recognized as valid by the dominant structures in society, but also to see and critique the ways in which these structures silence different voices.

Even for those who strive to critique discourses of power, having been taught to think that the need to acquire cultural capital is in many ways a bad thing, privileging one kind of habitus over another, it remains difficult to argue that individuals, in this case students, should not need to access socially sanctioned forms of cultural capital. When one comes from a position of privilege, where cultural capital is a given, it is easy to criticize the acquisition of and fetishization of cultural capital as an oppressive practice, but when one has historically been denied such access, this is a much harder argument to make. It's no surprise, then, that in my opening example it is a Midwestern public university that is worried about the implications of removing Shakespeare from the curriculum rather than an Ivy League institution whose intellectual bona fides are given. Anxiety about status reveals itself in anxiety about knowledge, about cultural capital.

Simone de Beauvoir provides a model for thinking about the individual as being subject to discourse but also having meaningful agency. She says that each individual experiences life as "an indefinite need to transcend himself," but that the situation of women is uniquely complicated by the fact that "an attempt is made to freeze her as an object and doom her to immanence, since her transcendence will be forever transcended by another essential sovereign consciousness."[17] In other words, women are having to strive for a condition that men already inhabit. This condition has its own challenges—the struggle to transcend oneself is real for everyone—but in the first instance women need to get to that place. There is a problematic and tender-hearted conservatism to de Beauvoir's point here, that once we eradicate patriarchy we can all be existentialists together. But the idea that self-transcendence is the highest good is itself riddled with class assumptions. Lorde critiques de Beauvoir's essay's assumptions in a speech she made at a conference on *The Second Sex* in 1979, "The Master's Tools Will Never Dismantle the Master's House." Lorde's point in this speech is to say that women need to look outside of patriarchal paradigms to successfully resist oppression. Following this logic, the question of whether working-class students benefit from exposure to the kinds of canonical texts that signify as cultural capital is an open one: how can these tools, the "master's tools," break down an oppressive system? I argue that Shakespeare shows us a middle way. The humanist subject, using the Master's language and cultural traditions, is a Foucauldian subject as well as a critical political force.

This is a hard point to articulate: for students who want to improve their economic standing, to "do better" than their parents, classic American-Dream style, the acquisition of cultural capital remains necessary; learning to think about the world in terms of canonical texts and stories is important. However, it looks likely that at least some students are not going to "do better" than their parents, given the current job numbers for recent graduates.[18] Furthermore, many if not most of my students are not going to use their college education to leap to the upper middle class; instead, they're using their college credentials to access jobs that would not have required a bachelor's degree fifty years ago: I'm thinking of the student who is going to take over the family's cattle ranch, the football player who aspires to work in mid-level management, the young woman who will work as a nurse's assistant in an orthopedic clinic. What does cultural capital, even imagined as some kind of nebulous social access, really do for them? My answer, imperfect and provisional as it may be, is that in the end it's vitally important to learn to see the ways in which the world is constructed, and most importantly to see the ways in which power relationships structure the world around us, no matter our class. Shakespeare then becomes a site through which one can examine the relationship between language and the discourses of power. Teaching Shakespeare—often in the context of survey courses—at a small, lower-tier institution (as I do), brings instructors into continual contact with first-generation students. For such students, the study of Shakespeare is part of a curriculum that enables them to identify and name themselves as both speaking subjects and subjected. They can learn to see the ways the mastery of language and rhetoric provides certain kinds of real social and political power while at the same time understanding that the wielding of this power comes at a cost, excluding other voices.

Shakespeare himself provides a case-study of exactly this point. Then, like now, pedagogues were expanding their definition of who qualified to attend school. Writers like Shakespeare, Dekker, and Webster benefited from an increased access to education in the late sixteenth century. The grammar school system imagined students as embarking on a project of subject-making that depended on a version of early modern cultural capital. As Enterline notes, "Humanist training in rhetorical *copia* was designed to intervene in social reproduction, to sort out which differences between bodies (male and female) and groups (aristocrats, the middling sort, and those below) were necessary to defining and producing proper English 'gentlemen.'"[19] Education in the sixteenth century then functioned as a site of habitus-formation. As Shakespeare's eventual knighthood reveals, he managed to adopt enough of the habitus of a gentleman to be formally recognized as such. Yet even while benefiting from this cultural capital, Shakespeare and others used the rhetorical tools they learned in the early modern classroom to critique the system of power under which they were formed. Enterline explains, "when Shakespeare creates the convincing effects of character and emotion… he signals his debt to the Latin institution that granted him the cultural capital of an early modern gentleman precisely when undercutting the socially normative categories schoolmasters invoked as their educational goal."[20] Over and over again in the Shakespearean corpus we find places where Shakespeare reflects on and critiques early modern pedagogical practices and, by extension, the social order of early modern England.

The value of an education comes up as a question in lots of Shakespeare's plays across his career. From Navarre's short-lived scholar's retreat in *Love's Labour's Lost* to Hamlet's scholarly demeanor, from Petruchio's taming (reframed by the play as "teaching") of Katherine to the recasting of Marina as schoolteacher in *Pericles*, from Jacques' impotent intellectualism to Prospero's literally magical knowledge, thinking through the value of education is important to Shakespeare.[21] Furthermore, he is not only interested in the value of education generally. Shakespeare is specifically interested in the class politics of education. In perhaps the clearest example of this, Shakespeare demonstrates working-class suspicion of education in *2 Henry VI*, when Jack Cade accosts Lord Saye: "Thou has most traitorously corrupted the youth of the realm in erecting a grammar school; and, whereas before our forefathers had no other books but the score and the tally, thou hast caused printing to be used and, contrary to the King his crown and dignity, thou has built a paper mill."[22] Cade's suspicion of education is located specifically in the printed word. The book-learning so prized by early modern humanists is here (anachronistically) dismissed by Shakespeare's champion of the lower class.

I want to move now, however, to two examples that dramatize Shakespeare's understanding of humanist education especially well: *Coriolanus* and *The Tempest*. *Coriolanus* holds out a limited hope that both the habitus and the rhetorical skills imparted by humanist education might make it possible for the masses to achieve meaningful, non-violent access to republican power. In the beginning, the play provides a largely dysfunctional picture of class politics, being set against the backdrop of class strife. The First Citizen outlines the parameters of this tension: "We are accounted poor citizens, the patricians good... The leanness that afflicts us, the object of our misery, is as an inventory to particularize their abundance; our sufferance is a gain to them."[23] In his account, the misery of the impoverished is imposed by the rich. Existing only to provide a kind of bar by which the rich can measure their relative or superlative success, the poor are driven to "revenge" (1.1.24). Furthermore, as Annabel Patterson points out, the citizens are not distinguished from one another; their "ordinal numbering" contrasts with Coriolanus' "commitment to a *name* as the sign of personal identity and self worth."[24]

The plebeians do have a certain amount of power. Patterson argues that Shakespeare "clearly shows us plebeians capable of reasoning from one thing to another, from a local corn shortage to economic injustice in general; and, as a consequence of the changes he made in the Roman historical pretext, he shows us that popular, food-centered protest could *work*, since it resulted in the creation of the tribunate."[25] In this reading, Shakespeare presents a picture of class politics that functions, where the plebeians really do have some opportunity to effect change, which is echoed in the historical reality that the tribunes created at this time were instrumental in the establishment and long success of the Roman republic.

At the same time, the plebeians seem unable to make effective use of their right to advise and consent to the election of the consul. The Third Citizen acknowledges that the power of the citizenry is still largely symbolic: "We have the power in ourselves to do it, but it is a power that we have no power to do" (2.3.4–5). The plebeians, when talking with Coriolanus, are unable to ask him the kinds of probing questions the tribunes suggest and instead grudgingly give him their assent. They lack the habitus of an informed political actor that education could provide. Given the opportunity to "giv[e] him our own voices with our own tongues," the citizens find themselves unable to articulate their grievances (2.3.41–42). Coriolanus does have to speak with each citizen individually and in theory hear their concerns. His reply to the Fourth Citizen, however, reveals his lack of interest in the process:

> And since the wisdom of their choice is rather to have my hat than my heart, I will practice the insinuating nod and be off to them most counterfeitly; that is, sir, I will counterfeit the bewitchment of some popular man, and give it bountiful to the desirers. (2.3.94–98)

Yet even this lukewarm and frankly insulting reply is enough for the citizens, who give him their votes, even though, as they later note, "He flouted us downright" (2.3.155).

One might say that this is because the ruling class has no intention of allowing the plebeians to make real use of the power they ostensibly possess. As Kai Wiegandt points out, Coriolanus regards winning the consent of the Citizens as pure pantomime, something like the British monarch's power to appoint the prime minister, a power that would be revoked if its wielder ever attempted to refuse it. For Coriolanus, "Nothing is as slight for him as a voice, even if it is to get him the consulship. It is telling that Coriolanus says that the citizens *are* voices, an anonymous plural referring to the use he may make of them."[26] Coriolanus resists the idea that in order to become consul he must curry favor with the citizens; in turn they are not sure whether or not to support his candidacy, questioning whether they have the power to oppose him in a productive way. The Third Citizen outlines the way in which the relationship of obligation is expected to work:

> For if he show us his wounds and tell us his deeds, we are to put our tongues into those wounds and speak for them; so if he tell us his noble deeds we must also tell him our noble acceptance of them. Ingratitude is monstrous, and for the multitude to be ingrateful were to make a monster of the multitude. (2.3.5–11)

In other words, the citizens are expected to show their gratitude for Coriolanus' military success by voting him in. It might be easy to write off the citizens as stupid and gullible here, but it is also clear that they are aware of the limitations of their electoral process and see Coriolanus as a decent choice, particularly given their lack of other options. They seem to have no real choice but to approve the man who meets the minimum requirement of going through the motions to win their approval, despite his evident distaste for the process and open disdain for them.

One might also argue, however, that what the plebeians lack is not power but the habitus necessary to make effective use of it. Although they demonstrate their rhetorical capability when speaking among themselves, they are tongue-tied in their interactions with Coriolanus. The tribunes scold them for voting, asking, "Could you not have told him / As you were lessoned"? (2.3.172–173). The tribunes, it turns out, had asked the citizens to try and draw out Coriolanus, to challenge him in the hopes of "putting him to rage" (2.3.193), and thus harm his chances of being elected. What stymies the citizens (and, in fact, also allows them also to be manipulated by the tribunes) is neither a lack of competence, nor the fear their power will be revoked, but a lack of confidence in their own capabilities: as the Third Citizen says, if the plebeians were to truly vote with their preferences, rather than being led (or coerced) into choosing a particular candidate, "all our wits…would fly east, west, north, south, and the consent of one direct way should be at once to all points of the compass" (2.3.19–22). The citizens do not insist on their right to choose because they worry that choosing their own candidates would end in chaos.

Furthermore, Coriolanus also lacks the *right* kind of cultural capital. He lacks the rhetorical polish to assuage the plebeians' doubts about him—his refusal to perform gracious speech leads to his expulsion from the city and, ultimately, his death. O'Dair argues that Coriolanus' distaste for the electoral process reveals another kind of shift in social power, in which "self-evident, absolute distinction based on blood will give way to constructed distinction based on style, which takes a great time and effort to establish and maintain and this is not available to most people."[27] In order to exert social power moving forward, according to this reading, an individual must develop a habitus of power, which is developed by the acquisition and concentration of cultural capital over time. Both Coriolanus and the plebeians lose in this reading; Coriolanus because he cannot adapt to new expectations of leadership, and the citizens because they will never have the time or opportunity to acquire the social markings of power.

Despite the possibility then that what motivates the tragedy in *Coriolanus* is the ruling class's refusal to grant the citizens more than purely symbolic political power, it is also possible to read the play as suggesting that what its characters need is more and better cultural capital, which a better educational system might provide. Possession of the habitus of power and the rhetorical polish afforded by humanist education might make possible a less dysfunctional and less violent version of class politics.

The Tempest offers another, different reading of humanism as a site of the student's potentiality. Scholars often read this play as being about colonialism and the colonial project,[28] but Shakespeare is here again interested in the way in which power is exerted through language. However, I'd like to think about the play's interrogation of language and power in the context of humanist education. In Caliban and Prospero we see both the possibilities and the limitations of humanist education. Caliban is left with nothing but symbolic resistance to his master, but symbolic resistance is not itself nothing. Prospero's spells, by contrast, associated with classical humanism via his imitation of Medea, give him the power to defeat and revenge himself on his political opponents; in addition, they have made him the consummate artist for whom he has stood as metaphor for generations of critics. Yet the scholarship that has given him such mastery also makes him a weak and ineffective political actor in Milan. In fact, Prospero represents for Shakespeare, and for students, both the possibilities and failures that the acquisition of canonical knowledge can entail. Enterline observes the failure of sixteenth-century writers to follow the Virgilian models so favored by their schoolmasters:

> Given the resonance between Virgilian civic duty and the school's announced goal of fashioning gentlemen by bringing Rome to England, there is something puzzling about the results of its training: poems written by former schoolboys rarely followed *anything like* the model of the *Aeneid*. Rather, as poetry in the 1590 s indicates, school training encourages an outpouring not of epic poetry, but of epyllia.[29]

In other words, we might say what the early modern classroom produced was versions of Prospero: not only docile political subjects who wielded their cultural capital to gain power and influence, but also poets and writers who used their skills in new and unexpected ways.

As a product of Prospero's humanist educational project, Caliban becomes an able speaker, but one who can only curse his master. Caliban must turn to Prospero as his teacher, expanding his field of knowledge from the practical to the linguistic. While Prospero teaches Caliban language, Caliban teaches Prospero about the island: "I loved thee / And showed thee all the qualities o'th'isle: / The fresh springs, brine pits, barren place and fertile."[30] Caliban develops an affective bond with Prospero, just as schoolboys were taught to love their masters.

Prospero's successful education of Miranda is contrasted in the play with his education of Caliban. As Caliban notes, when Prospero first came to the island he taught Caliban "how / To name the bigger light and how the less / That burn by day and night" (1.2.335–337). Miranda and Caliban are imagined to be schoolmates; even though she is the younger of the two, Miranda occupies the role of the superior student, or prefect, who monitors other students' behavior for the teacher.[31] Miranda describes their relationship in pedagogical terms:

> Abhorred slave,
> Which any print of goodness wilt not take,
> Being capable of all ill; I pitied thee,
> Took pains to make thee speak, taught thee each hour
> One thing or other…
> But thy vile race
> (Though thou didst learn) had that in't which good natures
> Could not abide to be with. (1.2.352–356; 359–361)

In her view, Caliban's failure as a student is a moral failure. Caliban should have reaped the benefit of a humanist education, which combined language learning with moral development, becoming a good citizen in Prospero's world (as Caliban notes, "I am all the subjects that you have" [1.2.342]), but instead Miranda argues that there is something innate in him that hinders his moral development, implying that his inheritance from Sycorax his mother is inherently inferior to her own humanist training by Prospero. Caliban has learned Prospero's and Miranda's lessons; after all, he has learned to speak properly. But whereas Miranda's education is coupled with her morality, Caliban appears to have rejected the moral aspects of humanism.

Yet the accuracy of Miranda's self-characterization as a superior pupil to Caliban is undercut by the rhetorical power of Caliban's speeches. While Miranda humanistically links education with moral development in her indictment of Caliban, Caliban's own description of his education arguably reveals him to be the more able student. Caliban's scene of education is first dominated by affection, "Thou strok'st me and made much of me" (1.1.334), "then I loved thee" (1.2.337). Caliban, however, soon shifts into the language of political authority, claiming that Prospero has usurped Caliban's rightful position: "For I am all the subjects that you have, / Which first was my own king" (1.2.342–343). Caliban recognizes his relationship to Prospero in political terms, a recognition that allows him to contest (however unsuccessfully) his own subordinate position. Paul Brown notes, "Paradoxically, it is the eloquent power of civility which allows [Caliban] to know his *own* meaning, offering him a site of resistance even as civility's coercive capacities finally reduce him to silence."[32] Caliban's "site of resistance" is not necessarily meaningless; as Dick Hebdige argues in his account of punk: "I would like to think that this Refusal is worth making, that these gestures have a meaning, that the smiles and sneers have some subversive value, even if, in the final analysis, they are…just so much graffiti on a prison wall."[33] Resistance, even futile resistance, is not necessarily meaningless.

Caliban is not the only wielder of a humanist inheritance in *The Tempest*. We can see the complicated nature of this classical inheritance when the Ovidian Medea appears in Prospero's speech in 5.1, where he explicitly imitates her invocation of the spirits in Ovid's *Metamorphoses:* "Ye elves of hills, brooks, standing lakes and groves" (5.1.33). (Golding's translation of this line in Ovid reads "Ye Ayres and windes: ye Elves of Hillles, of Brookes, of Woods alone / Of standing Lakes, and of the Night."[34] It is the dissociation of Medea's speech from her actions—a move characteristic of the humanist schoolroom, in which grammar and style were emphasized over content—that allows Shakespeare to invoke her in the character of Prospero. Jonathan Bate describes this use of Medea as a model: "To imitate [Medea's speech] was to assert its continuing relevance; humanist imitation was based on the premise that classical texts were appropriate patterns or models because they embodied fundamental, enduring truths."[35] These enduring truths are not necessarily identical. Medea's speech in Ovid is an incantation; she calls upon the spirits in order that they might help her "To flowring prime of lustie youth old withred age reduce."[36] Prospero, by contrast, invokes Medea's language to relinquish his magical powers; he calls upon the elves so that he might "abjure" his "rough magic" (5.1.33, 50–51). Prospero's use of Medea here represents

Shakespeare's recuperation of a positive version of Medea's words and power, as opposed to the threatening mother figure, familiar in the sixteenth century from Seneca's *Medea*, which in this play is located in the character of Sycorax. Powerful as Medea is, in her Ovidian iteration her power is used for good (in the moment Prospero imitates she is preparing to rejuvenate Aeson). Shakespeare is going against the grain of a traditional understanding of the Medea story. Rather than a murderous mother figure, Shakespeare reimagines Medea as a healer, both of bodies and the social order.

The uneasy relationship Prospero has with Medea, and by extension the literary canon of the humanists, complicates our understanding of his role in *The Tempest*. We might think of Prospero as the consummate humanist, a master of texts and an expert manipulator of language (since his magic powers are all grounded in his books), but he is in fact a political failure.[37] The picture of him "neglecting worldly ends, all dedicated / To closeness and the bettering of my mind" (1.2.89–90) is reminiscent of a medieval scholastic rather than a humanist prince. Prospero has not mastered the ability to be both learned and effective in the world, a fundamental goal of humanist pedagogy. His imitation of Medea is his most "humanist" moment; a piece of formal imitation, it marks his resolution to reintegrate himself into the political world. After this he returns to the stage dressed "As I was sometime Milan" (5.1.86), ready to take up his dukedom which he mentions repeatedly, (see, for example, 5.1.107, 133, 159, 168; Epilogue.6). Despite his magical maneuvering, however, Prospero does not succeed in rectifying the political situation. Antonio remains silent after Prospero's appearance, and we have no evidence to justify thinking that he has repented of his usurpation, the threat of which hangs over the end of the play; although Prospero says "I could pluck his highness' frown upon you / And justify you traitors!" (5.1.127–128), he does not tell Alonso, nor is there any evidence that Antonio takes this as a chastisement. In fact, Prospero's resolution that he will "retire me to Milan, where / Every third thought shall be my grave" (5.1.311–312) does not bode well. Even without his books, Prospero's plan is to meditate and reflect rather than involve himself in the social world. As an exemplar of humanism, he falls short. The perfect humanism that early modern educators would like their students to attain is imagined here as an impossible goal. Instead, however, what Shakespeare gives us is the possibility that one's cultural inheritance might be utilized in new and unexpected ways.

What I am suggesting in this essay then is that Shakespeare remains an important site for uncovering the relationships between power and education. Students can benefit from seeing the way that Shakespeare thinks through the benefits and costs of his own educational inheritance, and he can perhaps model the ways in which students might interrogate their own experiences of education. When I started writing this essay, in the summer of 2016, it felt like a different time. It was easy to feel sure that I knew what was best for my students, that I could show them what kind of knowledge is important, and why. Now I'm not so sure. That position feels like hubris. However, if my own optimism has turned to ambivalence, that ambivalence is mirrored in Shakespeare. And what Shakespeare teaches about education is that ambivalent benefits are still benefits. The twenty-first-century educational system, like the sixteenth century's, is designed both to help students get for themselves a better place in the world and to keep them in their place. One thing academics sometimes forget is that escaping from poverty by being enfolded in the discursive tendrils of the middle class is not, in fact, an unalloyed bad thing. One still gets to escape from poverty. But furthermore, and more importantly, Shakespeare shows us that an education designed to keep people in their place can, albeit grudgingly, also provide the very tools needed to subvert the system of places itself.

Notes

1. Pierre Bourdieu, *Distinction: A Social Critique of the Judgement of Taste*, trans. Richard Nice (Cambridge, MA: Harvard University Press, 1984), 1–2.
2. Patrick Brantlinger, "Who Killed Shakespeare? An Apologia for English Departments," *College English* 61, no. 6 (1999): 681.
3. R. W. French, "Shakespeare and the Common Reader," *College English* 38, no. 1 (1976): 87.
4. Geoffrey Galt Harpham, "From Eternity to Here: Shrinkage in American Thinking About Higher Education," *Representations* 116, no. 1 (2011): 45.
5. Ibid., 45.
6. Ibid., 45.
7. Sharon O'Dair, *Class, Critics, and Shakespeare: Bottom Lines on the Culture Wars* (Ann Arbor: University of Michigan Press, 2000), 3.
8. Walter Benn Michaels, *The Trouble with Diversity: How We Learned to Love Identity and Ignore Inequality* (New York: Metropolitan Books, 2006), 10.

9. Ruby K. Payne, *A Framework for Understanding Poverty: A Cognitive Approach* (Highlands, TX: Aha! Process, Inc., 2013).
10. O'Dair, *Class, Critics, and Shakespeare*, 11.
11. Bourdieu, *Distinction*, 54.
12. Richard Halpern, *The Poetics of Primitive Accumulation: English Renaissance Culture and the Genealogy of Captial* (Ithaca: Cornell University Press, 1991), 29.
13. Ibid., 29, 38, 42.
14. Timothy Hampton, *Writing from History: The Rhetoric of Exemplarity in Renaissance Literature* (Ithaca: Cornell University Press, 1990), 19. Of course, Renaissance pedagogues did not explicitly theorize the effects of imitation in this way. Instead, imitation was conceived of as a basis for imaginative thinking. For an extensive discussion of this, see Thomas M. Greene, *The Light in Troy: Imitation and Discovery in Renaissance Poetry* (New Haven: Yale University Press, 1982).
15. Rebecca Bushnell, *A Culture of Teaching: Early Modern Humanism in Theory and Practice* (Ithaca: Cornell University Press, 1996); Lynn Enterline, "Rhetoric, Discipline, and the Theatricality of Everyday Life in Elizabethan Grammar Schools," in *From Performance to Print in Shakespeare's England*, ed. Peter Holland and Stephen Orgel (Basingstoke: Palgrave Macmillan, 2006), 173–190.
16. Bushnell, *A Culture of Teaching*, 74.
17. Simone de Beauvoir, *The Second Sex*, trans. Constance Borde and Sheila Malovaney-Chevallier (New York: Vintage Books, 2009), 17.
18. Teresa Kroeger, Tanyell Cooke, and Elise Gould, *The Class of 2016: The Labor Market Is Still Far from Ideal for Young Graduates* (Washington, DC: Economic Policy Institute, 2016).
19. Lynn Enterline, *Shakespeare's Schoolroom: Rhetoric, Discipline, Emotion* (Philadelphia: University of Pennsylvania Press, 2012), 1.
20. Enterline, *Shakespeare's Schoolroom*, 1.
21. See Elizabeth Hutcheon, "Imitating Women: Rhetoric, Gender, and Humanist Pedagogy in English Renaissance Drama" (PhD diss., University of Chicago, 2011).
22. William Shakespeare, *King Henry VI, Part II*, ed. Ronald Knowles (London: Thomson Learning), 1999, 4.6.29–34.
23. William Shakespeare, *Coriolanus*, ed. R. B. Parker (Oxford: Oxford University Press, 1998), 1.1.14–15, 18–21. All further references are to this edition and will hereafter be parenthetical.
24. Annabel Patterson, *Shakespeare and the Popular Voice* (Oxford: Basil Blackwell, 1989), 130.
25. Ibid., 143.

26. Kai Wiegandt, *Crowd and Rumour in Shakespeare* (Farnham, Surrey: Ashgate, 2012), 86.
27. O'Dair, *Class, Critics, and Shakespeare*, 82.
28. See O'Dair, *Class, Critics, and Shakespeare*, 30–31.
29. Enterline, "Rhetoric, Discipline," 183.
30. William Shakespeare, *The Tempest*, ed. Virginia Mason Vaughan and Alden T. Vaughan (London: Thomson Learning, 1999), 1.2.338–339. All other references are to this edition and will hereafter be parenthetical.
31. See Enterline, "Rhetoric, Discipline," 176 for a description of the duties of the monitoring student.
32. Paul Brown, "'This Thing of Darkness I Acknowledge Mine': *The Tempest* and the Discourse of Colonialism," in *Political Shakespeare: New Essays in Cultural Materialism*, ed. Jonathan Dollimore and Alan Sinfield (Ithaca: Cornell University Press, 1985), 61–62.
33. Dick Hebdige, *Subculture: The Meaning of Style* (Padstow, England: TJ International, 1979), 3.
34. Ovid, *Ovid's Metamorphoses: The Arthur Golding Translation*, 1567, ed. John Frederick Nims (Philadelphia: Paul Dry Books, Inc., 2000), 7.265–266.
35. Jonathan Bate, *Shakespeare and Ovid* (Oxford: The Clarendon Press, 1993), 9.
36. Ovid, *Ovid's Metamorphoses*, 7.285.
37. Richard Strier describes Prospero's amazement at Antonio's political powers in "'I am Power': Normal and Magical Politics in *The Tempest*," in *Writing and Political Engagement in Seventeenth-Century England*, ed. Derek Hirst and Richard Strier (Cambridge: Cambridge University Press, 1999), 12–13.

Creativity Studies and Shakespeare at the Urban Community College

Katherine Boutry

Can you make no use of nothing, nuncle?
The Fool to Lear (2.4.130)

'Tis still a dream, or else such stuff as madmen
Tongue…
Or senseless speaking, or a speaking such
As sense cannot untie.

In Act V of *Cymbeline*, Posthumus utters these lines as he awakens to find a tablet placed on his chest, not by a human prankster, but by Jupiter, a superhero among gods. It is a miracle, a thing amazing, and a thing completely incomprehensible to him. Although its value is clear (Posthumus has been promised that the writings on the god-endorsed tablet will predict his future happiness), its meaning is not. And thus, Posthumus feels vulnerable, frustrated, and afraid, staring at a locked door to understanding he desperately wants open, but for which he is not certain to possess the key.

K. Boutry (✉)
West Los Angeles College, Culver City, CA, USA

S. O'Dair and T. Francisco (eds.), *Shakespeare and the 99%*,
https://doi.org/10.1007/978-3-030-03883-0_7

This is the experience of most community college students upon first approaching the works of Shakespeare. One of my students at West Los Angeles College, who has since transferred to UC Irvine, explained: "My exposure to Shakespeare prior to that class was little to none. One fear many have (that I can surely attest to) is not being able to understand the text at face value." Most have heard of the Bard; they have been told that he is important and valuable, that studying him may be the academic benchmark of a student on her way somewhere with keys to an executive bathroom ("Studying his works is simply the foundation of a good education" observed another student), but they know little else. If they took honors or AP English in Los Angeles public high schools, they may have been required to read *A Midsummer Night's Dream* or perhaps *Romeo and Juliet*, but likely they read a modern translation. Thus coming into a class devoted "only" to Shakespeare feels both limiting and daunting to them, akin to boarding a darkened subway car. It *may* take them to a brave new world, but it looks disquietingly claustrophobic and vaguely unsafe. Certainly, one must be courageous and a little foolhardy to enter therein.

So who is this dauntless 99 percent at West Los Angeles College? The demographic of this urban two-year community college in Los Angeles is made up of underrepresented minorities, primarily Latino and African American. In a student body of 19,000, 76 percent are students of color. Fewer than 13 percent are Caucasian. We have over five hundred veterans, not all of them honorably discharged, and a significant majority of our students are the first in their families to attend college and to speak English. And they are largely underprepared for college. On entering, 65 percent place below college-level in English and writing skills; only 6 percent place as math-ready.[1] A food pantry on campus serves those in need; many of the recipients of that food are our students. Several report being homeless. It is accurate to say these students face multiple challenges on every level: material, physical, emotional, intellectual, and spiritual. Whether providing an education or a hot meal, WLAC does not turn students away, but recognizes the truth in Pisanio's soliloquy that "Fortune brings in some boats that are not steer'd."[2] It does indeed, but that does not make those boats less sound, nor less seaworthy. If anything, the fact that they have made it this far, drawn by currents, proves their promise as much as their fortune. My experience at West has borne this out.

An awareness of the mitigating factors affecting our students' progress is an important starting point. Because finances are tight, most of our students must simultaneously work one or more jobs while enrolled full time. Part-time studies would be more manageable for them, but if they drop below full time, they find themselves no longer eligible for financial aid. Many are also responsible for the care of children and dependent elders. As a result, time is their most precious resource. Hence our students' classes must necessarily be leading them somewhere quickly: either to transfer or to better employment.

Unlike "traditional" students, they do not generally indulge in the luxury of classes for personal growth, exploration, or pure pleasure. They are rarely English majors, nor is English always their first language. Many worry quite reasonably that Shakespeare is literally not worth their time. Who wants to bother reading Shakespeare when you are intermittently homeless and hungry, and have trouble simply making it to campus? As it turns out, they do. They show up after a grueling day of work to sit in my classroom every week. I asked my students (after grades were submitted, with no pressure to oblige), if they would be willing to share with me any difficulties or obstacles they faced in pursuing their education at West. Contrary to what I expected, their answers came pouring in. It turns out that they were very eager to share their stories.

A single father and Navy veteran wrote,

When I decided to return to college, my son was three and I was working a full time graveyard shift at Fed Ex ground. The commute to work was an hour. This schedule made going to school very difficult. I would go to work at 10 pm, get off at 7 am, rush home to take my son to day care for 8 am, head to school for my 9:35 am class, then after I finished school at 2:00 pm, go pick my son up from day care, go home and do it all again. Notice I left something out: sleep. It is nearly impossible to get quality sleep with a three year old running around the house causing havoc.

Another student wrote,

When I was eight, my mother passed away from lung cancer. Then, shortly after, my father died. I felt alone and desolate. I was an orphan who had nothing to give to the world and no potential. I never knew how I was able to get past my difficulties but I know that I owe my success to my teachers who would stay after hours with me to help me. I always supported myself. Since 10th grade I have worked three jobs and I go to school full time.

One student shared,

I had to take on another job, which was difficult since I was taking four classes on campus and one online. I would wake up at 7 AM and get ready to go to my job at the mall, get off at 12, rush to school, change in my car, and get to class by 12:15. I would be finished with my classes around 7:15 PM,

> so I would jump in my car and rush downtown to catch another shift at work from 8 PM to 1 AM, then go home and repeat. This left me with virtually no time for my online class, let alone homework from my classes on campus. I wish I could tell you how I did it, but I really don't know. I think my mind just had to rise to the occasion and make the most of my time to make sure I was still getting at least a majority of my homework done. It was an awful cycle and it left me exhausted. Somehow, I managed to get straight As. I'm very proud of how I managed to make things work. Whenever I'm going through a hard time with work or school I just remind myself that if I could handle all that, I surely have it in me to handle whatever is happening at the moment.

I find these statements and these students profoundly inspiring. Rather than feel defeated and overwhelmed by their challenges, these students rose to meet them, showing the creativity traits of flexibility, resiliency, resourcefulness, and perseverance. And these are not students barely scraping by, these are "A" students who sit in the front row, and participate, and come on time to every class. If I had not asked, I would never have imagined their struggles. (Two of these students are now at Berkeley, one at UCLA.)

Given these challenges, it becomes incumbent upon the community college professor to make Shakespeare useful and relevant to students' already over-burdened lives. A professor who intends to capture and hold the intellectual interest of this demographic must be prepared not only to teach and to entertain, but also to reassure and to inspire. A Shakespeare course has to be *worth* it.

This realization led me to blend my two interests in the classroom.

Two years ago, inspired by the creative potential in my students to overcome personal obstacles, I started the first Creativity Studies initiative in a community college anywhere in California. I became convinced that my students, not in spite of, but *because* of their life challenges, were inherently creative, and that creativity could be a source of pride and an advantage in the workplace. If designer George Lois is correct that "Creativity can solve almost any problem,"[3] it follows that in order to be creative, you *need* the problem. The research suggests that it is precisely when limits are imposed that creativity can flourish; thus limits allow creativity to happen. In other words, there is no "outside the box" without the box.

The majority of our students have always been outside of their comfort zones. And that is where growth happens. What do you do when you lack resources? You become resourceful. You adapt. You become resilient and self-sufficient. What do you do when you have no model? If no one in your extended family has ever attended college? You must create a new model where none has existed before—and isn't that the very definition of creativity?

A student of mine explains,

> I'm the first to graduate high school. I know I have the drive to excel in college, but given no one in my family ever did, it took countless affirmations that I was good enough and deserved an opportunity to thrive. As I look back I think of all the struggles; and I think to myself, it is all worth it! I chose to believe in myself and be my own definition of success.

And if challenging life experience is indeed an advantage when it comes to creativity, it also makes my students more mature and better able to access the emotional depth of Shakespeare and to relate to characters facing challenges. Indeed, his or her particular obstacles and response to them define so many characters in Shakespeare's plays: they must adapt creatively or end tragically. According to psychologist Mihaly Csikszentmihalyi, creativity may have developed in human beings as an evolutionary response to a constantly changing and hostile environment.[4] Every character in Shakespeare reacts to environmental pressures and adversity, and thereby demonstrates a creative response. My students can relate; they adapt to environmental stressors continually. And those who make it to college have certainly demonstrated creativity traits and maturity beyond their peers. It turns out, also, that these traits lend themselves to the reading and analysis of Shakespeare and a deeper understanding of character.

When I inherited the sole Shakespeare class taught once a year at our college, I was thrilled, and then I panicked. The last time I had taught Shakespeare was quite literally to the 1 percent: a graduate section of the well-loved Harvard University Core course taught by Marjorie Garber. At the time, I had just finished my Ph.D. there and was working as a lecturer in English. West certainly proved a change of demographic and culture, but not in the ways I expected. It would probably not be possible to find two more diametrically opposed Shakespeare-studying populations. My Harvard seminar had been comprised of sixteen students, now my class cap was forty. On the first day of class at Harvard years ago, students had asked which Shakespeare anthology I preferred, which Folio we would be studying in class, and whether

I was an Oxfordian (I am not). Before the first night of class at West, one of the students came to my office hours and looked at me panicked, deer-in-the-headlights style, until he finally admitted with a tinge of hostility bred by shame that he had "No idea what these words mean. It's like a foreign language, or something." He was afraid. So was I.

So on the very first night of class, I took them on a field trip.

Performance

Although the summer season was over, the Griffith Park Free Shakespeare Festival put on by the Independent Shakespeare Company in Los Angeles happened to be doing an extended run, one special encore performance of *Romeo and Juliet* on the very night our first class met. This was great good luck and also an enormous risk. Griffith Park is up in the Hollywood Hills and many of our students don't have cars, but carefully-arranged carpooling with my family minivan and helpful students could work, if they would take a leap of faith and make the effort to attend. Asking them to deviate from a very carefully-balanced schedule where there is precious little margin for change is challenging even at the end of a semester. It is unheard of on the first night of class. But this was the last performance of the season. It was our only chance. I held my breath as these students found their way to Griffith Park, put down blankets, and settled in. As our numbers grew and the crowd fell silent, I sent up a silent smoke signal to the gods of education: *Please, let this be good.*

It was. The atmosphere could not have been better for this first experiment with live performance and with Shakespeare. Plays for the Free Shakespeare Festival take place in the Old Zoo in Griffith Park on a hilltop overlooking Los Angeles. Los Angeles weather seems designed for viewing Shakespeare outside. Cool, dry evenings with the smell of eucalyptus trees make it feel removed from the bustle of the city. The Independent Shakespeare Company (#shakespearesetfree) takes "Free Shakespeare" to heart. The plays not only cost nothing to attend, but they are free in spirit as well. The actors and directors take liberties with the clothing, music, set design, and direction. It is not unusual for them to play with gender and race in assigning roles. Their musical version of *Romeo and Juliet* incorporated an original rock score and design that their promotional materials proclaimed "equal parts fairy tale and punk." (In their version of *The Tempest*, Trinculo throws real fish into the audience). They do this all while remaining absolutely true to the letter and the language of the plays. Shakespeare is hence freed of the stuffiness some associate with attending a performance today, and made accessible to those with financial constraints. (L.A. Opera also put on *Macbeth* featuring Placido Domingo at the Dorothy Chandler Pavilion, but at $199 per ticket, that was out, and I suspect it may have been a lot less fun.)

Attending this live performance had an impact that far exceeded my expectations. Although we live in a city full of actors and playhouses, most of the students in the class had never before attended a professional play of any kind. A student described her profound experience:

> Our first class set the tone and taught me that 'true art is not a masterpiece unless it is experienced, spoken and felt.' We watched the play *Romeo and Juliet* held at Griffith Park outside, under the stars, and we could hear the crickets. Hearing the words spoken was magical and enchanted my soul. The poetry I heard confirmed the idea that Shakespeare's words are meant to be heard in order to feel the magic of the art.

Back in the classroom, several students confessed a similar enjoyment and mentioned repeatedly how seeing the play performed made it much easier to understand. This led me to believe that performances early in the semester, if the stars align, can set the tone in a positive way for the entire course.

And I must acknowledge their part in this. They didn't yet know me; they didn't know Shakespeare; and they had never been to a play or Griffith Park, *but they did it anyway.* In his research conducted in housing projects in 1969, Creativity Studies pioneer Paul Torrance found creativity traits such as having a higher tolerance for the unknown, flexibility, and the ability to take risks and be adventurous more prevalent in economically-challenged demographics.[5] My students' creativity traits served us very well, both that night, and in the course as a whole. I quickly learned to expect a lot from them.

The Bar: A Word About Expectations

When teaching community college students underprepared for college and facing difficult personal circumstances, an instructor might be tempted to "lower the bar," or to ease up on the course requirements. This was a fundamental mistake I made in my second semester teaching. My first semester, I taught as I always had at Harvard, but I was new and a little unsure of myself. My students sensed this and complained vociferously about workload. In retrospect, it was one or two students out of eighty, but they were loud. And I was too inexperienced to know that it is the students' job to sniff out lack of confidence in a professor and decide that too much has been asked of them. Not yet realizing that, in my second semester, I reduced my expectations. I sincerely regret the disservice I did my students that semester. Whenever I set a level of expectations, I find 80 percent will rise to meet it. When that bar lowers, 80 percent will still rise to meet it, but they will have gotten much less done. In other words, students rely on the professor to set the pace and to anticipate the distance. Moving the finish line closer only ensures that less learning will occur. It is doing the students a grave disservice to deny them a learning experience by deeming them incapable. I make a point of telling them this in the beginning of the semester.

Cymbeline contains a similar lesson about reducing the world for someone else out of a misguided desire to protect them. Although their adoptive father, disgusted by his unjust banishment, and rightly so, decries the city and society in vituperative terms, his sons Guiderius and Arviragus feel cut off from something they desperately want to experience. For them, being in the wilds of Wales is akin to being locked in a "cell of ignorance" (3.3.33). By leaving the segregation of a landscape in which they've been "protected" for too long, the brothers meet their destiny and come into their own only once they find the courage to leave the protection of the familiar and take a risk. Only once they, too, "fear no more," are they able to step into their birthright as heirs to the throne. Underestimating their capabilities similarly keeps community college students locked in a "cell of ignorance (4.2.258)." Students can break through these limitations (in addition to those that are self-imposed) with the help of an instructor who never doubts their strengths.

That was the last semester I ever expected anything less than their best effort. I now demand the same level of comprehension and reading that I would at Harvard, but I need to cheerlead a bit and to acknowledge the growing pains at the beginning of the semester as they make strides to catch up. I will often say things like "I know this is hard, but I also know you can do it. Every semester students struggle, and every semester students succeed, and they never see the world quite the same way again." I occasionally give them two minutes at the beginning of class to "share their pain" and vent all they want about how hard the workload is and how unreasonable I am. They smile and complain and realize that they are not alone; that it is normal to struggle when faced with a worthy challenge; that I am not surprised; that they will be fine, and that they owe this experience to themselves, to be one of the few who has read Shakespeare and understood his work in a way that makes him theirs.

Moreover, there is a realism to this approach that cannot be denied. Those students who cannot read the work with understanding will not go on to do well in four-year colleges, and giving them easier material would be giving them false expectations of what studying in a four-year institution is like. I prefer they get that hard lesson from me, in a safe environment in which I am prepared to help them through it and give them the skills they need. At the same time, those students who take on the challenge find themselves comfortable with other English classes once they transfer. And they are grateful for those high expectations. As one student wrote on an anonymous survey, "It allowed me to step outside my comfort zone and really challenge myself. I am grateful. I feel like I really accomplished something this semester. PS: I learned a great deal from your class and plan to take another as soon as my mind is ready!" If we aren't teaching the very best our language and discipline has to offer, how can we ever hope to convey why literature is worth loving in the first place?

Universal Experience, the Great Equalizer

Up to this point, I have focused on the disadvantages community college students face when compared to the 1 percent. But in one very significant area they have an enormous advantage: maturity. One of the ways we discuss literature most effectively is to correlate it to our everyday, universal experience. And this is where community college students excel. They may not have read a lot about life, but they have lived it. Their experience is firsthand.

If we can agree that the brilliance of Shakespeare is not only in the linguistic play, but perhaps more profoundly, in the dimensionality of Shakespeare's characterizations, human motivations, and his recognition of the dark side of every character when thrust into circumstances beyond his or her control, the distinction that sets his characters apart is their *action*: their choices and responses to what the world brings their way. Our students unquestionably face adversity and obstacles that would stop many of us in our tracks just in making it to campus each day. But rather than a deterrent to reading Shakespeare, this life experience serves as an invaluable advantage to understanding the meanings of the plays. Who better to understand the vicissitudes of fate Shakespeare depicts than someone who has experienced them firsthand? Creativity Studies, in which we study specific creativity personality traits and methodologies in problem solving, allows us to apply this framework in the context of literature through the lens of characters who continually face complex problems.

Creativity, Maturity, and the Making of Meaning

Frederika Reisman's "Diagnostic Creativity Assessment" identifies markers of creative problem-solving ability. These are applicable both to characters who solve problems and students who close read. (After all, what is difficult literature but a complex problem to be "solved"?) Those creativity traits are the following:

- Originality: Produces unique and novel ideas
- Fluency: Generates many ideas
- Flexibility: Generates many categories of ideas
- Elaboration: Adds detail
- Tolerance of Ambiguity: Comfortable with the unknown
- Resistance to Premature Closure: Keeps an open mind
- Divergent Thinking: Generates many solutions [or readings/interpretations]
- Convergent Thinking: Comes to closure [Chooses the best possible readings among the options]
- Risk Taking: Adventuresome
- Intrinsic Motivation: Inner drive
- Extrinsic Motivation: Needs reward or reinforcement[6]

The first four markers (Originality, Fluency, Flexibility, and Elaboration) are the instructor's to model and for students to practice in the classroom. For instance, when a professor puts up a difficult Shakespeare passage, she must allow the students to "play," by throwing out ideas and possible interpretations. She must be careful in this process not to shut anyone down, nor to leap too quickly into the other side of the human brain and the one more typically exercised in college, critical thinking. Rather she must allow sufficient time for the creative, idea and interpretation-generating part of the students' minds to develop. This is what creativity experts term the "incubation phase." In this stage, all ideas are possible. Judgment is suspended and there is not yet any talk of "good" or "bad," but rather "Yes, *and*..." ways of encouraging the ideas to flow, with more elaborate, original, and multiple interpretations welcome.

But while the professor can demonstrate these first four traits by teaching close reading and developing textual analyses, the rest of the creativity traits must be found within the student, and this is where the 99 percent may have an advantage over the 1 percent. Our students demonstrate "Risk Taking" and "Tolerance of the Unknown"[7] continually. Many are not only the first in their families to take a Shakespeare class, but also the first to attend *any* college class. They are "Risk Takers" because it takes enormous courage to break with tradition, to risk a loss of income to take college classes, and to tolerate failure. Our students tolerate failure repeatedly. One student wrote "Although I couldn't complete the course due to personal matters, I wanted to finish, and so I retook it, and the plays were easier to read and understand, and the language was easier to grasp." Unlike traditional students, our students have a high rate of failing classes and retaking them until they succeed. As this testimonial illustrates, our students have a strong drive to "get it right" and to prove themselves capable despite temporary setbacks. This demonstrates persistence and an impressive degree of intrinsic motivation (i.e., those not moved exclusively by extrinsic motivation such as grades and requirements, but rather by the inner drive to complete a task). This is what Csikszentmihalyi calls an "autotelic personality," that is, someone who engages in a task or activity because they find it valuable and worthy in and of itself. He mentions this as one of the single most important traits in a person capable of finding their "flow" and ultimately lasting happiness in "the making of meaning."[8]

If the goal of any literary interpretation (and any life) is ultimately the ability to find meaning and to make sense of the events that have transpired, then our students are getting valuable practice in that endeavor both in the classroom and without. The maturity students demonstrate in empathizing with a character and in sensing the nuance in an interaction may be more profound in the community college student. Whereas my traditional students might be content to "get" what the scene is about, my community college students as a whole tend to be more sensitive to subtler readings of emotions and motivations, to the undercurrents in character interactions. In one example among many, my Harvard students accepted that Romeo and Juliet were in love. My community college students immediately recognized, however, that Romeo and Juliet are immature young teenagers in love with the *idea* of love. They hone right in on the meteoric transfer of Romeo's affections to Juliet from the deep and painful love he professes for Rosaline a scene before. Rather than seeing the play as "the ultimate romantic love story," they are more prone to read it as a cautionary tale, and this demonstrates a wiser, more experienced perspective.

Like Pisanio, in *Cymbeline*, they judge for themselves. Our students very often have more work and life experiences under their belt than the traditional college sophomore. They trust their own instincts in interpretation, whereas traditional students might be more apt to spout conventional (mis)information they have heard about the plays through popular culture. Likewise, my community college students are able to relate to a young Hal seen as a misunderstood rebel, biding his time patiently, gathering information and experience. He finally unveils his true potential only once he has sufficiently studied those from every walk of life: both society's "dregs" and those in power who quickly dismissed him for hanging out "with the wrong crowd." Our students know how it feels to be misjudged on poor appearance, to be found wanting, but to be harboring greatness within. They are quicker to recognize that Hal has the advantage of knowing the tavern clowns and Falstaff at the same time that he is able to get along in his father's court when the time comes. In short, he's been taking notes, and like them, he can pass between both worlds, widening his experience, his emotional intelligence, and hence his ability to rule effectively.

Perhaps not unrelated to this, I noticed early on in quizzes that the moments of human interaction were much more important and memorable to the students than the characters' names. This became even clearer to me when I looked at the results of a passage identification exam where students were required to recognize key passages, and to name the play, which character was speaking the lines, and describe the significance of the passage as well as its context. Repeatedly, students would write detailed pages on the interaction, putting it into the context of the larger work, but forget the name of the character or even the title of the play. It was clear to me that the essence of the character interaction was far more important to them than the characters' names. Although I was attached to the titles and names, and continue to be, I realized that they were almost defiantly not so. This may be consistent in a demographic for whom labels have been neither helpful nor accurate markers of worth. They may have been discouraged in the past by instructors who miscast them as "bad" Young Hal-like students and did not see them for the intelligent and resourceful scholars they are becoming.

Like most students, mine react strongly to the racist verbiage and stereotypes surrounding Othello at court. But when they read he wooed Desdemona with his war stories, they recognize what he doesn't: that she could not have loved him had he been anyone else. She loves him *because* his difficult experiences and pain make him attractive and complex. They are sensitive to stereotypes—as in Shylock's "If you prick us, do we not bleed?" (*Merchant*, 3.1.6)—while they are quick to condemn unproductive responses like revenge because they know that it is not easy to make the right choice, but that like Pisanio's refusal to kill Imogen, the right choices lead to success and a clearer conscience. In my teaching career, the most profound discussions of the plays have taken place in the community college classroom, ones that leave the instructor as moved as the students because there is a greater foundation of personal experience upon which the students have to draw.

Having studied hundreds of subjects, Csikszentmihalyi makes clear that happiness does not come from having an easy, stress-free life, but rather from the satisfaction of overcoming life's challenges and finding meaning in them. This is where creativity, maturity, and Shakespeare fully intersect. Shakespeare's characters do not have an easy lot in life; indeed, conflict is the basis for all drama by definition. But in every Shakespearean Act V, whether tragedy, history, romance, or comedy, the characters who remain on stage and the audience members who remain in their seats are left to make meaning of the events that have just transpired. Csikszentmihalyi develops the idea that what makes life worthwhile (and what the value of his own life's work has been), is the ability for individuals to "make meaning" of their experiences and to identify "life themes."[9] Creativity Studies encourages students to uncover their own life themes and to decide what gives their own lives meaning, and what better context in which to engage in this exploration than Shakespeare?

Shakespeare's power for them is that even in the face of the deepest tragedies—*Hamlet, Othello, Macbeth, Romeo and Juliet*—there is a story to be told and a lesson to be learned through which painful experiences are made meaningful. Our students live tragedies every day, witnessing gang violence, drug addiction, and incarceration. Shakespeare allows us to recognize, however, as these students have, that we get to choose the story we tell about our lives through the actions we take. Man's search for meaning, as Viktor Frankl put it so eloquently,[10] is the best adaptive strategy there is. Shakespeare gives us a pattern to impose over the chaos, and that pattern is our design. But it requires a creative response.

Teaching Shakespeare Through Creativity Studies: *King Lear*

King Lear provides a useful test case for teaching Shakespeare through the lens of Creativity Studies. Lear's lack of creative vision causes his kingdom to stagnate while it allows other characters to demonstrate variously their own creative responses to adversity. This all starts from nothing; or more precisely, Lear's fear of nothing.

In *The Creative Mind: Myths and Mechanisms*, Margaret Boden notes that "The dictionary definition of 'creation' is 'to bring into being a form out of nothing.'[11] It is hence the space of "nothingness" that allows the creative act to flourish. Because Lear fears the "nothingness" of his impending mortality, he feels he must act to fill the void he finds so uncomfortable. Indeed, Lear's hasty plan to divide the kingdom displays an ignorance of the true issue in need of a creative solution. The King's "problem" isn't dividing his lands; there's no reason he needs to do that before his death. If he is tired of ruling, as he says he wishes to "Unburthen'd crawl toward death" (1.1.41), he could simply have asked his children to step in as proxies. Lear's real problem is his lack of sovereignty over death's nothingness. If children provide parents an immortality of sorts, it makes sense that Lear reaches reflexively for his. Their sworn love and devotion promises he may also live on in memory. Lear simply needs reassurance from his children. But he sets out to solve the wrong problem (the division of lands rather than the sharing of love) in an effort to get there. Solving the wrong problem is a common and costly creative problem-solving mistake according to creativity experts Gerard Puccio and Susan Keller-Mathers.

By contrast, Puccio and Keller-Mathers have identified a specific creativity type, the Clarifier, who pauses in the action to be sure he or she is answering the correct question and considering solutions from all angles.[12] Cordelia recognizes Lear's precipitous and faulty reasoning in divesting himself of his kingdom and power and expecting to maintain the power these have conferred upon him once they are lost. The role of the Clarifier is often a thankless one, and it requires slowing down to "get it right." Indeed, Kent urges Lear to pause before acting, just as Edmund warns Gloucester. The clarifiers are the Hamlets of the world, carefully considering the consequences of actions before solving the problems with which the world presents them. Lear jumps to solutions, and hence reveals himself to be an "Implementer" in the Creative Problem Solving (CPS) model.[13] The Implementer jumps to solutions and gets things done, but often too precipitously, and at great cost to the organization. This is because he neglects to consider all of the facts or properly research the situation before acting. Indeed, Lear proves this to be true.

But Cordelia, faced with the problem, comes up with a much more creative response. She sees that her father is moving too fast in the wrong direction. In an aside, she says "Love and be silent"(1.1.63). Recognizing the infinite creative possibilities in nothing (Indeed, God created the universe *ex nihilo*), she prefers silence as containing the potential for *all* feeling. Cordelia knows what Bronx criminal defense attorney Murray Richman notoriously tells his clients, "Keep your mouth shut. When the words are in your mouth, you're their master. Once they're out, you're their slave."[14] Avoiding the creative constraints that quantifying an abstract emotion like love would impose, Cordelia says "Nothing" (1.1.87). Indeed, the play is obsessed with "Nothing" to the point of verbal tic.

While this has dire consequences, Kent also prefers the limitless creative possibility in "nothing": "Freedom lives hence, and banishment is here" (1.1.181). And the play immediately delivers on the creative promise of nothingness. Cordelia's seeming tragedy in Act 1, being disowned as she is on the verge of making a promising match, ends up being the "nothing" space—no dowry—that allows France to "get creative" by marrying her anyway. He even loves her the more for it, thus distinguishing himself from Burgundy as the better suitor. From nothing, *because of nothing*, Cordelia experiences unconditional love.

But creativity, while highly desirable, can lead to maladaptive traits like dishonesty or creating alternate realities, as Tomas Chamorro-Premuzic has observed in a *Harvard Business Review* article, "The Dark Side of Creativity."[15] Edmund, the bastard son of Gloucester, introduced and described repeatedly as the "Bastard," is defined by lack, his lack of recognized paternity or paternal nothingness. This creative space allows him to reinvent himself as the "good" son, but for evil ends. He capitalizes on "nothing," gaining legitimacy and power, if only temporarily, as a result.

Powerfully, Edmund warns Gloucester against jumping to "uncreative" well-worn conclusions and the harm that this will do (and indeed, these untested assumptions lead ultimately to Gloucester's demise just as the same failing leads to Lear's fall):

> If it shall please you to suspend your indignation against my brother till you can derive from him better testimony of his intent, you should run a certain course; where, if you violently proceed against him, mistaking his purpose, it would make a great gap in your own honor and shake in pieces the heart of his obedience. (1.2.79–85)

Like Lear's, however, Gloucester's mind is closed, predisposed to accept only the first interpretation and to mold the circumstantial evidence to support it: "These late eclipses in the sun and moon portend no good to us. …There's son against father… Machinations, hollowness, treachery, and all ruinous disorders" (1.2.104, 110–114). Like Lear, he does not, if you will, go through the incubation phase of testing hypotheses as a creative thinker would. If he did, he would realize that his assumptions have led him to the wrong son.

Edmund is contemptuous of Gloucester for blaming the stars, and for refusing to see the possibilities rather than the limitations in the nothingness of a bastard. But while the eclipses (the blotting out of the sun and the making of "nothing") have prescribed consequences to Gloucester and become a self-fulfilling prophecy, Edmund can make *anything* of nothing. This creative space allows Edmund to tell Edgar to stay away from Gloucester, thus enabling him to construct alleged parricide out of the nothingness of Edgar's absence. He asks Edgar, "Have you nothing said / Upon his party 'gainst the Duke of Albany?" (2.1.25–26). Edgar hasn't, but out of "nothing," Edmund encourages Edgar to flee so that in his absence Edmund can weave a new and impressively-wrought tale of very detailed slander, all entirely fabricated. This is a creative, maladaptive mind at work. Similarly, Goneril and Reagan step into the nothingness Cordelia's answer has provided by reinventing a new world order starring themselves.

The Fool tells Lear "I am a Fool, thou art nothing." But the wiser Fool recognizes the creative possibility in it, asking Lear, "Can you make no use of nothing, nuncle?" and Lear answers, "Why no, boy, nothing can be made of nothing" (1.4.184–85, 128–129, 130). How wrong Lear is in Acts 1 and 2. Ironically, Lear needs to sit with being "nothing" in order to realize the maturity that will allow him to accept mortality. At this stage in the play, however, devoid of the external markers—power, title, retinue, and robes—Lear needs someone else to fill in the "nothing" gap for him, "Who is it that can tell me who I am?" (1.4.230). While creative characters capitalize on nothingness, Lear lacks the imagination to fill it. Until he becomes creative, he is incapable of reinvention.

Similarly, when Lear comes across Kent in the stocks, he refuses to believe the truth in front of his eyes. If Csikszentmihalyi posits that creativity is an evolutionary adaptive response to an ever-changing and hostile environment,[16] Lear, in his unevolved state, cannot, as a non-creative, adapt to changing circumstances. He can only deny them, just as he lacks the creativity to comprehend either Cordelia's goodness or his other daughters' evil. Lear has such limited imagination that when he complains to Regan about Goneril's treatment of him and his men, he refuses to believe Regan when she tells him she will do the same. As Lear progressively loses all that is familiar, he cries out, "I'll do such things– / What they are yet I know not—" (2.4. 280–281). He cannot even imagine his revenge.

But Lear evolves. Lear's evolution into a creative character starts in 3.2. after ranting (and yet taking his first lesson from Cordelia), "I will say nothing" (3.2.38). His first creative spark comes when he has been stripped of everything in the storm. This is the first time he can express empathy and imagine "What [homeless] wretches feel" (3.4.34) and chide himself for his previous lack of imagination. It is the nothingness of the stripping that allows it. Indeed, as my students have shown, this adversity causes creativity to flourish. Upon meeting Edgar in disguise, Lear starts using the rhetoric of nothingness himself. "Coulds't thou save nothing?" (3.4.17).

Following Lear's lead, other characters evolve into creatives in the same way. The disguised Edgar invents an alter ego full of vices and lusts, an imagination he previously lacked and which got him into trouble for taking Edmund's story at face value. Moreover, Gloucester transforms as dramatically as Lear. It is precisely at the moment that Gloucester is blinded and experiences visual "nothingness" that he learns what he was incapable of imagining before (but should have): that Edmund is false. He admits that "I stumbled when I saw" (4.1.19). But in a beautiful moment my students found particularly compelling, it is when one has literally hit rock bottom that things can only improve. Edgar says "The lowest and most dejected thing of fortune, / ... lives not in fear" (4.1.3). Like Lear, Gloucester experiences empathy for the first time and maligns "the man that will not see / Because he does not feel" (4.1.68–69). Gloucester strips himself of his money and now favors "nothingness" so much that he craves suicide on the cliffs of Dover. He now *prefers* the true nothingness of his own death, when earlier he was stricken by the idea that his son wanted him dead. Edgar saves Gloucester's life by forcing him to use his imagination and create an alternate reality: that he is climbing the cliffs of Dover. Edgar provides a detailed, imaginary landscape that allows Gloucester to embrace nothingness for the first time: "This world I do renounce" (4.6.35). Had Gloucester not lost his vision, he would not have experienced the depths of filial love Edgar exhibits. "Thy life's a miracle" says Edgar to Gloucester after the "near death" pretend fall, and Gloucester sees it that way for the first time (4.6.55). Edgar's and Gloucester's new-found creativity saves Gloucester's life, where Edmund's would destroy it. Gloucester can now say "I see feelingly" (4.6.149), his synesthetic creative transformation complete.

Notably, it is in the thunderous and raging storm that Gloucester and Lear find their creativity, an external manifestation of both the political and mental chaos swirling within them, but not before it leads to profound insight and growth. Bedecked in flowers and embracing the madman's role in Act 4, Lear asks for an ounce of civet to "Sweeten my imagination" and pays money for it (4.6.131). Like Gloucester, for the first time in the play and in direct contrast to the Lear of Act 1 who feared death, he now prefers the nothingness of death: "You do me wrong to take me out o' th' grave" (4.7.44). Tellingly, it is only when Lear becomes "mad"—a charge leveled at many creatives—that he begins to see the situation clearly and in the frame of mind that would have led to a positive solution. Margaret Boden notes the similarities between creativity and madness: "So is chaos as such creative? There is novelty in madness too."[17] Madness thus leads to vision and "insight," a theme that the Gloucester blinding subplot echoes quite literally when Lear regains his "vision" in finally recognizing Kent.

Once Lear and Gloucester begin to make moral progress and to gain insight into their real problems, the antagonists kill each other in rapid-fire succession. I point out to students that this is a comparable situation to identifying the correct problem in Creative Problem Solving: once the real problem is identified and addressed, the obstacles to finding and implementing a workable solution dissolve and become irrelevant.[18]

Finding his creativity earlier could have averted Lear's tragedy by giving him a better framework with which to view his mortality. Indeed, Shakespeare returns to the idea that creative expression is the only antidote to the universal fear of mortality throughout his work:

> O fearful meditation! where, alack,
> Shall Time's best jewel from Time's chest lie hid?
> Or what strong hand can hold his swift foot back?
> Or who his spoil of beauty can forbid?
> O, none, unless this miracle have might,
> That in black ink my love may still shine bright (9-14).

Sonnet 65, Shakespeare's meditation on "sad mortality's" (2) unstoppable power over every element but the "miracle" of literature and its meaning making, underscores his faith in creativity's ability to defeat tragedy. It is a faith my students and I share, and one that several had tattooed "in black ink" on their bodies.

Shakespeare and Student Tattoos

While I was surprised by the powerful impact my students had had on me, I was astonished to discover that Shakespeare had left an indelible mark on them as well. Five students from separate classes got tattoos that read "Fear No More," from *Cymbeline*. "Fear no more the heat of the sun, / Nor the furious winter's rages" is the funeral dirge for Imogen/ Fidele (4.2.258–259). It is a song that, in the words of Hallett Smith, comprises "quite possibly the most resonant lyric lines Shakespeare ever composed."[19] The lines make the radical suggestion that we needn't fear death, that we might even welcome it as a restful promise rather than as a threat. Virginia Woolf's Clarissa Dalloway comforts herself with these same lines as she makes her way through post-war London and contemplates her own mortality. Clarissa extracts the essence of these lines—the core of the comfort, the anti-cliché, the beauty and meaning that only creative expression can convey alongside a life fully lived. Despite her lack of an education (she admits to receiving only "dry sticks" of knowledge from an incompetent tutor), she has found comfort through creative expression (indeed the lines themselves are creative, but Clarissa (and Woolf through her) works her own creative magic on them by re-contextualizing them for herself in the 1920s as a balm to her own obsession with mortality.[20]

I'm proud that my students got tattoos, if they took that with them—to "fear no more"—Shakespeare, creativity, the unknown, and death—because isn't that one of the gifts literature gives us? A sense that we are not alone? That no matter how desperate we may feel, that someone else somewhere in time has felt what we are feeling?—if that is the meaning they derived, then I count their class experience a success. "Fear no more" tattoos are tangible proof that Shakespeare's words had a visceral impact on the students, and that they wanted to carry that talismanic reminder with them forever—to literally embody Shakespeare's poetry. This was their creative response to the fear of nothingness. My students find the creative promise in "nothing," and they make beautiful use of it every day. In his ending benediction, King Cymbeline urges:

> Laud we the gods,
> And let our crooked smokes climb to their nostrils
> From our blest altars (5.5.476–478).

For all of us invested in community college learning and pedagogy, student and professor alike, we can hope for nothing less: the recognition that our smokes *may* be crooked, but our altars the more blessed and creative because of it.

Notes

1. "College and Student Profile," *West Los Angeles College Research* (2016): http://www.wlac.edu/WLAC/media/documents/research/planning/Student_Profile_Fall_2016.pdf. Accessed October 2, 2018.
2. William Shakespeare, *The Riverside Shakespeare*, ed. G. B. Evans (Boston: Houghton Mifflin, 1974), 4.3.46. All further references to Shakespeare's plays and poems are to this edition and will hereafter be parenthetical.
3. George Lois, *Damn Good Advice (For People with Talent!)* (London: Phaidon Press, 2012), 1.
4. Mihaly Csikszentmihalyi, *Flow: The Psychology of Optimal Experience* (New York: Harper Row, 2009), 8, 24.
5. E. Paul Torrance, "Creative Positives of Disadvantaged Child and Youth," *Gifted Children Quarterly*, 13, no. 2 (1969): 71–81.
6. Reisman Diagnostic Creativity Assessment (RDCA), Apple iTunes/iPhone App, 2010.
7. Ibid.
8. Csikszentmihalyi, *Flow*, 83–90.

9. Ibid., 214, 230.
10. Victor Frankl, *Man's Search for Meaning* (New York: Simon & Schuster, 1959).
11. Margaret Boden, *The Creative Mind: Myths and Mechanisms* (London and New York: Routledge, 2005), 13.
12. Gerard Puccio and Susan Keller-Mathers, "Enhancing Thinking and Leadership Skills through Creative Problem Solving." in *Creativity: A Handbook for Teachers*, ed. Al-Girl Tan (Singapore: World Scientific Publishing Co. 2007), 281–301.
13. Ibid.
14. Murray Richman, interview by Errol Morris, *First Person*, "The Only Truth," Bravo, 2001.
15. Tomas Chamorro-Premuzic, "The Dark Side of Creativity," *Harvard Business Review*, November 2015: https://hbr.org/2015/11/the-dark-side-of-creativity. Accessed October 2, 2018.
16. Csikszentmihalyi, *Flow*, 8, 24.
17. Boden, *The Creative Mind*, 13.
18. Puccio and Keller-Mathers, "Creative Problem Solving," 281–301.
19. Hallett Smith, "Introduction to *Cymbeline*," in *The Riverside Shakespeare*, ed. G. B. Evans (Boston: Houghton Mifflin, 1974), 1520.
20. Virginia Woolf, *Mrs. Dalloway*, with a foreword by Maureen Howard (New York: Harcourt, Inc., 1981), 7.

Poverty and Privilege: Shakespeare in the Mountains

Rochelle Smith

Allegany County lies in the western part of the state of Maryland, folded into the Appalachian Mountains that roll from southern Pennsylvania through Maryland on their way toward West Virginia. This is, as we like to say out here, the mountain side of Maryland, perhaps the state's most beautiful region. It is also among the state's most isolated and economically depressed regions; indeed, our largest city, Cumberland, was recently named the poorest city in Maryland.[1] Our local students grow up largely disconnected from the vibrant Shakespeare culture that enriches the lives of many of their peers downstate. We are 150 miles from the nearest metropolitan area—too far for a casual visit to the Baltimore Shakespeare Factory, the Folger Shakespeare Theatre, or the Shakespeare Theatre Company in Washington, DC. Allegany County had been coal mining country, and Frostburg State University, where I teach Shakespeare ten miles up the mountain from Cumberland, was built on land purchased by donations from Frostburg's coal miners. Founded in 1898 as State Normal School Number Two, the university has a strong presence in a community that, in so many other ways, is sorely lacking in resources.

R. Smith (✉)
Frostburg State University, Frostburg, MD, USA

S. O'Dair and T. Francisco (eds.), *Shakespeare and the 99%*,
https://doi.org/10.1007/978-3-030-03883-0_8

So, while this region may not seem like the best place for a strong community Shakespeare program to flourish, about fifteen years ago I began organizing a local Shakespeare festival, a cooperative project involving both our university and the area high schools from western Maryland, southwest Pennsylvania, and West Virginia. In this essay, I will explore what it means to teach Shakespeare in an isolated and depressed rural community, situating the work of our local Shakespeare Festival within the larger context of the role "Shakespeare" has played in American life. I will consider what it is about Shakespeare, both the plays themselves and America's relationship with these works now over four hundred years old, that makes Shakespeare so important to a community such as mine. I argue that Shakespeare's immense power as a marker of cultural capital, his privileged place in a contested canon, turns out to have great value for places like this that are distinctly lacking in privilege.

* * *

Western Maryland has not always been isolated and depressed. In fact, the early history of this region is one of persistent efforts to connect, both to the urban centers in the east and to the western frontier. During the French and Indian War in 1755, General Braddock built his famous road connecting Cumberland to Pittsburgh in his failed attempt to oust the French from Fort Duquesne. This same road became the starting point for America's first National Highway in 1806, an oxcart and covered wagon turnpike that originated in Cumberland and followed much of Braddock's route as it headed west to the Ohio River, eventually extending west almost to St. Louis and then back east to Baltimore.[2] By mid-century, the steam locomotive had arrived with the Baltimore and Ohio Railroad, linking Baltimore to Cumberland in 1842, soon followed by the Chesapeake and Ohio Canal in 1850. All of this construction was, of course, economically driven, fuelled by the desire to bring the region's valuable resources east.

Western Maryland's key resource was its clean-burning, world-famous "Big Vein" coal. It was coal mining that brought many of the region's English, Scottish, Welsh, and Irish immigrants here during the nineteenth century.[3] By 1850, there were close to thirty coal companies in the region, which produced over 64 million tons of coal during the next fourty years,[4] enough coal to build a foot-wide path to the moon and back. Big Vein coal was so highly prized that a 5-ton block of it was put on display at the 1924 International Fair in Milan, Italy.[5]

As coal production declined in the first half of the twentieth century, mining jobs were replaced by factory jobs. Cumberland, known as Maryland's "Queen City," by the 1920s had become a manufacturing town, producing beer, glass, acetate fiber, and tires. But by the late 1980s, Cumberland's last major industry, Kelly-Springfield Tires, was finally closed down. Ironically, the national transportation system that did so much to connect this region to the rest of the country in the first half of the nineteenth century turned out to be equally effective in isolating these mountains in the second half of the twentieth century. In 1956, the year President Eisenhower's Federal-Aid Highway Act initiated the national interstate system, travel from Frostburg to the nearest metropolitan areas of Baltimore and Washington took over five hours by car on two-lane roads. The highway would eventually cut that time in half, but it was not until the very late date of 1991 that the interstate finally reached western Maryland. By that time, almost all of the area's industries had either relocated or closed their doors.

Today, with a poverty rate of 19.2 percent, Cumberland ranks as the fifteenth poorest city in the country.[6] Only 17 percent of people over age twenty five in the county have a bachelor's degree, compared with 29 percent in the United States, and 37 percent in Maryland.[7] Mining and manufacturing jobs have mostly disappeared, replaced only partially by the new prison industry: maximum-security state and medium-security federal prisons. Cumberland suffers from problems similar to those of other Appalachian regions: the closing of coal mines and industries; a brain drain; and the crisis of opioid addiation. In 2015, the percentage of drug and alcohol deaths in the county was 44 percent higher than the state average.[8]

Nevertheless, or possibly as a result of such grim present realities, ours is a community that regards its past history with great pride. The engraved stone that once marked the mileage on Braddock's road in the 1750s is proudly on display on Main Street in Frostburg, in front of the local museum. Route 40, the original National Road, is still referred to as the National Pike, and its round toll house from 1835 remains standing by the side of that road. Frostburg is still proud of its miners who, according to local historian Tom Robertson, "saw mining as a skill and a craft."[9] Cumberland businesses today find ways to incorporate "Queen City" into their names, while Frostburg residents continue to point out the booth in the Princess Restaurant on Main Street where President Truman and his wife Bess stopped to dine on Father's Day in 1953, as they traveled the National Road from their home in Missouri to the White House.

The nostalgia for a more glorified past is almost palpable around here, and Shakespeare, who is as canonical an author as they come, somehow fits right in. In a community wary of change, a community proud of its working-class character and suspicious of intellectual elitism, a major exception is made for Shakespeare. Shakespeare feels familiar, in part because we have been reading him for so long. In the years before the Civil War, some of Frostburg's coal miners were certainly reading Shakespeare, as one of them, Andrew Roy, reminisces: "We used to meet after our day's work in the mine and read aloud to each other, 15 minutes alternatively. In this manner we read … a number of Shakespeare's plays."[10] Shakespeare has long been a part of the high school curriculum in Cumberland. For example, at the Frederick Street School, which served African American students in the community from 1922 until desegregation in 1959, students "studied Shakespeare and read from *Hamlet*, *Macbeth*, and *Othello*."[11] Shakespeare even found his way into local commerce, as we see in a mid-twentieth century poster advertising the Queen City Brewing Company, where a selection of local beers is promoted with the caption, "As you like it."[12]

Western Maryland is not unique in this respect; Shakespeare has always held a special place in American culture. Although the early settlers, if they carried books with them, were more likely to bring a copy of the Bible than of Shakespeare's works, by the colonial era, Shakespeare had a firm foothold in the New World, at least with the elite segment of American culture. Contrary to scholarly legend, Cotton Mather, the Puritan minister infamous for his role in the 1692 Salem witch trials, probably did not own a Shakespeare First Folio.[13] But the Virginia planter who founded Richmond, William Byrd II, definitely did, a Fourth Folio that he brought to America in 1696, and James Franklin, Benjamin's older brother, purchased a full set of Shakespeare's works for his newspaper in 1722.[14] The first record of a professional performance of Shakespeare in America occurs as early as 1750, with five performances of Colley Cibber's adaptation of *Richard III* in New York and Williamsburg.[15] There were 166 performances of Shakespeare from 1750 to 1776,[16] making Shakespeare the most popular playwright in the American colonies.[17] Thus it should not be surprising that George Washington, in Philadelphia during the summer of 1787 presiding over the Constitutional Convention, was able to stroll over to the Opera House to catch a performance of *The Tempest* while taking a break from drafting the United States Constitution.[18]

Indeed, many of America's founding fathers were bardolaters. Our second president, John Adams, praised Shakespeare in his diaries, calling him "that great master of every affection of the heart and every sentiment of the mind as well as of all the powers of expression."[19] Our third president, Thomas Jefferson, agreed, reflecting in 1771 that "a lively and lasting sense of filial duty is more effectually impressed on the mind of a son or daughter by reading *King Lear*, than by all the dry volumes of ethics and divinity that ever were written."[20] A few years later, in 1786, Jefferson and Adams made a pilgrimage to Shakespeare's birthplace and indulged in what seems to have been the requisite act of bardolatry. Abigail Adams wrote in a letter that Jefferson, arriving in Stratford, "fell upon the ground and kissed it," while Adams "not quite so enthusiastic, contented himself with cutting a relic from his [Shakespeare's] chair, which I have now in my possession."[21]

The founding fathers may have been extreme in their admiration, but by the early nineteenth century, Shakespeare had clearly found his way into every corner of American life. The French historian Alexis de Tocqueville, while touring America in 1831, remarked, "There is hardly a pioneer's hut which does not contain a few odd volumes of Shakespeare."[22] On the Mississippi River, in 1858, the young Mark Twain was apprenticed to a riverboat pilot who "would read Shakespeare to me; not just casually, but by the hour, when it was his watch, and I was steering."[23] As Lawrence Levine has demonstrated, in nineteenth-century America, Shakespeare's plays were known and loved not only by those Americans wealthy enough to purchase his works but also by the average citizens who attended and participated in performances of his plays just about everywhere, "from the large and often opulent theaters of major cities to the makeshift stages in halls, saloons, and churches of small towns and mining camps." For nineteenth-century Americans, Levine emphasizes, "Shakespeare *was* popular entertainment."[24]

As the century progressed and Americans expanded westward, Shakespeare went with them, turning up in some unexpected places. W. T. Hamilton, a fur trapper in Wyoming, records receiving a copy of Shakespeare's works from a fellow trapper in 1842.[25] The mountain guide, Jim Bridger, meets a group of settlers heading west on the Oregon Trail in 1863, and he swaps a yoke of cattle worth $125 for a copy of Shakespeare's works. Then, because he was illiterate, he spends another $40 a month to hire a German boy from one of the wagon trains to read to him, and all this because his companion at that time,

Captain J. Lee Humfreville, had told him that Shakespeare's was "the best book that had ever been written." Listening to Shakespeare wasn't always easy for Bridger. Humfreville relates how, at times, Bridger "got the thread of the story so mixed that he would swear a blue streak, then compel the young man to stop, turn back, and re-read a page or two, until he could get the story straightened out." Although Bridger was illiterate, he was soon able to quote Shakespeare, in his own fashion, as Humfreville explains: "He could give quotation after quotation, and was always ready to do so. Sometimes he seasoned them with a broad oath, so ingeniously inserted as to make it appear to the listener that Shakespeare himself had used the same language."[26]

Stories of mountain men in the Rockies trading cattle for Shakespeare are not as surprising as they may at first seem, given Shakespeare's theatrical dominance of the western frontier. As Helene Wickham Koon has shown, Shakespeare was hands down the most popular playwright during the California Gold Rush of 1849–1865. Many of these performances took place in mining camps where the average miner, according to Koon, had at least a sixth-grade education and "was familiar with Shakespeare, either because he had learned long passages from *McGuffey's Reader* or had seen a traveling theater company."[27] Reminders of this frontier passion for Shakespeare can still be found in the names these early settlers gave to the places they discovered. As Jennifer Lee Carrell has observed, Shakespeare's name can be found "scattered all over the West," attached to towns, canyons, mountains, reservoirs, and glaciers from New Mexico to Alaska. But Carrell asserts that "it was the miners who most often staked Shakespeare to the earth. Nineteenth-century claims called Shakespeare dotted the landscape of Colorado and spilled into Utah." Christening one's claim "Shakespeare" may not indicate more than a passing acquaintance with the Bard, but Carrell has also found nineteenth-century mines out west named Ophelia, Cordelia, Desdemona, and even, most appropriately, Timon of Athens, named after one of Shakespeare's rarely-performed tragedies where the protagonist, exiled in the wilderness, digs in the forest for roots and discovers gold.[28]

When it comes to rural America's response to Shakespeare in the nineteenth century, perhaps the most memorable depiction comes from Mark Twain's *Adventures of Huckleberry Finn*, when two con-artists, claiming to be an English duke and the French dauphin, hitch a ride with Huck and Jim down the Mississippi. They stop along the way in small rural towns in Arkansas to perform a sword fight from *Richard III*, along with the balcony scene from *Romeo and Juliet*, and an unforgettable rendition of "Hamlet's Immortal Soliloquy!" that begins:

> To be, or not to be; that is the bare bodkin
> That makes calamity of so long life;
> For who would fardels bear, till Birnam Wood do come to Dunsinane.[29]

The duke is disappointed that only 12 people show up for the performance, and those who do laugh the actors out of town. The duke complains that "these Arkansaw lunkheads couldn't come up to Shakespeare."[30] But Twain has readers laughing with the "lunkheads" at the two "Shakespearean tragedians" and their outrageous pretensions of European nobility and culture. Even Twain's rural Arkansas audience seems to know the difference between Shakespeare and the garbled nonsense that these two con artists try to foist off on them.

By the end of the century, Shakespeare was right up there on the shelf next to the Bible, as Karl Knortz, visiting America in 1887, observed, declaring, "there is certainly no land on the whole earth in which Shakespeare and the Bible are held in such high esteem."[31] Shakespeare was literally placed on a pedestal in New York City's Central Park, where his statue was unveiled in 1872. Then, early in the twentieth century, Shakespeare captured prime real estate in Washington, DC. when the Folger Shakespeare Library, housing the world's largest collection of First Folios, opened in 1932 on the east end of the Washington Mall, right across the street from the Library of Congress and a block away from the Supreme Court. The bronze statue on a granite pedestal in Central Park, and the white marble building occupying sacred space on the Washington Mall are both indicative of how America's response to Shakespeare changed at the turn of the twentieth century. As Levine, who traces Shakespeare's transformation in this period from popular to high culture, points out: "By the turn of the century Shakespeare had been converted from a popular playwright whose dramas were the property of those who flocked to see them, into a sacred author who had to be protected from ignorant audiences and overbearing actors threatening the integrity of his creation."[32]

What, if any of this, has filtered down to rural America at the beginning of the twenty-first century? Certainly one clear benefit to teaching Shakespeare, as opposed to, say, Chaucer or Milton, is that one can pretty much count on everyone's having heard of him. This goes beyond simple name recognition, though. I remember one warm spring morning at the end of the semester, grading papers at my kitchen table while the appliance repair man worked on my broken freezer. When he had finished, he caught sight of the half-graded papers on the table, asked what I did for a living, and in response recited, "Is this a dagger which I see before me, the handle toward my hand?" He had Macbeth's entire speech by heart. I have been the willing audience more than once for such impromptu recitations, always by an older member of the community. Sometimes the soliloquy is Antony's funeral oration, sometimes Portia's lecture on the quality of mercy, and often it is Macbeth's dagger speech. Shakespeare continues to occupy a special place in the minds and, I think, hearts of the parents and grandparents of my students.

As for the current generation of students, a generation often assumed to be more visual than aural, the name "Shakespeare" is likely to evoke not a recitation but one of the visual images of the Bard so pervasive in our culture: either the white marble bust placed high up on some library shelf looking down from his perch next to Plato and Aristotle—cold, distant, and firmly situated within the highest circle of academic culture; or a cartoonish version of the famous Droeshout engraving—that overly large, shiny, and balding head, a floating egg of a head sitting awkwardly on a white plate of a collar, in other words, the ultimate egg head. At best, Shakespeare epitomizes the apex of an elite literary culture that demands at least a nod of recognition and approval. At worst, Shakespeare, for the typical high school and even college student today, stands for all that is old and dull, incomprehensible and surely irrelevant. These two iconographic images—the marble bust and the balding Bard—represent cultural preconceptions that turn out to be invaluable for teachers of Shakespeare in rural America: the first, because of the cultural prestige associated with the name "Shakespeare,"[33] and the second because of the widespread expectation of dullness and irrelevance, which makes overturning those expectations so easy to do, this, after all, being Shakespeare. It is, I would argue, the overturning of expectations that gives that much more power to our students' realization that the work *is* actually great: immensely entertaining, powerful, and even—and maybe this is what surprises students the most—still relevant.

The Shakespeare festivals that have been so popular all over America tend to be either professional, offering a series of plays performed by theater companies, or amateur, situated within high schools where teachers require their students to perform a play or a few scenes. Our festival is definitely of the amateur variety, but it may be unique in being organized as a community outreach program where I place our college students in local high schools as mentors to work with groups of ninth to twelfth graders. The college student mentors who participate are not education majors or student teachers; any interested college student can sign up. Throughout the semester, we meet regularly as a group to discuss approaches to teaching and performing Shakespeare, and meanwhile my college mentors visit their high school class once a week. I choose a scene for performance that fits each class, edit the scene, and provide scripts. The mentors spend the first two weeks with their high school group doing a careful read-through of the scene. Then for the rest of the semester, the student performers are up on their feet working on issues of staging, which, naturally, leads to questions of interpretation and more close reading. For example, when students first read the scene early in *Romeo and Juliet* where Lady Capulet speaks to her daughter about Paris's marriage proposal, they rarely pause over Lady Capulet's line, "Nurse, give leave awhile. / We must talk in secret.—Nurse, come back again."[34] It is not until they begin to block the scene that they question why Juliet's mother tells the nurse to leave, and then summons her again in the very same line. This question sends students back to a close reading of the text, as they try to determine the nature of Juliet's relationship with a mother who seems uncomfortable at the prospect of an intimate talk with her daughter. My college mentors also write two papers: a research paper comparing various stage performances of the play containing their scene and a final reflection on the experience. At the end of the semester, everyone—all 200 high school students, their teachers, my college mentors, and interested family and friends—comes up to our university's Performing Arts Center for the Shakespeare Festival, a day of scene performances interspersed with Shakespeare-themed games and contests.[35] The university provides transportation, lunch in our dining hall, and an FSU Shakespeare Festival t-shirt for every participant, each year in a different color and graced with a different Shakespearean quote.

This sounds like a simple and feasible plan but, in reality, my college mentors have their work cut out for them when they first walk into that high school class and try to interest their 14–17 year olds in performing Shakespeare. The strong resistance to all things Shakespeare that they confront initially is a point my mentors clearly want to impress on me in their final reflection papers. One mentor explains, "My students were high schoolers so the first problem I encountered was getting the kids motivated. … Many of them had no real interest in Shakespeare let alone in acting."[36] Another is blunter, recognizing that her tenth graders "were not at all eager to participate in this program. … During our first few visits to the school, the students were unruly. It was extremely difficult to make them listen to us politely and attentively." One advantage my college students possess, however, is that they themselves are only a few years out of high school, and so it is easy for them to empathize. One mentor remembers, "As a high school student, I genuinely despised Shakespeare." Another confesses, "In high school, it is safe to say that I loathed reading Shakespeare. I found it difficult to understand and, more often than not, I would give up before really attempting to appreciate any of his plays."

Once my mentors convince their group that this project is not only worthwhile but also *will* be fun, the next problem they encounter is getting their students to actually engage with the scene because, predictably, the only way their high schoolers can imagine having fun is by turning their scene into a burlesque or parody. They reason that although Shakespeare is old and musty and dull, they are young and funny and full of life. Much like the veneration of Shakespeare, the burlesquing of the Bard is also an abiding American tradition. A few years before George Washington slipped out of the Constitutional Convention to see *The Tempest*, a Tory sympathizer wrote a political parody of Hamlet's soliloquy in order to mock the demand by the First Continental Congress that colonists sign an agreement to boycott British goods, a parody that begins, "To sign, or not to sign? That is the question."[37] Over the next two centuries, Hamlet's soliloquy continued to be a favorite target for burlesque: in an 1882 version, Hamlet asks, "To be or not to be, (that is the question,) / Relieved of an attack of indigestion"; and in 1879, a truncated version of Hamlet's soliloquy is set to the tune of "Three Blind Mice."[38] Other notable burlesques include the one by the American performer, Richard Buckley, whose stage persona as "Lord" Buckley surely marks him as a successor to Twain's duke and dauphin. In 1955, he offered a jazzy riff on the famous soliloquy that asks:

> Is it hipper for the wig to dig
> The flips and drags of the wheel of fortune
> Or to come on like Kinsey
> Against this mass mess
> And by this stance cover the action.[39]

There is certainly nothing wrong with having fun with Shakespeare; in fact creating a brilliant parody requires a thorough understanding of whatever is being skewered. But instead of asking my mentors to make such arguments about parody with their high school groups, I urge them to work with their students to discover what is puzzling or surprising, relevant or strange, emotionally gripping and overall amazing about their particular scene, and then to run with that. I do assign a large number of comic scenes, and even the tragic scenes often contain comic moments. But I try to emphasize that if a group is doing the final scene from *Hamlet*, for example, they will have more fun playing the scene for all of its potential drama and irony and swift violence than by turning it into a joke. Tell them, I say, that their goal is to get the audience to watch this sequence of events play out on stage with rapt attention, to watch with fascination and with horror; their goal is to evoke an audible, collective gasp from the audience at the climax of the scene. Trying to accomplish this and possibly succeeding—now *that* would be an accomplishment.

Our insistence that the starting place must be the text itself does not preclude an openness to interpretation. Creative interpretations and modernizations are welcomed, although modernized language is not permitted. Thus, for example, one group recast the Capulet–Montague feud as high school jocks vs. geeks, another performed a Peter Pan *Hamlet* because, as the group argued, Hamlet has a problem with growing up, and one memorable performance featured Macbeth's witches dancing around the cauldron to Lady Gaga's hit song of that year, "Bad Romance," because bad romance, they explained, aptly describes the relationship between Macbeth and his lady. When it comes to freedom of interpretation, I like to keep in mind the words of my own high school English teacher who told us, "You can do things *with* Shakespeare, and you can do things *to* Shakespeare." We encourage the former and discourage the latter.

By the end of the semester, many expectations have been overturned. The college mentor who complained about her students' unruly behavior at the beginning of the project marvels at how, by the end of the semester, "They changed from completely disinterested to comparing insights on how they interpreted the language independently of what was asked of them in class, showing off their characterizations, and seeking opinions on acting choices from one another." Another mentor writes, "To see the expression of my students when they got to the Performing

Arts Center and knew that it was time to perform was something that will stick with me forever. I cannot express it enough how great my students felt after leaving the stage." One high school performer, riding the bus back to his school in southern Pennsylvania, tweeted, "We just rocked the Willy Shakesfest!" The comments by high school students after the festival do express a change in perspective. One ninth grader explains, "I used to think Shakespeare was nothing but a bunch of big, boring words and that the stories weren't interesting but now that we did the festival all that changed. I see now that you can look at Shakespeare in a lot of different ways and if you have fun you can understand them." A tenth grader states more simply, "He is much cooler than I ever thought."[40] What these students have discovered was, perhaps, best articulated by the poet Robert Graves, who wryly observed, "The remarkable thing about Shakespeare is that he is really very good—in spite of all the people who say he is very good."

The students who participate are not the only ones whose expectations have shifted. Parents often seem just as surprised by their sons' and daughters' new-found enthusiasm. One mother related with a mixture of bafflement and pride in her voice how her daughter had spent the past several weeks walking around the house reciting her lines from *Macbeth*. A father whose son attended our local Career and Technical Center approached me at intermission to tell me proudly that his son "really likes Shakespeare." It is the marble bust Shakespeare these parents seem to be envisioning as they speak, and what they are saying is that their child is "up to Shakespeare."

There is certainly much healthy debate about Shakespeare's privileged place in the canon. But the cultural capital attached to Shakespeare can have an unexpected payoff in parts of the country where poverty is all too prevalent and "privilege" something that often seems permanently out of reach. When high school students discover that they can read Shakespeare and even enjoy him, they start to wonder what else they might be up for. As one mentor explains, "Shakespeare Fest gets students interested in Shakespeare, in literature, and in college. … If those participating can understand Shakespeare, they can do anything."[41] It may be true that Shakespeare's firm position in the canon and his status as the ultimate "dead white male" author appeals in ways not necessarily admirable to the strongly conservative streak in regions like this one. Kim Sturgess, in *Shakespeare and the American Nation*, notes how Shakespeare was championed in the late nineteenth century by those Americans feeling threatened by the growing number of immigrants. Their response, Sturgess explains, was to promote "cultural symbols and traditions thought to represent Anglo-American monoculture. ... Appropriated to this political and cultural project was the most recognised and respected playwright in America ...William Shakespeare."[42] But the very qualities in his work that have led to Shakespeare's rise to the top of the literary hierarchy—not the least being his ability to dramatize with astounding empathy the vast range of human experience—are the same qualities that have precluded his work from becoming the possession of any one particular cultural group. Shakespeare is the example par excellence that demonstrates how exceptional literature can transcend cultural barriers, as evidenced by the immense popularity of Shakespeare's work all over the world, from Mexico and Brazil to Africa, India, and China.[43]

That Shakespeare's appeal is unquestionably diverse is something that even our western Maryland Shakespeare Festival has witnessed over the past decade, as our student population at the university has become increasingly diverse as well, currently with a minority population of 40 percent. My student mentors who are not white sometimes encounter additional challenges as they leave our campus to visit the largely white local schools. As one mentor explains, "As an African American student, I am fully aware of the predominantly white region I have chosen to pursue my degree in. When I walked into the door (on the first day), I know that was the first thing the students noticed. It was written all over their faces." Her response—"diving right into the work and always remaining focused on the goal"—reminded her class that "the play's the thing," and, by the end of the semester, she writes, her "students opened their minds and hearts." For her part, she reflects, "Never have I taught a predominantly Caucasian group of students." But she concludes, "I learned that I can teach anybody. What really matters is working with the wide range of personalities and skill levels of the students. I was happy to walk away from this experience with something new."

As this student's reflection suggests, the afterlife of an experiential learning project like this one exists not only for the high school students who perform but for their mentors as well, and this was the final thought that my college students voiced in their final papers.[44] One writes, "Visiting the classroom and watching the students become interested in Shakespeare and knowing that I had some part in it amazed me. I had never had that much influence over anyone before and I swelled with pride after nearly every classroom visit." Another reflects, "I think I gained more from the Shakespeare Festival than any of my students … . I learned something about how to teach. Something you can't do with your nose in a book like I've been doing for years. This was a real-world experience. … I learned that to make someone willing to learn you have to pour your heart into your words."

The success of this program is due in large part, of course, to Shakespeare's great talent, especially in that his work has power even in the hands of the most amateur of performers. Ultimately, though, I would have to give the most credit to my college students, who really do pour their hearts into this experience. I have emphasized to our assessment-conscious administration that the results of a program like this cannot really be measured. But I was pleased last fall when one of my high school teachers who had missed the application deadline emailed me a few weeks later saying that he had a class who really wanted to participate and asking if it was too late. I emailed back saying, yes, you can definitely participate—and, no, it is not too late. A few minutes later, he replied, "I just read your email to the class and they cheered!" Here in western Maryland, in one of the poorest school districts in the state, our kids are cheering because they get to do Shakespeare. Those of us who are not from these parts, who have preconceptions about what poor, rural students are capable of doing, might be surprised. But the nine hundred local residents who donated their savings to establish a college in Frostburg over hundred years ago would not be surprised.[45] Although most were coal miners, many of whom had not themselves finished high school, they clearly valued education and had no doubt about their children being "up to Shakespeare." Fortunately, Shakespeare turns out to be up to them as well. In an era of budget cuts in higher education, especially in the humanities, we need to look harder for ways to make the turn to a more public humanities. We teachers of Shakespeare have quite a bit going for us: a rich history of Shakespeare's very public place in American life, a wider audience than we may have thought, and a playwright who never underestimated any segment of his own audience, showing us how to reach all of our own rich and varied publics.

Notes

1. Stephen Peters, "America's Poorest Cities," *24/7 Wall Street*, October 7, 2016: http://247wallst.com/special-report/2016/10/07/americas-poorest-cities-3/. Accessed November 19, 2016.
2. "History of the Road," Maryland Historic National Road, Maryland National Road Association: http://marylandnationalroad.org/history-of-the-road/. Accessed November 25, 2016.
3. Harry I. Stegmaier, Jr., et al., *Allegany County: A History* (Parsons, WV: McClain Printing Co., 1976), vii. See also Katherine A. Harvey, *The Best-Dressed Miners: Life and Labor in the Maryland Coal Region, 1835–1910* (Ithaca: Cornell University Press, 1969), 19.
4. "Maryland Mines," Mining Artifacts & History: http://www.miningartifacts.org/Maryland-Mines.html. Last modified October 23, 2016. Accessed November 19, 2016. See also Harvey, *Best-Dressed Miners*, 9.
5. Tom Robertson, *Frostburg* (Charleston, SC: Arcadia Publishing, 2002), 37.
6. Peters, "America's Poorest Cities."
7. "Allegany County, Maryland Educational Data," TownCharts, (2016): http://www.towncharts.com/Maryland/Education/Allegany-County-MD-Education-data.html. Accessed November 20, 2016.
8. "Drug- and Alchohol-Related Intoxication Deaths in Maryland, 2015," Maryland Department of Health and Mental Hygiene: http://bha.dhmh.maryland.gov/OVERDOSE_PREVENTION/Documents/2015%20Annual%20Report_revised.pdf. Last modified September 2016. Accessed November 20, 2016.
9. Robertson, *Frostburg*, 32. Robertson also notes that the area miners were unusual in owning their own homes (32). He points out that the "whitewashed stone and picket fences of these small, but functional homes made quite a contrast to the stereotype of squalid living conditions found in some other company towns in other coal mining regions" (107). Harvey emphasizes this point as well in her history of coal mining in the region, a work that takes its title from a comment made in 1905 by a United Mine Workers' organizer: "Taken as a whole, this is a community of the best-dressed miners I have ever seen" (*The Best-Dressed Miners*, vi, 95–98). See also Stegmaier, *Allegany County: A History*, 208–210. This factor may have been significant in shaping the community's sense of itself as working class as opposed to "poor." As Nancy Isenberg argues in *White Trash: The 400-Year Untold History of Class in America*, class hierarchy in America, "begins and ends with the concepts of land and property ownership: class identity and the material and metaphoric meaning of land are closely connected" ([New York: Viking, 2016], xvii). As a result, she explains, land ownership in

America was often what separated the working poor from the "terminally poor" (xiii).

10. Andrew Roy, *Recollections of a Prisoner of War*, 2nd ed. revised (Columbus, OH: J. L. Trauger Printing Co., 1909), 148.
11. Western Maryland Historical Library: http://www.whilbr.org/itemdetail.aspx?idEntry=3399&dtPointer=4. Accessed September 6, 2017.
12. Dave Tabler, "They all drink Cumberland beer in the same popular barroom," *Appalachian History*, June 5, 2017: http://www.appalachianhistory.net/2013/06/they-all-drink-cumberland-beer-in-the-same-popular-barroom.html. Accessed December 20, 2017. Lawrence W. Levine, in *Highbrow / Lowbrow: The Emergence of Cultural Hierarchy in America*, gives other examples of America's fondness for using Shakespeare to sell products, including a memorable ad referencing Lady Macbeth's hand-washing problem:

"It's Duncan's blood," the man replied,
"She strives the fearful stains to hide."
"Why don't she wash her hands, b'gosh!
With Ivory Soap?" cried Uncle Josh.

([Cambridge, MA: Harvard University Press, 1988], 54).

13. James G. McManaway repeats this claim in "Shakespeare in the United States," *PMLA* 79, no. 5 (1964): 513. Kim C. Sturgess, however, refutes this as a myth (*Shakespeare and the American Nation* [Cambridge: Cambridge University Press, 2004], 123).
14. Alden T. Vaughan and Virginia Mason Vaughan, *Shakespeare in America* (Oxford: Oxford University Press, 2012), 11–12.
15. Ibid., 15.
16. Sturgess, *Shakespeare and the American Nation*, 57.
17. Levine, *Highbrow / Lowbrow*, 16.
18. Vaughan and Vaughan, *Shakespeare in America*, 7.
19. Ibid., 12.
20. Barbara A. Mowat, "The Founders and the Bard," *The Yale Review* 97, no. 4 (2009): 7.
21. Ibid., 1.
22. Alexis de Tocqueville, *Democracy in America*, ed. Phillips Bradley, vol. 2 (New York: Vintage Classics, 1990), 55.
23. Mark Twain, *Is Shakespeare Dead? From My Autobiography* (New York, NY: Harper & Brothers, 1909), 5.
24. Levine, *Highbrow / Lowbrow*, 20, 21.
25. McManaway, "Shakespeare in the United States," 514.

26. J. Lee Humfreville, *Twenty Years Among Our Hostile Indians* (1903; repr., Mechanicsburg, PA: Stackpole Books, 2002), 468.
27. Helene Wickham Koon, *How Shakespeare Won the West: Players and Performances in America's Gold Rush, 1849–1865* (Jefferson, NC: McFarland & Co., 1989), 4.
28. Jennifer Lee Carrell, "How the Bard Won the West," *Smithsonian* 29, no. 5 (1998): 2, 101.
29. Mark Twain, *The Adventures of Huckleberry Finn* (1884; repr., New York: Penguin, 1985), 150.
30. Ibid., 165.
31. James Shapiro, ed., *Shakespeare in America: An Anthology from the Revolution to Now* (New York: Literary Classics of the United States, 2014), xxv.
32. Levine, *Highbrow / Lowbrow*, 72.
33. As Michael Bristol recognizes, Shakespeare's "position as the representative of durable literary value has been affirmed as a natural fact within the United States for a considerable time" (*Shakespeare's America, America's Shakespeare* [London: Routledge, 1990], 1).
34. William Shakespeare, *Romeo and Juliet*, in *The Complete Works of William Shakespeare*, 6th ed., ed. David Bevington (New York: Pearson, 2009), 1.3.8–9.
35. The inspiration for many of our games and contests comes from the annual Shakespeare Festival held at the Folger Shakespeare Library for high school students in Washington, DC.
36. The quotes from Frostburg students are taken from the final reflection papers they write at the conclusion of the experience.
37. Shapiro, *Shakespeare in America*, 3.
38. Stanley Wells, ed., *American Shakespeare Travesties (1852–1888)*, vol. 5 of *Nineteenth-Century Shakespeare Burlesques* (Wilmington, DE: Michael Glazier, Inc., 1978), 26, 208. For additional nineteenth-century examples of burlesques of Shakespeare, see Levine, *Highbrow / Lowbrow*, 3–16; and Frances Teague, *Shakespeare and the American Popular Stage* (Cambridge: Cambridge University Press, 2006), 79–110.
39. Shapiro, *Shakespeare in America*, 517. For additional, recent examples, see Vaughan, "American Shakespeare Today," in *Shakespeare in America*, 191–203.
40. Comments from high school students are from a 2008 survey administered by a grant from the Maryland State Arts Council and the National Endowment for the Arts.
41. Another benefit of this program may be its success in connecting local students with students from all over the state pursuing their college degrees. As J. D. Vance reflects in *Hillbilly Ellegy: A Memoir of a Family*

and Culture in Crisis, "living in a place where most of your neighbors are poor really narrows the realm of possibilities. ... It means that you don't have people to show you by example what happens when you work hard and get an education" ([New York: HarperCollins, 2016], 242). In reflecting on the examples of those in his community who did eventually succeed, he explains, "Each benefited from the same types of experiences in one way or another. ... they saw—from a family friend, an uncle, or a work mentor—what was available and what was possible" (241).

42. Sturgess, *Shakespeare and the American Nation*, 2.
43. For a discussion of film adaptations of Shakespeare's plays from these countries, see Mark Thornton Burnett, *Shakespeare and World Cinema* (New York: Cambridge University Press, 2013).
44. See Sidonie Smith on the "afterlife" of what she calls "real work" that engages students in the larger world, in "The English Major as Social Action," *Profession* (2010): 200.
45. Elizabeth and Howard Adams, eds., *A Century of Commitment: Frostburg State University 1898–1999* (Frostburg, MD: FSU Foundation, 1997), iii.

How the One Percent Came to Rule the World: Shakespeare, Long-Term Historical Narrative, and the Origins of Capitalism

Daniel Vitkus

Theory, Historiography, and the Rejection of Long-Term Historical Narratives

New Historicism, reacting to humanist and universalist approaches to the study of literature, sought to reconstruct the past in ways that defined that past as radically different. So much so, that sometimes the perceived strangeness of past cultural practices functioned to disconnect that strange past from the familiar present. If contextualization is the key to a text's original and primary meaning, and if we must "Always historicize!", then only those erudite few who can embed Shakespeare within "a highly specific life-world" can understand his plays properly.[1] According to this logic, without detailed knowledge of the Essex rebellion, for instance, readers simply cannot grasp the meaning of Shakespeare's *Richard II*. Without knowing about the shipwreck of the *Sea Venture* or reading William Strachey's "A True Reportory of the Wracke and Redemption of Sir Thomas Gates, Knight," it will be impossible to understand *The Tempest*.

D. Vitkus (✉)
University of California, San Diego, CA, USA

S. O'Dair and T. Francisco (eds.), *Shakespeare and the 99%*,
https://doi.org/10.1007/978-3-030-03883-0_9

At about the same time that Stephen Greenblatt coined the term "New Historicism," post-structuralist theorists were rejecting "meta-narratives" and maintaining instead that there could only be a multiplicity of micro-histories and no valid overarching historical structures or processual continuities.[2] Despite their continuing influence on current critical practice, both New Historicism and Post-Structuralism have been called passé and have given way to new approaches and trends in early modern studies. And yet the critical opprobrium heaped on long-term historical narratives as "teleological" or narrowly Eurocentric continues to hold sway.

Jean-Francois Lyotard declared in 1979 that one symptom of the postmodern condition was an "incredulity toward metanarratives," but he followed this observation with an important political question: "Where, after the metanarratives, can legitimacy reside?" His answer was to propose that metanarratives should give way to *petits récits*, or more modest and localized[3] narratives, which can throw off the grand narratives by bringing into focus the singular event. By rejecting any and all overarching structural frameworks, Lyotard leads us down a path toward the fragmentation of both theory and history.

The delegitimization of long-term historical narratives has been two-fold: first, by seeking to undermine the project of reconstructing coherent historical narratives that span the *longue durée*; and second, by dismissing all (so-called) "grand" theories that have an explanatory, enabling utility for said narratives. In their stead, new historicists and post-structuralists would limit inquiries to a myriad of specific local contexts and would celebrate the incommensurable diversity and heterogeneity of human life—not its unity, coherence, or shared experience. It is certainly the case that some meta-narratives have been fashioned to justify or reinforce oppressive power structures, so there are good reasons to challenge certain types of reductive or distorting historical narrative—Whig history, American imperial triumphalism, or various theories of modernization and secularization, to name only a few. The problem, though, is that this all-out and indiscriminate attack on long-term narratives has had some unintended political consequences: most importantly, it has a disintegrative effect on our ability to understand, organize, and connect to the past or to understand our inevitable linkage to long-term, large-scale historical processes. And if the yet-unfulfilled "master idea" that grounds our understanding of history is the achievement of human rights for all, the struggle to defeat exploitation, tyranny, and superstition, and the reduction of human suffering, then perhaps it is a mistake to withdraw from that "grand" Enlightenment program to a place of suspicion or incredulity, where we may peer out from the smug and familiar safety of a snug local niche, ensconced (or perhaps even mired) somewhere in the micro-historical archival matrix.

History in its fullness is a vast and largely irrecoverable mass of events, thoughts, feelings, and experiences. And yet it is the job of scholars and experts to make some sense of the past, examining and analyzing the existing archive in order to reconstruct the shapes of time and organize history in a meaningful way that helps us to understand our relationship to earlier societies and to the potentialities of the future. Since economic systems are the primary mechanisms of social reproduction that organize human societies, they comprise the appropriate objects of description for a basic understanding of long-term historical change.

The time has come to return to large-scale historical narratives, or at least to that one sweeping historical process that connects us to the early modern past in a way that serves an ethical, political purpose today. This "grand" narrative is the Marxian conception of historical change, stretching from the early modern period to the postmodern, as a *longue durée* predicated on the emergence and rise of capitalism. Reconstructing the long story of how the new capitalist classes wrested power from the old aristocratic elites, and tracing the changing shape of the class system, allows for a better understanding of the forms of social injustice, wealth disparity, and uneven development that haunt us to this day but find their origins in the emergence of capitalism during the early modern era. Nonetheless, since they have become so widely accepted in the humanities, I need to address two sorts of objections to such a long-term narrative—the epistemological and the anti-Eurocentric.

As seen from various philosophical points of view, any large-scale framework to describe the past is doomed to be a falsification of history's complexity and contingency—at the very least, such history-writing may be accused of concealing the past's ontological un-representability. It may also be guilty of a distorting teleology, or of endorsing a hegemonic totalization. Bruno Latour, Jürgen Habermas, Hayden White, and others are right to point out that there is too much interpretation and narrativity in the work of history-writing for it to be accepted as an unmediated account of the past. The validity of this skepticism about comprehending or organizing the past is undeniable at a certain level of analysis: the gap between past events and our current reconstruction of those events, between the fragmentary, surviving archival evidence and "what really happened" is unbridgeable. But taken too far, such skepticism becomes (at best) myopic and (at worst) a paralysis. A historical methodology that allows a description of historical change with some measure of long-term linearity, linking the present to the distant past, is a necessary ethical undertaking. If we do not take up this task, other stories about "history" deployed by conservative ideologues and right-wing popularizers will triumph over our niggling skepticism. The political consequences of this Bartleby-esque withdrawal from Big History are all too apparent today. For instance, conservative authors of best-selling books (like William J. Bernstein's *A Splendid Exchange: How Trade Shaped the World* or Niall Ferguson's *The Ascent of Money: A Financial History of the World*) do not hesitate to present grand, sweeping accounts of capitalism that celebrate finance as the foundation of human progress and civilization—or to link today's global economy to "the first fragmentary evidence of long-distance commerce during the Stone Age."[4] Ferguson goes so far as to declare, "the ascent of money has been essential to the ascent of man."[5] Such authors are apparently immune to Lyotard's "incredulity": they are quite happy to trumpet their triumphalist apologies for neoliberal power, and to celebrate the virtues of Western capitalism in a grand narrative about development, growth, and the spread of global economic interdependence.

The other objection to the Marxist meta-narrative is based on an accusation of Eurocentrism, and here the important work of Jack Goody and Dipesh Chakrabarty comes to mind first. Again, this is a valid complaint when directed against many of the traditional narrations of modernity. It is certainly true that the idea of "modernization" has been linked with Reason, with the West and its empires, and with "civilization." And this brand of "modernity" has been forced upon the world—used to justify unjust wars, imperial tyrannies, and today's virulent neoliberalism. Nonetheless, it is hardly a gross distortion to claim that Western Europe played a crucial part in the dynamical global matrix that generated modern capitalism. Try telling the indigenous peoples of the western hemisphere or Australia just how "provincial" the Europeans were! But a proper understanding of the important role of the Western empires in a global history of capitalism must include an acknowledgment that Europe's contribution to that process was only made possible by its connectedness to other parts of the world through the commercial world-system. After the Eurocentric world histories of the past, and their tendency to locate the origins of capitalism, modernity, and "the rise of the West" solely within an "exceptional" western Europe, were rightly challenged by Goody, Chakrabarty, and the California School (the latter argue for the Chinese economy as the true center of global history), a variety of counter-theories and historiographies have emerged, offering new, alternative narratives that displace the historical center from imperial Europe to other systems and locations: Janet Abu-Lughod (Eurasia, the Pax Mongolica, and the Silk Road), Samir Amin (the Mediterranean and the Arab-Islamic world), Dipesh Chakrabarty (South Asia), and John M. Hobson (China). More recently, neo-Marxist historiographers have responded to these debates by attempting to develop a truly global approach that sees multiple, shifting centers located throughout a global capitalist system as it emerged and evolved. One of the most promising examples of this new Marxist historiography is Alexander Aneivas and Kerem Nişancioğlu's *How the West Came to Rule: The Geopolitical Origins of Capitalism*, where they "call for a recognition of how the *interactively generated* socio-economic and political differences between Europe and other societies played a part in the former's eventual rise to global pre-eminence."[6] At the same time, Aneivas and Nişancioğlu seek to describe the long-term history of capitalism as part of an even larger story about a world containing a variety of economic structures that make up a truly global, geopolitical system In doing so, they substantiate and enable an understanding of specific early modern texts and events in relation to proto-capitalism and within an inclusive narrative account of capitalism spanning the centuries from its origins to its present-day manifestations.

Shakespeare and the Emergence of Capitalism

Shakespeare began to write plays in a time and place where capitalism was first emerging and where feudalism was still well established. It was not yet recognized as "capitalism," of course, but early modern writers were keen observers of its harmful effects on the 99 percent and of the ways it enriched the new bourgeois members of the ruling class. The capitalists' economic practices were frequently condemned as avaricious sin or as un-Christian usury, and sometimes ridiculed as an outrageous new form of greed and corruption. For instance, in 1609 Robert Mason, in *A Mirror for Merchants*, writes,

> [u]sury is set up as an universal Trade. This is the cause, that Charity growth cold, loving affection between friends and allies, turned into hatred, hospitality decayed, and the service of God despised…; This is the cause that the alms to the poor are neglected, the dish of neighborly hospitality not provided, the ordinary and necessary servants turned off, and the gate of pity and compassion fast locked and sealed up.[7]

The early modern usage of the word "usury" denoted not only exorbitant interest rates, but the full range of innovative capitalist practices involving investment, speculation, credit, debt, currency exchange, and other ways to breed money from money. As the capitalist classes gained power, however, they sought to make usury morally justifiable. Dante put usurers in the same circle of hell as the inhabitants of Sodom and others who were condemned for what were considered "unnatural" vices. Later, the Lateran Council of 1515 clearly condemned usury as unearned income, declaring that usury occurs "when gain is sought to be acquired from the use of a thing, not in itself fruitful (such as a flock or a field) without labour, expense, or risk on the part of the lender." A century later, however, usury had "passed from being an offence against public morality which a Christian government was expected to suppress to being a matter of private conscience. [A] new generation of Christian moralists redefined usury narrowly as excessive interest" while blessing the debt-based economy in general.[8] Shakespeare lived and wrote at a time when this transition from abhorrence and condemnation to acceptance and naturalization was taking place.

Now we read Shakespeare in an age when postmodern capitalism has gone global and when the charging of excessive interest on loans is a normalized practice that ensnares so many of the 99 percent. If today's critical practice in reading and teaching Shakespeare is going to find a correspondence with the current struggle against the power of the 1 percent, it must focus on our linkage to Shakespeare's time through the history of capitalism's expansion, from the end of the feudal order to the triumph of global capital today. The story of how capitalism and its class system began in Shakespeare's day is part of the much bigger story of which we are a part as disenfranchised citizens of a neoliberal world system (that last "we" excludes the 1 percent, of course).

In Shakespeare's drama, the onset of capitalism was often identified with transnational entities and exchanges: initially, capitalist practices and effects were blamed on outsiders—Jews and Italians, for the most part. This perception was based on a longstanding tradition of anti-Semitism and ethnocentrism, but the old racism and xenophobia were motivated in new ways by the transmission of capitalist practices from the Mediterranean to Northern Europe, and by the arrival of Italian merchants and Jewish *converso* refugees in London. Shakespeare and his contemporaries were also affected by the rise of the Western empires, by the cultural and socio-economic changes wrought by the expansion of long-distance foreign trade after 1570, and by the economic crises that brought on widespread hunger and suffering in both rural and urban England.

In fact, the joint-stock theater companies themselves were some of the first capitalist undertakings in England. And as these new commercial playhouses were being built in London, many characteristics of English theater also developed and changed with the times: to cite just one example—the traditional form of personification allegory was employed less frequently over time. Characters called "Mankind," "Lady Lucre," or "Lady Conscience" appear more rarely on the stage, and audiences begin to meet more naturalistically individuated figures. Nonetheless, in many cases these newly individuated figures retain, in names like "Sir Bounteous Progress," or "Justice Greedy," an affiliation with a moral type or stock character. These changes in how dramatic character was imagined and presented correspond to a shift in London's culture from a sense of community and commonality toward an increasingly individuated subjectivity marked by the ideology of emergent capitalism with its new forms of possessive individualism and commodity fetishism.

In the work of Shakespeare and other London playwrights, the commercial life of the city grew to become a persistent point of focus. This was especially the case for a new form of comedy called "city" or "citizen" comedy, which represented urban life and the vigorous energies of commerce in its traditional center and marketplace, the City of London. The critical, satirical note is very strong in these plays; their plots were structured around commercial and marital transactions, and the main male characters are obsessed with the pursuit of wealth, and often with the goal of securing a lucrative marriage to an heiress.

Shakespeare's *The Merchant of Venice* is an important early version of the city comedy genre.[9] The setting is shifted, however, from London to the city of Venice, a place that represented, in the minds of many English subjects, a polity based on trade where commerce allowed for cross-cultural and inter-religious exchange. *The Merchant of Venice* is typical of the city comedy form in the way that it combines and conflates the erotic and the commercial. Debt and credit define the characters in this play and drive the action. The young gallant Bassanio's effort to obtain the hand of Portia (and in doing so, to take control of her wealth and property) depends on a strained and dubious system of credit and debt that has already rendered Bassanio desperate. He confesses to Antonio:

> 'Tis not unknown to you, Antonio,
> How much I have disabled mine estate
> By something showing a more swelling port
> Than my faint means would grant continuance. (1.1.122–125)

His "chief care" is "to come fairly off from the great debts / Wherein my time, something too prodigal, / Hath left me gaged" (1.1.127–129). All of Bassanio's "plots and purposes" involve "How to get clear of all the debts [he] owe[s]" (1.1.133–334) so that he can continue his excessive and parasitical way of life. His marriage with the rich heiress Portia is a means to this end. The play demonstrates the truth of the adage that Portia's companion Nerissa invokes to admonish Portia for complaining that she, like Antonio, is unhappy despite her prosperity: "they are as sick that surfeit with too much as they that starve with nothing" (1.2.5–6). Here, Shakespeare hints at the connection between the excesses of those who enjoy great wealth by exploiting others and the deprivations suffered by members of the lower classes who must serve the elites for low wages or else starve. To be a "merchant" engaged in trade in this text is to be a part of the new capitalist system in which capital is raised and increased, not by the honest sale of goods for a fair price, but by means of a "trade" that is really speculation and usury made possible by the underhanded manipulation of debt and credit networks. In fact, the play takes as one of its central themes the commodification of human beings, and of human flesh, which is the consequence of the radical new capitalist system that relies on investment, risk, credit, and debt to increase the wealth and power of the merchant class.

The play's pattern of commercial transaction as aggressive swindle is quite clear. As in other city comedies, *The Merchant of Venice* features the triumph of witty, clever characters who prevail through deceptive and improvisational performances, through the tactic of disguise, and through timely unveiling and unscrupulous seizing of opportunity, as well as by means of verbal play that exploits the slipperiness of law and language in order to pull the wool over the eyes and ears of their victims. Honest bargain, firm contract, and fair and equal enforcement of the law all must give way to a moral malleability that is laced with sadistic laughter. A pattern unfolds as a series of cruel swindles takes place in the comedy: in the trick pulled on Shylock when his property and daughter are stolen; when Bassanio presents himself as a wealthy young man of means and then later has to confess to Portia (after he has won her) that he is "worse than nothing" (3.2.259), a financial zero; when Bassanio plays the casket game and wins because Portia bends the rules by providing him with strong hints and clues that give away the correct casket (something she does not do for the other suitors, whom she mocks and humiliates); and finally, when a legal game of bait-and-switch deprives Shylock of his religion and wealth at the end of the trial. All the while, the interanimation of erotic and commercial language is fundamental to the structure of this play, as it was to other comedies like it. Portia herself speaks eloquently of how her intrinsic worth as a human being must become an itemized quantity of fungible commodities for Bassanio's sake—"to stand high" in Bassanio's "account," she must become a "sum of something" (3.2.158). The wordplay here suggests that she must be reduced from her power and autonomy as an unmarried heiress and "lord" (3.2.167) of Belmont to become a mere part of a possessed thing. Her transformation speaks to the reifying power of capitalism.

The uneasiness produced by Shakespeare's *The Merchant of Venice* indicates a strong ambivalence about the new economic practices of the day. For the audience, there is an excitement to be had in identification with the romantic heroes who win out and claim the prizes that come with comic closure, but at the same time there is an uncomfortable sense that theft and trickery, a distasteful fraud, are essential elements of economic life in this imaginary city. The competition for wealth, property, money, and inheritance in Shakespeare's problem comedy exposes the proto-capitalist system as a problem. Such a text offers its twenty-first-century interpreters an opportunity to look back at the late sixteenth-century in London as a time and place where capitalism was beginning and thus where some of the origins of today's postmodern crisis of global capitalism may be located.

By the middle of the next decade, Shakespeare had gone on to write *King Lear*, a play that bears clear marks of the socio-economic trauma that England had experienced during the preceding decade. As Chris Fitter has recently argued, *Lear* is a "radical" play, one that refers to the suffering of the poor and the failure of the 1 percent to relieve that suffering. "Take physic, Pomp," demands Lear: "Expose thyself to feel what wretches feel, / That thou mayst shake our superflux to them, / And show the heavens more just" (3.4.34–37). And once Gloucester is also dispossessed and tossed out on the road, he agrees with Lear. If the "superfluous and lust-dieted man" were himself to feel the agonies of material want, that could mean that "distribution should undo excess, / And each man have enough" (4.1.67–71). In *Coriolanus*, probably written just after *Lear*, Shakespeare's starving plebeians would point out that "What authority surfeits on would relieve us. If they would yield us but the superfluity while it were wholesome, we might guess they relieved us humanely" (1.1.13–15). These plays clearly identify the relationship between the ruling classes and the lower classes as one of exploitation, injustice, and cruel indifference. This radical strain in the London theater of the early seventeenth century, which pointed to the inequity of the class system and suggested that a fair redistribution of resources was the solution to that problem, was by no means the dominant mode for representing proto-capitalism and its class conflict. As the drama of early modern England moved from "medieval morality" toward modern character psychology, this transformation was accompanied by a shift in the theatrical treatment of poverty and its causes. Often the Jacobean and Caroline theater obfuscates or misrepresents socio-economic injustice and the unfair distribution of wealth—an ideological move. While many of these plays expose the excesses and follies of Pomp, they do not always reveal the direct connections between the sufferings of the lower classes and the vices of the middle and upper classes. Rather, they tend to misrepresent the poor in three different ways: as parasites, as criminals, or as jolly, amusing beggars. Those patterns of misrepresentation have continued through the centuries and, sadly, are still widely disseminated today. Pointing to instances of this kind of misrepresentation and demonization of the working poor is one example of how teachers can connect early modern literature to a long-term history of capitalism and its ideology—and to today's socio-economic crisis of income and wealth inequality.

Teaching Shakespeare in the Undergraduate Classroom: Connecting Early Modernity to Postmodernity

As I hope was made clear in the previous section of this essay, when we read plays like *The Merchant of Venice*, *King Lear*, or *Coriolanus*, we find ample evidence of how proto-capitalism was affecting and disturbing early modern England. We need not force this view onto the texts: economic changes and new forms of economic behavior are present at the center of the action in many plays performed at the commercial playhouses in the commercial city of London, which was rapidly becoming a world city.[10]

Reading Shakespeare in this manner is to read Shakespeare through a politics that is critical of capitalism. We must be critical of capitalism because it is a socio-economic system that has produced inequality, human suffering, and environmental destruction on a planetary scale. Our efforts to restrain capitalism offer our only hope to make a better, more just world in which we might work to confront, for example, the coming crisis of climate change, a tangible consequence of capitalist patterns of aggression, consumption, and profit-taking. If we fail, and the neoliberal accumulation of capital continues without restraint, then the crisis will be exacerbated tremendously. According to Naomi Klein, "any attempt to rise to the climate challenge will be fruitless unless it is understood as part of a much broader battle of worldviews, a process of rebuilding and reinventing the very idea of the collective, the communal, the commons, the civil, and the civic after so many decades of attack and neglect."[11] To accomplish this challenging but necessary goal, we must fight a battle against free market, neoliberal ideology on every possible front, and to succeed we must restrain and disempower the 1 percent while informing, empowering, and motivating the 99 percent.

This view of capitalism, and the political project of recovering and writing a cultural history that reveals and resists an exploitive and unjust political economy, must not be limited to a critical discourse that exists solely within the circuits of academic exchange through lectures, conferences, and publications. While it is important for experts to speak to experts in order to exchange ideas and strengthen our disciplines by constantly questioning and re-theorizing what we do, that is not enough. If nothing else, the crisis in the humanities demands our robust engagement with persons outside the academy. Other forms of intellectual work, public activism, and communication are crucial: these include engagement with the 99 percent through free online culture and the digital humanities, through public activism and community engagement, through the curation of exhibitions that are accessible to the public, and through theatrical productions and other forms of performance that reach audiences beyond the academy. But within the context of higher education, we must also bring the larger concerns of our time to bear on our teaching. Our teaching can convey to students of all kinds, whatever their major, in specialized seminars or in general education required courses, a critical way of understanding the long history of capitalism. Tenured faculty, in particular, might play a leading role, exercising what power and choice they have, in shaping curricula and engaging with the general education curricula at their institutions, and in promoting broader conversations with colleagues outside their home institutions—rather than turning entirely toward the kind of hyper-specialized scholarship and publication that are rewarded in the status economy of the elite academy, especially.

In the remainder of this essay, I will describe a few examples of how Shakespeare's plays can be taught in a historical framework that is not only about the early modern context in which the plays and poems were produced but also about how we see Shakespeare at the other end of a historical process that touches the present. This kind of critical pedagogy is not necessarily limited to a chronological leapfrogging whereby we jump from the Elizabethan to the Trumpian period in order to show the uncanny correspondences, relevancies, or analogous situations that link the past to the present. We can do that, and with very positive effects, but we can also stress our connectedness to the early modern past through a continuous history of capitalism's economic and cultural development that unfolded by means of a globalization that began at the end of the fifteenth century.

To accomplish this pedagogical goal, the earliest meetings of a Shakespearean drama class, and many of the initial reading assignments, must include not only a survey of the "historical context" for early modern drama but also a discussion of periodization, of how we might understand and organize the history that separates and yet connects us to Shakespeare's time. This might include the use of a timeline and a dialogue with students about the meaning of terms like *ancient, medieval, modern, postmodern, early modern, Renaissance, humanism, feudalism, capitalism, eurocentrism*, and so on. This discussion can initiate a process that will last throughout the course whereby each play is understood in terms of a dialectic between past and present, linked by the long-term history of capitalism, to a potential future. To avoid the pitfalls of a narrow Eurocentrism, there should also be a discussion about capitalism and globalization that underscores the place of London in a changing system of economic and imperial activity that was increasingly globalized (especially after 1492).

While an emphasis on the long-term history of capitalism and globalization is crucial, the linkages to the past through historical narrative can also focus on other strands of the historical fabric that are woven into the history of capitalism but may be unraveled in order to direct classroom discussion in other ways. In the three plays I mentioned already (*The Merchant of Venice*, *King Lear*, and *Coriolanus*), commercial swindling, the unjust distribution of wealth and resources, and class struggle in the context of famine are all present as indications of economic crisis and change. In additional plays, the discussion could be focused on other concerns that link early modern and postmodern times. Within the limits of this article, I will offer three examples of this kind of historicist-presentist dialectic as it might be enacted in the classroom.

My first example is *Julius Caesar*, a play that asked Elizabethan playgoers to consider the political dilemma that citizens of a republic must face when powerful elites, rallying behind a single, potentially autocratic leader, threaten to destroy democratic rights and replace democracy with tyranny. It also represents assassination and political violence as a possible solution to tyranny. By dramatizing the assassination of Caesar and the consequences that follow, Shakespeare's tragedy suggests that political violence in the name of democratic rights may be counterproductive because when the people are unable to seize power themselves, such violence may lead to disorder, unrest, and political revenge rather than justice, peace, or stability. The assassination of Caesar leads not to a republican revival in Rome, but to civil war and dictatorship under the triumvirate. Then as now, citing the threat of assassination (or today what is often called "terrorism"), a demagogue can bring to power a tyranny that is the same or worse than the tyranny that was initially threatened. It is a tragedy that comes about in a society in which the plebeians, the proletariat of Rome, are manipulated by deceptive rhetoric and brought to support leaders who do not represent their basic interests or rights. Finally, it is a play that revives the distant past and its political history in order to speak to present political concerns and ask that audiences learn from the past in order to understand their present and future.

Students today look back at ancient Rome and early modern London through a long history of political struggle that resisted and eventually overturned the power of the monarch enthroned atop a God-given social hierarchy. This struggle brought the concepts of democracy and human rights to ascendancy, establishing laws upholding those principles within the modern nation-state, only to see those hard-fought gains in rights and democratic institutions undermined and thwarted by the 1 percent through the corruption of traditional party politics and the triumph of corporate power, as seen in the US judiciary's authorization of corporate control over government through political contributions in the case of Citizens United. That history can be sketched out in the classroom, and then specific reference can be made to the rise of corporate power, the shrinking of the middle class, and the history of the Occupy movement that popularized the concept of the 1 percent, making clear, in the wake of the 2008 financial collapse, that Wall Street, neoliberal corporations, and their accomplices in political office were to blame for the sufferings of the 99 percent.

This kind of careful consideration of the recent crisis in American democracy can launch the historicist-presentist dialectic so that, when discussing scenes from *Julius Caesar* featuring the plebeians, students can consider the role of public demonstrations and protests in effecting change or communicating grievances to those in power. The class can be shown images of the Occupy movement (for example, they can watch a documentary film like *99%: The Occupy Wall Street Collaborative Film* [2013]); they can consider the movement's history, its slogans, its manner of bringing its grievances into public spaces, its ways of collectively organizing and discussing, its repression by the police and the authorities, and its failure to bring the needed changes to the system—all of these can be connected to *Julius Caesar* and its representation of the plebeian crowds filling the streets of Rome, occupying the stage, but then losing control as costly civil wars were prosecuted and as a populist leader, Mark Antony, comes to power who speaks the rhetoric of democracy but acts very differently behind the scenes. Furthermore, the class can view film clips of the 2017 Public Theater production of *Julius Caesar* that was directed by Oskar Eustis and performed for free at the Delacorte Theater in Central Park. The director, Eustis, set up a very clear analogy between Caesar's triumph over Pompey in Rome and Donald Trump's triumph over the electoral college. The production featured a Julius Caesar, played by a red-haired, coifed Gregg Henry, swaggering about with a cigar in one hand, the other hand pawing his wife Calpurnia's crotch. Calpurnia, for her part, wore a flowing designer silk dress, spoke in a heavy Slavic accent, and stumbled around the stage in stiletto heels. This Caesar was clearly a version of America's pussy-grabber-in-chief who appeared to be naked in a bath tub as Calpurnia attempted to dissuade him from attending the Senate on the Ides of March. Students can also read some of the reviews and journalistic coverage of the production, which created controversy and provoked some Trump supporters to loudly interrupt the performance with their own protests against a play that staged an assassination of a Trump look-alike. A discussion of this production, and the controversy that it inspired (including the withdrawal of financial support by Delta Airlines and Bank of America, two corporate donors to the Public Theater free summer productions), can lead to further understanding of how Shakespearean tragedy could instigate a radical questioning of undemocratic political machinations by the 1 percent, as well as a discussion of how conservative demagogues from the 1 percent can pretend to populism in order to manipulate the common people—then and now.

Eustis's interpretation of *Julius Caesar* associated the political power of a Trump-like Caesar with sexual sleaze, but another play by Shakespeare, *Measure for Measure*, gives teachers of Shakespeare a chance to trace the long history of sexual harassment, abuse, and assault that links the early modern period to our own time through the continuous history of patriarchal power. The words and actions of the magistrate Angelo, and his treatment of the virginal Isabella, provide a chance to consider the play in relation to the #MeToo movement. Isabella's courage in confronting Angelo requires the support of another powerful man, the Duke himself, in order to speak out against Angelo without being punished for it. Without the Duke's support, Angelo's chilling question, "Who will believe thee, Isabel?", would have rung true, and Isabella's accusations would have been ignored or worse. *Measure for Measure* makes it clear that women are subordinated and manipulated by men who hold power over them, that sexual misconduct is facilitated by sexual hypocrisy, and that harassed women are rarely believed, or if believed, the punishment of the harasser or abuser is difficult to enforce—and that this why it can be so easy to victimize them.

There are a number of productions of *Measure for Measure*, recent or planned for the near future, that have chosen to stage the play in order to connect its sexual politics to our current #MeToo context and to the empowerment of fourth-wave feminism through social media. One such production was mounted off-Broadway in Manhattan by Elevator Repair Service, opening in October of 2017. It was reviewed in *Vox* by Tara Isabella Burton, who wrote,

> "It was another time." "People didn't care about harassing women until now." "He's an old dinosaur learning new tricks." As more and more publicly influential men continue to fall from grace as a result of sexual harassment accusations, one of the most common excuses for their actions is that it was different back then.
>
> Defenders of Harvey Weinstein, of Roman Polanski, or of Roy Moore often use temporal moral relativism as an excuse. Sure, they admit, nowadays, women are so sensitive about these things. But they treat consciousness of sexual harassment as a uniquely post-feminist phenomenon: the result of politically correct brainwashing. But all too often, many critics of feminism can be as ahistoric [sic] as the "left" they despise, imagining a past blissfully bereft of any potential for sexual misconduct, in which no woman would ever think to "speak up" because nothing was worth speaking up against. But that era did not exist. I was reminded of this last week at the Public Theater, at Elevator Repair Service's production of *Measure for Measure*, one of Shakespeare's most perplexing — and powerful — plays.[12]

It is not only that we see, in this case, Shakespeare's powerful "relevance" to our own time, but even in Burton's account of the play and its meaning, there is a sense of the *longue durée* of the feminist struggle, encompassing the struggles of women in early modern England, the current effort to obtain justice for victims of sexual harassment, and all of the centuries in-between. The teaching of the play can incorporate an understanding of gender ideology, laws, and the sexual regime of Shakespeare's day, and that context can be connected to our own time and the ongoing effort to seek gender equality. This can also involve a consideration of the limits of an identity politics that does not acknowledge how political economy is connected to gender oppression through the constraints and limits put on the labor and legal status of women, and to the ways that the patriarchal system of heteronormative marriage served to control women and their bodies. These larger biopolitical concerns are also present in *Measure for Measure* through the subplot involving Mistress Overdone and Pompey Bum, comic sex workers who speak out against the efforts of the 1 percent to control their bodies and restrict the sexual freedom of the Viennese population.

Finally, I want to discuss Shakespeare's late comedy *The Tempest* (1609). The last thirty years or so have seen a huge interest in this play as a kind of postcolonial text, a play that prefigures the postcolonial condition, and questions the power dynamics that were beginning to develop between colonizer and colonized during a time that the Western empires were expanding and new colonies and commercial outposts were being established all over the world. This critical attention produced a rich variety of insightful political interpretations of the play: critics urged us to read *The Tempest* in the context of English settlement and plantation in the New World, and to see Caliban and Ariel as representatives of the indigenous colonized subject under European empire. Such readings continue to be valid and useful, and discussion of the play's relationship to the colonial enterprise and to the origins of European possession in North America and elsewhere continue to be an important way to contextualize the play and connect Shakespeare's art to the long history of Western empire.

In addition to these (post)colonial readings of *The Tempest*, another interpretation of the play that asks us to span the centuries would focus on Prospero's "art"—his ability to raise a storm and effect control over nature by means of his book-based knowledge. A connection can be made between early modern fantasies and aspirations about acquiring a technology that could control the elements, and the rise of a scientific knowledge that defined the earth, not as a living biosphere, but as a repository of raw materials to serve economic ends and to enable technological development. The long history of science, technological knowledge, and petrochemical capitalism leads from the emergence of Baconian empiricism in the seventeenth century to our own anthropocene or capitalocene era.[13] Today we see how, in time, the force and trajectory of our technological development, driven and shaped by capitalism, has raised an unstoppable "tempest" in the form of climate change.

One could, as I have been doing, begin class on *The Tempest* with an image of Hurricane Irma, the vast storm system that struck the eastern Caribbean and the southeast United States during the hyperactive hurricane season of 2017. I then ask my students, "What is this?" and then, "who conjured up this tempest?". The connection between human activity as cause and the current effects of climate change, and an understanding of that phenomenon as something resulting from centuries of capitalist-driven extraction and consumption—this is perhaps the single most important lesson that can be learned today, within and without our educational systems.

Next, one could ask students to consider that the human race, armed with its knowledge, power, and technology, has conjured up, over time, a series of tempests that "have put the wild waters in this roar" (1.2.2) of storms and hurricanes that are already flooding our coastal cities. Furthermore, our students can be referred to the arguments made by various environmental historians about the continuing causes of climate change. These arguments have recently been popularized by Naomi Klein: that the primary cause and source of our global climate crisis and the destruction of the environment is capitalist ideology, corporate power, and the neoliberal drive for short-time profit and wealth accumulation, forces that have driven the human race to rape the earth, mine and consume petrochemical fuels, and by doing so destabilize the balance of aery elements that compose our atmosphere.

A discussion of Prospero's motives, as a colonizer and slavemaster, and as a man whose goal is to abandon the island so that he can regain the power and wealth of his dukedom, is also an important conversation to hold in class. The play can be seen as a kind of uncanny, prophetic parable about knowledge, technology, and power: the power that comes with Prospero's magic (his control of nature) must be "abjured" because it is "rough"—it has been used to raise the dead and to force nature to unravel its natural order. But the purpose of Prospero's magic is clearly not to pursue knowledge in a disinterested or altruistic manner—it is to gain revenge on his enemies, to subdue them, and to force them to submit. The imperial impulse visited upon Caliban is also present in Prospero's Continental ambition to retake his rightful place in Milan at the top of the 1 percent.

If current critical practice in reading and teaching Shakespeare is going to find a correspondence with the contemporary struggle against the 1 percent, then one way to accomplish that is to focus on our linkage to Shakespeare's time through the continuous history of capitalism's expansion, from the end of the feudal order to the triumph of global capital today. The story of how capitalism and its class system began in Shakespeare's day is part of the much bigger story of which we are all a part as disenfranchised citizens of a neoliberal world system: plays like *The Merchant of Venice* or *The Tempest* offer, from our postmodern purview, intimations of our current situation—when more than half of the world's wealth is in the hands of 1 percent of the population and (at latest count) eight multi-billionaires possess the same amount of wealth as the world's poorest half. The need to interpret and discuss Shakespeare's plays in this manner, and to situate them within a long-term historical narrative that connects our current situation with that of Shakespeare and his contemporaries, can and should be energized and motivated by the economic injustice that we now face. The struggle of the 99 percent against the power and greed of the 1 percent is a struggle for the future of the planet itself. The lessons of the 2008 financial crisis are clear, but the neoliberal powers have not heeded them; instead they have carried on with business as usual. The gap between rich and poor continues to grow as capitalism enriches the 1 percent, shrinks the middle class, and inflicts additional deprivation and suffering on the working poor. The evidence of climate change and its human causes, based on the capitalist economy and its ideology, is also utterly apparent. The stakes could not be higher, and the role of the human sciences is a crucial one in making sure that we understand the past as prologue to our present crisis, and consider its cultural artifacts as part of a greater whole, the story of capitalism. According to *The Heart of the Matter*, the 2013 report of the American Academy of Arts & Science's Commission on the Humanities and Social Sciences to the U.S. Congress, "The humanities—including the study of languages, literature, history, jurisprudence, philosophy, comparative religion, ethics, and the arts—are disciplines of memory and imagination, telling us where we have been and helping us envision where we are going." Our ethical mandate is to use our expertise and knowledge of texts and histories in a way that reveals and relies on a long-term historical narrative, the tale of how capitalism arose and became a powerful force that changed human society and sacrificed the ecological balance of the planet for the sake of profit and the interests of the 1 percent. A better world is possible; a more just economy can be created through radical reform.

This is no time for scholars and students to turn away from the current crisis—to find refuge in a micro-historical archival narrowness, in a historicism that sees only difference in the culture of the past, in an empty formalism, or in the study of the past as a source of an aesthetic pleasure and transcendent timelessness that serve to insulate us from a harsh and unjust present. Our universities are some of the last institutions where resistance to the neoliberal system, and a properly critical understanding of its history, can still take place. Higher education, even in Research I universities, in privileged private liberal arts colleges, or in the heavily endowed private mega-universities like Stanford, Duke, and the universities of Ivy League, cannot ignore this struggle, and even there, where the 1 percent are often trained and the ruling class reproduces itself, scholars working in the humanities, including those who study Shakespeare, must strive to question the status quo by making connections between early modernity and our postmodern crisis.

Notes

1. "Always historicize!" is a famous critical dictum delivered by Frederic Jameson in *The Political Unconscious: Narrative as a Socially Symbolic Act* (Ithaca: Cornell University Press, 1982), ix. Stephen Greenblatt, on being appointed University Professor of the Humanities at Harvard in 2000, was quoted as saying, "My deep, ongoing interest…is in the relation between literature and history, the process through which certain remarkable works of art are at once embedded in a highly specific life-world and seem to pull free of that life-world. I am constantly struck by the strangeness of reading works that seem addressed, personally and intimately, to me, and yet were written by people who crumbled to dust long ago" ("Greenblatt named University Professor of the Humanities." *The Harvard Gazette*, September 21, 2000: https://news.harvard.edu/gazette/story/2000/09/greenblatt-named-university-professor-of-the-humanities/. Accessed April 1, 2018).
2. Greenblatt first used the term "New Historicism" in his introduction to a special issue of the journal *Genre*. See "The Forms of Power and the Power of Forms in the Renaissance" Genre 15, nos. 1–2 (1982): 5.
3. Jean-François Lyotard. *The Postmodern Condition: A Report on Knowledge*, trans. Geoff Bennington and Brian Massumi (St. Paul: University of Minnesota Press, 1984), xxiv–xxv.
4. William J. Bernstein, *A Splendid Exchange: How Trade Shaped the World* (New York: Grove Press, 2008), 16.
5. Ibid., 4.
6. Alexander Aneivas and Kerem Nişancioğlu, *How the West Came to Rule: The Geopolitical Origins of Capitalism* (London: Pluto Press, 2015), 250.
7. Robert Mason, *A Mirror for Merchants* (London: T Creede, 1609).
8. Roger Ruston, "Does It Matter What We Do with Our Money?" *Priests & People* (1993), 173–174.
9. All quotations from Shakespeare's plays in this essay are taken from Stephen Greenblatt, et al., ed., *The Norton Shakespeare* (New York: W. W. Norton, 2015).
10. On the "global Renaissance" in England, see the essays in Barbara Sebek and Stephen Deng, eds. *Global Traffic: Discourses and Practices of Trade in English Literature and Culture from 1550 to 1700* (New York: Springer, 2016) and Jyotsna G. Singh, ed. *A Companion to the Global Renaissance: English Literature and Culture in the Era of Expansion* (Oxford: John Wiley & Sons, 2009).
11. Naomi Klein, *This Changes Everything: Capitalism vs. The Climate* (New York: Alfred Knopf, 2014), 397.

12. Tara Isabella Burton, "What a lesser-known Shakespeare play can tell us about Harvey Weinstein," *Vox*, November 15, 2017: https://www.vox.com/culture/2017/11/15/16644938/shakespeare-measure-for-measure-weinstein-sexual-harassment-play-theater. Accessed December 15, 2018.
13. "Capitalocene" is a term that was coined and defined by Jason W. Moore. See the usage of the term throughout Moore's *Capitalism in the Web of Life: Ecology and the Accumulation of Capital* (London: Verso, 2015).

Hal's Class Performance and Francis's Service Learning: *1 Henry IV* 2.4 as Parable of Contemporary Higher Education

Fayaz Kabani

The State of Contemporary Higher Education

Despite rancorous debates surrounding Title IX and campus sexual assault, civil rights, free speech, tenure, and the use of contingent faculty, Americans on the right, center, and left tend to agree about the benefits of higher education. Conservative Patrick Garry writes that "the most important social mobility function a government can perform—or promote—is education. In an open society, education gives each citizen the opportunity to advance on his or her own merit,"[1] while the Hamilton Project, launched by the nonpartisan Brookings Institution, asserts in a policy memo that "Over the past fifty years, policies that have increased access to higher education, from the GI Bill to student aid, have not only helped lift thousands of Americans into the middle class and beyond, but also have boosted the productivity, innovation, and resources of the American economy."[2] David Bergeron and Carmel Martin of the progressive Center for American Progress propose college for all "to ensure that the United

F. Kabani (✉)
Allen University, Columbia, SC, USA

S. O'Dair and T. Francisco (eds.), *Shakespeare and the 99%*,
https://doi.org/10.1007/978-3-030-03883-0_10

States has the skilled workforce and educated citizenry to achieve inclusive prosperity and economic growth."[3]

Since the end of World War II, Americans have come to believe that economic advancement can be achieved by increasing educational access. Given the consensus of experts across the political spectrum about the value of a college degree, ramped-up competition among colleges and universities, and working-class anxieties, it is no surprise that "Americans have been bombarded with a steady barrage of media stories showing the growing differential lifetime earnings between those with a four-year college degree and those without, and about the disappearance of manufacturing and the accompanying loss of well-paying jobs that do not require a college degree."[4]

While policymakers propose to offer diverse populations better access to educational opportunities and solutions to help at-risk students increase their rates of completion, many people no longer see a college degree as guarantor of economic success or social mobility. Many high school graduates we aim to help by encouraging their college attendance, especially nontraditional students, fall through the cracks, racking up debt, failing to complete degrees that may or may not be relevant, and navigating the world with neither a practical skill set nor an education. Higher education, thus, often further stratifies the social divides it claims to bridge.[5]

Increasingly, students are weighing the benefits of a four-year education against the costs, averse to taking on crippling amounts of debt.[6] Recently, college enrollment numbers have declined nationally.[7] Though some of this can be attributed to the graying of America—numbers of high school graduates are decreasing, although graduation rates are at all-time highs[8]—student enrollment at for-profits and community colleges is dropping at sizeable rates, and enrollment in four-year publics and privates has stagnated.[9] Although Heidi Schierholz of the Economic Policy Institute claims, "Falling college enrollment indicates that upward mobility may become more difficult for working-class and disadvantaged high school graduates,"[10] it seems just as or more likely that prospective students and their families no longer see a college education as a cost-effective path up the social ladder. Is it social mobility if one ends up only marginally better off financially? Or not at all?

The prevailing image of the college student is still one of the fresh-faced eighteen-year old headed, immediately after prom, to the big state school or to a private institution across the country. However, the traditional student today is becoming overwhelmingly nontraditional, as "single-parents now make up 26 percent of the country's undergraduate student population," and single parents, we know, "are also the largest demographic group living below the poverty line."[11] Given the obstacles these students face—students I am going to call "new traditionals"—such as familial expectations of making good, living off-campus, and working, often to support a family, it should not surprise that their completion rates are poor. Further, because student loans are easy to obtain, "students with a high probability of dropping out of college...borrow on the same terms as good students."[12] Unwittingly, perhaps, institutions that primarily serve lower income students may contribute to their future economic hamstringing via steep loan repayments[13] or the destruction of their credit.

Along with skyrocketing costs and changing demographics, the educations offered at four-year colleges might not be relevant to most of today's college students, since "a four-year college degree isn't necessary for many of tomorrow's good jobs."[14] Yet many students who would be better served by other career paths set out to earn a four-year degree because, as I have noted above, "America clings to the conceit that four years of college are necessary for everyone."[15] While "the number of good jobs held by workers with no more than a high school diploma has declined by over 1 million since 1991[,] [g]ood jobs have shifted primarily to workers with Associate's degrees, who have gained more than 3 million net new jobs during that same period."[16] Current data from the Bureau of Labor Statistics suggests that the demand for employees in "skilled services industries,"[17] which include financial and health services,[18] will continue.[19] Despite increased expense and students' desire that education result in employability and adequate future earnings, many colleges and universities continue to focus on the value of the liberal arts or a broad general education curriculum and its soul-enriching consequences.[20]

Shakespeare's *1 Henry IV*, particularly the beginning of scene 2.4, when Hal, in a giddy mood, waits for Falstaff to arrive after the botched Gadshill robbery, offers insight into the problems of higher education today and ways it can better serve the new traditional student. As Terry Eagleton has said, "it is difficult to read Shakespeare without feeling that he was almost certainly familiar with the writings of Hegel, Marx, Nietzsche, Freud, Wittgenstein, and Derrida."[21] If, as Eagleton suggests, Shakespeare's writings have anticipated the foundations of modern thought, they may prove useful to think through the tensions and contradictions surrounding higher education in this century. The first one-hundred lines or so of *1 Henry IV* scene 2.4 precisely address the problems of access, power, privilege, and social mobility that plague the current American system, particularly in their representation of our traditional notions of the college student. They provide a critique of the privileges inherent in that vision and an illustration of the difficulties faced by our new traditional students. In what follows, I am going to offer a parable, if you will, about those problems, casting Eastcheap and the Boar's Head Tavern as an institution of higher education, and Francis and Hal as, respectively, the "new traditional student" and the self-determining "traditional" student of yore. More high school students today share qualities—weaknesses and strengths—with Francis than with Hal, and institutions of higher learning need to market differently to the Francises of America by scrapping the rhetoric of an education that leads inevitably to "leadership"[22] and instead focus more on employability in a rapidly changing economy that benefits the highly skilled. If the American system of higher education hopes to satisfy current students' needs, it should (1) refocus on community college for many, if not most, low-income first-generation students, and (2) do away with or greatly reduce liberal arts or general education requirements at most four-year institutions.[23]

The Old Vision

Americans have imagined the college student as a young person with unlimited potential and aspiration, unfettered by restraints except final exams or twenty-page term papers. Students socialize, plays sports, join performing arts clubs, and volunteer to help the needy. Sometimes, they get into trouble by partying too hard or failing to study. In the end, however, they find themselves enriched by the experience, literally and figuratively. This self-determining traditional student corresponds to Hal's portrayal of himself in his soliloquy in scene 1.2 of *1 Henry IV*, in which he claims he will easily "throw off" his "loose behaviour" (*1 Henry IV*, 198) "when he please…to be himself" (190).[24] By play's end, he has bested Falstaff in jest, Hotspur on the battlefield, and Henry in political machinations. Just as we have long imagined of our young people going off to college, "Shakespeare seems to show…above all in the figure of Prince Hal in *Henry IV* and *Henry V*, something contrary to the determinism of contemporary theory: that it is what we do and wish to be which shapes the universe we live in."[25] We thus "desire Hal" because of the sovereignty he represents as an unspotted ego ideal. Hal's emergence can be read as "the dreamed-of success of the arriviste," "a middle-class ego ideal."[26] While "arriviste" seems pejorative when applied to college students trying to make better lives, I wish to posit analogies, which of course are not exact, between our old vision of the American college student and Hal: young, talented, "coming of age,"[27] and hungry for success. While being "upper middle-class" himself—well, really, quite a lot more than that—Hal, in our contemporary context, represents the dream of unconstrained self-determination and actualization, which so many working-class people have been inculcated with. Thus, schools that target nontraditional student populations, such as historically black colleges and universities (HBCUs) and public regionals, often also employ the marketing strategies of elite institutions, portraying themselves as molding future leaders. These schools, at the same time, want to lure more students like Hal, ensuring high retention and graduation rates, future notoriety for the school, and alumni donations. Schools "desire Hal" and students desire *to be Hal.*

Given colleges and universities' targeting of privileged and high-achieving students, it is not surprising that the rhetoric used to describe educations at private Ivy League research universities or highly selective liberal arts colleges has filtered into the discourse used by public research universities, regional public universities, and even minority-serving institutions and HBCUs as they all compete to attract more "college-ready" and easily retainable students. The two largest public research universities in my home state, the University of South Carolina and Clemson, have websites whose rhetoric illustrates how entrenched are the expectations of success via a four-year degree. If one hovers the mouse over the "Study" tab on the University of South Carolina homepage, one reads, "Our academic programs will challenge, inspire and spur your intellectual curiosity."[28] The "Experience" tab explains, "Expand your mind. Then expand your horizons." The "Research" tab promises more about one's potential future than it does about one's research: "You begin with a question. The possibilities of *where you end up have no limits*" (emphasis added). Although that statement may mean that one's research will take lead one to unexpected results, new questions, and the like, I read "research" here not as an inquiry into one's field of study but as a metaphor for life achievement, a life unfettered by limitations.

Curiosity and tenacity will lead one to a boundless future. It is almost as if the language on the university's homepage were designed to persuade Lisa Simpson, alternately interested in attending the Ivys or the Seven Sisters, into reneging on her denial, "I will not be a Gamecock."[29] The language, in fact, mirrors the rhetoric of self-actualization employed by the prestigious liberal arts college Amherst: "Our story is your story. Since 1821, we've been helping our students *find their own voices*, *discover their own truths* and *forge their own paths* in the world" (emphasis added).[30] Rather than deliver some definite outcome to students, the education offered provides them the tools needed to explore and blaze a successful trail for themselves.

Clemson's homepage echoes similar promises of self-actualization. The "Admissions" tab reads, "Since 1889, Clemson University has built a proud heritage of attracting intelligent, competitive students and helping each one reach his or her full potential. We are dedicated to *intellectual leadership*, *collaboration*, *public service*, *innovative research and a winning spirit—in academics*, athletics *and life*" (emphasis added).[31] Here too, one is told that becoming a successful scholar will result in the winning spirit to succeed in life. This education, ennobling minds and spirits, will not be limited to personal success or New Age-y self-actualization but will lead to "collaboration" and "public service." The sentiment that one's private pursuits will benefit the public pervades the marketing discourse of large public and private research universities. This logic of education as self-actualization and as public service reinforces the putative divide between four-year institutions that develop the brain and the character and technical schools and community colleges that provide blue-collar skills. Thus, Clemson hides the success of its athletic programs, including its 2017 National Championship football team, embedding the term "athletics," because excelling at the bodily and college sports' ability to drive campus culture might tarnish the school's academic reputation. One's future success cannot be guaranteed at a school that is good at sports, at least one overly proud of its achievements.

These university websites imply that prospective college students desire a specific kind of success that follows attendance at a four-year institution. A Shakespearean can remind us all that such institutions talk to *all* of their students, regardless of background, as if they were Hal. I suggest that one can analogize the denizens of Eastcheap either as instructors coming from a wide range of backgrounds and personal experiences or a diverse student body from whom the Prince learns. Eastcheap—obviously a party school—provides Hal with a wonderful general education. He learns hotel, restaurant, and tourism management from frequenting the Boar's Head, criminal justice by dealing with sheriffs and thieves, anthropology by observing the Boar's Head's clientele and wait staff, performance from Falstaff and Poins, rhetoric from everyone he deals with, and perhaps, most importantly, languages from the drawers. This general education's broadening of his mind, as promised by many colleges and universities, is part—even a large part of—Hal's (or the traditional college student's) success. As Hal tells Poins—shortly before Falstaff, Gadshill, Bardolph, and Peto arrive from their beating by the highwaymen—he is now at the apex of his powers, in command "of all humours that have showed themselves humours since the old days of Goodman Adam to the pupil age of this present twelve o'clock at midnight" (2.4.90–93). He has expanded his mind and his horizons (to use the USC homepage's language) through his education here. He understands, or so he claims, everything one could possibly know about the temperaments of all people who have ever lived.[32] His well-roundedness and thorough understanding of human nature will serve him well in his future role as king, and the education provided at the Boar's Head by instructors such as Poins and Falstaff, and yes, even Francis, has direct bearing on his future success.

Hal distinguishes himself from the simple-minded Francis and the single-minded Hotspur:

> That ever this fellow should have fewer words than a parrot, and yet the son of a woman! His industry is upstairs and downstairs, his eloquence the parcel of a reckoning. I am not yet of Percy's mind...he that kills me some six or seven dozen of Scots at a breakfast, washes his hands, and says to his wife, 'Fie upon this quiet life! I want work.' (96–102)

Francis's repetition of "anon" parallels Hotspur's focus on violence. Hal prides himself on the rhetorical facility Francis and Hotspur lack, but Hal is more than just gifted in speech. He is "the omnicompetent young politician."[33] Hal will be more successful than his rival Hotspur because of his ability to see multiple perspectives and speak from those points of view. Hotspur is only "credentialed" to wage war, much as Francis has learned only a certain skill set in his apprenticeship. Because he has a deeper understanding of the world, gained from his broad general education, Hal is destined to master both, to succeed beyond the dreams of either.

This description of Hal is one Americans recognize in their imagining of higher education. High school graduates become masters and mistresses of their destinies by getting into college, putting effort into their studies and extracurricular activities, and, like Hal, persevering despite the difficulties they face. Today, too, these students in addition become open-minded, empathetic individuals who can foster a rapidly diversifying society's engagement with a shrinking world. All of us have probably read justifications of the humanities and liberal arts suggesting that "colleges should focus less on making sure we cover the content and more on teaching students how to become self-regulated learners" because "without critical thinking, discernment and reflection, democracy retreats from the sound of the loudest voice."[34] In addition, "literary fiction" (and the humanities in general), "teach[es] us values…such as the importance of understanding those who are different from ourselves."[35]

Shakespeare's portrayal of Hal, however, disrupts these otherwise inspiring stories of the humanities' empathy-inducing and assumption-questioning abilities. Moreover, it punctures our long-standing image of traditional students, who, through their own merits, attend schools, receive degrees, and become successful. I would like to suggest that a close look at *1 Henry IV* 2.4 both represents *and* critiques the privilege required to access such educational opportunities in the first place. That education, while marketed as socially enriching, primarily benefits those privileged enough to receive it, who may then further entrench their privileged positions, blinding them to the experiences of others.[36]

Privilege

Large public research universities, focused on attracting elite students to improve their rankings, their enrollments, and ultimately, their donations, often style the educations they provide as pathways to global citizenship and power-brokering, all the while ignoring that their "narratives about wealth creation—such as education and hard work as the key to success…leave out the important truth that wealth begets wealth."[37] Necessarily, then, they also disregard that many of the low-income students they also try to recruit will not complete their degrees[38] because of inadequate academic preparation.[39]

As Robin Hanson wrote in 1990, "Academia is still largely a medieval guild, with a few powerful elites, many slavelike apprentices, and members who hold a monopoly on the research patronage of princes and the teaching of their sons."[40] So, while some see Hal, the "traditional student," as free from circumstance, it is his very circumstances (being heir to the English king, his subsequent inheritance, access to court, and adoption of his father's *realpolitik*) that are in large part responsible for his ability to learn anything worthwhile in Eastcheap.

Poins, at the beginning of scene 2.4, unaware of Hal's whereabouts and the "field work" he is conducting, asks "Where hast been, Hal?" (2.4.4). Hal, of course, has been in the cellar with the tapsters, "an experience reserved for favoured customers."[41] While it is possible that Hal has a special relationship with the Boar's Head's servers, it is likely that his social position has allowed him privileged access to the cellar and the tapsters' language. Poins, a "second brother" (*2 Henry IV*, 2.2.64),[42] is gentle himself. His orchestration of the Gadshill prank on Falstaff suggests that Poins is as clever as the Prince, and, thereby, could have earned "favored customer" status with the servers. But his being born gentle rather than noble and second rather than first presumably causes him to miss out on this opportunity, as he sits in a "fat room" (*1 Henry IV*, 2.4.1) instead of the cellar, partaking of much good wine.

Shakespeare's portrayal of Hal in 2.4, especially when contrasted with his portrayals of Poins and Francis, undermines the logic provided by many institutions that one's individual knowledge will have positive effects on society at large. Hal's knowledge is useful insofar as he can deploy it later in his future occupation, namely in earning the loyalty of his subjects before his accession, rather than having to coerce it from them after the fact. Knowledge is not always or entirely valuable in itself, as defenders of the humanities or general education like to assert, but it is almost always valuable in its performance and practical applications. Hal brags to Poins that he has mastered the drawers' language "in one quarter of an hour" (17). Hal's primary goal in crowing about his proficiency is performing for Poins his qualifications as an honorary tapster, almost as if Poins were a job interviewer reviewing Hal's application. Hal *seems* to know what he is talking about, successfully demonstrating his knowledge by explicating the drawer-phrases "play it off" (16) and "dyeing scarlet" (14–15). Regardless of its depth or superficiality, his knowledge of tapster culture yields desired results. Because of his privilege, Hal does not attempt to identify with his social inferiors but desires for them *to identify with him*. He "sound[s]" "the very bass string of humility," which can mean, "I have behaved with as much humility as possible,"[43] to endear himself to them. His display of their language also indicates that he does indeed "sound" like them. He can *parrot* them effectively without being reduced to a parrot.

Hal's knowledge of the tapsters and their preferred modes of behavior seems personally beneficial since

> They take it already, upon their salvation, that, though I be but Prince of Wales, yet I am the king of courtesy, and tell me flatly I am no proud jack, like Falstaff, but a Corinthian, a lad of mettle, a good boy—by the Lord, so they call me—and when I am King of England I shall command all the good lads in Eastcheap. (8–14)

He has passed his exam with distinction. His drawer-instructors praise his manners and attitude, as someone of Hal's social station arguably would exhibit undesirable affectations when dealing with inferiors. They call him a "good *boy*," "a *lad* of mettle," and a "Corinthian" (emphasis added), epithets seemingly diminishing and unworthy of one's future king, but enviable for a young man aspiring to achieve fraternity with the Eastcheap crowd. Hal's exhibition of Eastcheap cultural styles causes them to treat him like one of their own, as evidenced in their calling him a "Corinthian," meaning "good fellow…here derived from the putatively riotous behavior of inhabitants of Corinth."[44] They regard him not only as an unpretentious person, but also as one welcome to participate in their social circle's rituals. Hal's proud and slightly incredulous "by the Lord, so they call me" (12) highlights his own surprised pleasure at how willingly they accept him as one of their own. It could be argued that Hal's inclusion into their peer group illustrates the benefits of "general education" because he has acquired the adaptability to relate to those unlike him. However, it is his social position that both grants him this educational opportunity and the ability to use his knowledge to advance his own agenda.

While much humanist writing urged the education of the nobility so that they might benefit the commonwealth, Hal's education at "Eastcheap U." seems to benefit him only; he brags to Poins that the tapsters have already guaranteed their loyalty to him when he becomes king. He will be the man in charge of the "leash" (6), all without having to break them. His education has taught him to feign fraternity with others, now his "sworn brother[s]" (6), in order to win their loyalty. As *Henry V* makes clear, no one benefits from Hal's knowledge nearly as much as he does. Hal's education protects social boundaries and further entrenches class privilege. The king, Archbishop of Canterbury, and some nobles and clergymen benefit from the invasion of France, while boys get slaughtered, loyal soldiers like Williams and Fluellen act as pawns, and scoundrels like Pistol miss saying their goodbyes to dying spouses.

While those familiar with *Henry V* know the personal gains acquired by Hal/Harry from his education—propagating his legacy as ruler and continuing the patrilineal line through marrying Katherine of France—we see Hal in *1 Henry IV* 2.4 exercising his privilege to access and master the tapsters' language *so that he might further exercise his privilege* in this very scene, namely in his condescension to his social inferiors. While feigning camaraderie with them, he makes it known repeatedly that he sees himself as unique, which, it might be too obvious to note, contradicts the assumption or promise that a four-year college education makes one more empathetic. Hal tells Poins he has been "With three or four loggerheads, amongst three or fourscore hogsheads" (4–5). The Arden 3 edition notes that "loggerheads" means "blockheads" and continues, "the Prince's contempt for his new *sworn* brothers...is apparent as he jokes with Poins at their expense."[45] Hal has ingratiated himself with his social inferiors who grant him the privilege of visiting the cellar, but, apparently, they have not been so successful ingratiating themselves with him. It might be argued Hal calls them "loggerheads" for the word play with "hogsheads," but his uncertainty as to whether there are "three or four" of them indicates how little he regards them. Calling his newly "sworn brother[s]" "a leash of drawers" (6–7), however jocularly uttered, reveals his contempt, comparing them to beasts of burden. Not only are they regarded as insufficiently human, presumably because of their social station and their lack of education, that is, they lack rational capability and so resemble instinctual beasts, but they must also be controlled, "leashed," by someone of Hal's standing and intelligence.

Hal believes his fifteen-minute "course" with the tapsters qualifies him to "drink with any tinker in his own language during my life" (18–19). Arguably, Hal either believes that they do not have much to teach him—they are not worthy of knowing or have nothing to know—or that he only needs enough knowledge of their sociolect to feign fraternity with them. In addition to trivializing the drawers' language and culture, he conflates tapsters with tinkers, two different and specialized trades. Although mending cookware greatly differs from working in a tavern, for Hal, one group of workers speaks in the same manner as the other; they are interchangeable. The working class, regardless of occupation, are the same to him, indicating the superficiality of his knowledge of their culture and his concern for their lives.

Perhaps some of this derision aimed at the drawers can be explained as a kind of gentlemanly fraternizing with Poins, someone closer to him in social status. In a sense, Hal seeks to bring Poins closer to him by insulting people of lower status than either of them, but, in bragging about knowing the drawers' first names, he refers to Ned as "Sirrah" (6). Hal could use this term in an affectionate manner, but, even so, he illustrates the difference in power between them. Hal could have invited Poins to the cellar, as it would seem unlikely the tapsters would have refused his request, and thereby, "increase access" to one not so privileged, but neglects to do so. Perhaps Hal neglects to do so because he "understands the *political value* of his association with the apprentices as a group"[46] (emphasis added), a value unavailable to Poins. Much of the seemingly trivial knowledge Hal gains in his anthropological excursion "sound[ing] the very bass string of humility" (5–6) will only serve someone like him when he takes over his father's "job" running the family "business," his broad general education providing his "management degree" supplemental benefits due to his already privileged position and access to power.

While many people have the opportunity to receive a good general education, they, like Poins, are not as privileged as Hal, and, thus, might not be well-served by this cornerstone of higher education since "Only at the uppermost stratum of the professional elite might the *cultural* capital offered by general education courses be translated into *social* capital."[47] If Hal is not "Everystudent" but supremely privileged, as I have suggested here, one can barely avoid the conclusion that higher education reinforces the social and class divisions whose gaps it claims to close. Higher education promises upward social mobility to almost all, including the most vulnerable, but often or even usually further exacerbates social and economic difference. As the Pell Institute has shown, students from well-to-do families not only have a better chance of attending college but also of graduating.[48] When authors declare, "liberal arts graduates are significantly more likely to take leadership roles in their careers, engage in lifelong learning activities, and (eventually) earn into the six figures,"[49] they fail to acknowledge that, as Joe Pinsker quips, "rich kids study English."[50] A four-year liberal arts education provides better economic security because a large percentage of those students already come from economically secure backgrounds. Hal, despite the supposedly empathy-enriching consequences of his education, remains blind to the agency of others: he fails to consider that the drawers' compliments might be their calculated humoring of him or that Francis's gift of sugar is his way of "networking" with Hal.

The New Traditional Student

While Hal's privilege and education, particularly his knowledge of "Anthropology," "Languages," and "Rhetoric," give him the ability to ingratiate himself with commoners, he fails to understand Francis, and others, of his social class or to see their humanity. This becomes evident in the prank he plays on Francis, performed even as Hal waits for the much more amusing revelation of the prank he and Poins have played on Falstaff. As readers will no doubt recall, Hal, having come back from the cellar with the drawers and looking for another exploit to while away the time before Falstaff's arrival, recruits Poins to

> Stand in some by-room, while I question my puny drawer to what end he gave me the sugar, and do thou never leave calling 'Francis!', that his tale to me may be nothing but 'Anon'. (28–31)

Francis has given the Prince some sugar, and for his kindness, Hal decides to reduce Francis to a parrot by engaging him in conversation while Poins simultaneously calls for service, setting at odds Francis's duty to his future sovereign and his duty to the Boar's Head's clientele.

Although this scene is often read and played for laughs—the simple waiter unable to keep up with the quick-witted prince—I will argue in my close reading that their interaction reveals not Francis's shortcomings, but Hal's failure to acknowledge Francis's humanity. Hal brags about his being "of all humours" (90), yet his knowledge of Francis seems limited to some of the verbiage the drawer uses on the job. Read as an analogy of the idealized student, Hal illustrates the lack of human understanding one may retain despite being trained in the humanities. Read analogically as what I have called the "new traditional student," Francis's inaction at the end of the set piece symbolizes the impossible dilemma the underprivileged often face between serving practical interests, represented by Poins' calls, or attending upon an almost unimaginable and unreachable social mobility, represented by Hal and his seeming interest in Francis's future. Despite Hal's assumption that Francis lacks opportunities for advancement and the desire for them, Francis illustrates in this scene his competence, agency, and aspiration. Hal, however, cannot recognize these traits in Francis despite the education that has, in the analogy I have proposed, supposedly broadened his mind.

Francis is much more than the simpleton Hal and directors of the play often portray him to be. Although Francis, immediately after being called, answers with the desired, "Anon, anon, sir!," he follows with, "Look down into the Pomegranate, Ralph" (36–37), showing that, though charged to serve, he manages other duties and delegates them to others. He takes charge in his service industry role (one often held by those working their way through the now standard *five years* of college). In addition to regarding Francis's waiterly formulae as evidence of his ignorance, Hal further (mis)understands Francis's apprenticeship, remarking to Francis, "Five year! By'r Lady, a long lease for the clinking of pewter" (44–45). He trivializes Francis's trade; like many today, Hal believes technical training is a dead end, not a road to a fulfilling future. He sees himself as having, not privileged agency, but a privilege on agency, and assumes someone of Francis's social rank to be the product of forces more powerful than he, later evidenced by Hal's advising Francis to serve out his indenture's full term.[51] Hal, like so many of us, reduces Francis, the equivalent of our working-class or first-generation student in my analogy, to one who is tossed on the waves of circumstance.

Thinking Francis's vocational training to be inferior, Hal asks if Francis "darest be so valiant as to play the coward with thy indenture" (45–46), suggesting that quitting his apprenticeship is the "valiant," masculine course of action and that Francis should, rather than settle for a practical course of action, perhaps, chase his dreams. In Hal's formulation, acting on one's own desires is the way to be manly, noble, or free. Service is feminine and unworthy despite the advantages it provides to Francis, providing him with food, shelter, and, presumably, a secure future occupation. Francis's reply, "I could find in my heart—" (49) suggests that Francis *would* consider pursuing something more rewarding than his apprenticeship *should* the opportunity present itself: "Francis seems, as Dover Wilson suggested…to take Hal's interest in his willingness to break his indenture as a sign that he might be offered a position in the Prince's household, a hope repeatedly interrupted by Poins's calls."[52]

Further confusing the situation, Hal, after encouraging Francis to break his indenture, asserts that doing so is theft, taking labor away from someone else more entitled to it, rather than seeing the employer's taking something away from the employee. Arguably, Hal is socially conditioned to a certain blindness on this score, the kind of blindness an elite general education should cure: his father's usurpation and his own noble birth result in his becoming Prince of Wales. Hal distances himself from this real theft in his two soliloquies of the Henriad but casts Francis's hypothetical contractual breach as a real crime. Although the nobility throughout these plays must face the consequences of their misdeeds, they rationalize their own actions while judging the socially disadvantaged to be deviant when they act out of their own self-interests.[53] Thus Hal's question, "Wilt thou rob this leathern-jerkin, crystal-button, not-pated, agate-ring, puke-stocking, caddis-garter, smooth-tongue, Spanish-pouch?" (68–70), is not important because of its class condescension toward the innkeeper, but because Hal states that Francis *would be robbing his employer* in looking for an opportunity to better his own life. Critical commonplace holds that Francis's question, "O Lord, sir, who do you mean?" (71), illustrates his ignorance of Hal's terms to describe the innkeeper, and that the joke, therefore, is on Francis who cannot keep up with Hal's wit. It should be argued, however, that the question confuses Francis because Hal has framed it in terms of Francis's *robbing* someone. Francis does not understand whom he would be *robbing*. Francis apprentices at the Boar's Head and serves real thieves because he wants to make an honest living. Had he sought a life of robbery, he could have learned under Bardolph and Falstaff.

Francis's attendance upon Hal illustrates his desire for the advancement Hal himself represents and that Hal, seemingly, believes is only reserved for people like himself. Do we hear irritation, or perhaps sarcastic servility, in that "Anon, sir!" (51) to Poins after Hal asks if Francis has considered a more ambitious course beyond apprenticeship? Does he see this "interview" with the prince as a potential opportunity? Why has Francis given Hal the sugar in the first place? Is this a naive act on Francis's part because he believes Hal is genuinely "like" him despite the disparity in social status, or is this a calculated attempt to gain favor with someone who could improve his life?

The end of the set piece, in which Francis is torn between answering Poins or Hal and reprimanded by the Vintner, is generally played for laughs and depicts Francis as simple-minded. I would argue, however, that this illustrates Francis's thoughtfulness. He must decide between his obligation to Poins, read contemporarily as students picking from the immediate payoff of entering the job market or training at a vocational school, and his attendance upon Hal, read contemporarily as striving for a less well-defined but potentially more rewarding education at a four-year institution. Alternately, the dilemma between serving Poins or Hal can be read as that between students' responsibilities to their jobs (*the* extracurricular activity of many students), loan providers, families, or other "real-world" obligations and their desire to be Hal, the dream of socioeconomic success that could instantaneously release them from their burdens. After commanding, "come hither" (38), Hal asks, "How long hast thou to *serve*, Francis?" (40, emphasis added). The question, coupled with the command, possibly reminds Francis of his low station and relative poverty, matters that may always be close to the surface of his mind. Hal takes Francis repetition of the phrase "Anon, anon" and his inaction for a lack of mental acuity when it really reveals a lack of mental bandwith.[54] Triggered into thinking about his economic insecurity, asked about his job by the future king, and "offered" a thousand pounds, all this suggests that Francis's indecision to attend upon Hal or serve a customer is much less comical.

While for decades the average college student has been imagined as Hal, the reality is that *our students are Francis*, torn between their dreams of social mobility and the obligations that interrupt or defer those dreams, especially now that the cost of an education is no longer a "pennyworth" but "a thousand pound." Despite his education, which should have expanded his capacities for empathy, Hal does not understand Francis's situation or how he himself might assuage it. Francis might put up with Hal's abuse because he tries to make the best of a *poor* situation. He might recognize that Hal puts him on for the sake of a joke, but given their social difference, Francis cannot dash off to serve another customer and ignore his future sovereign. He might know the promise of the thousand pounds is not intentional, but, because folks like Hal are well-to-do and well-connected, and, on a whim, might bestow unmerited favor, Francis shows himself a good sport to leave standing the possibility of unmerited reward.

Conclusion

Students today are not homogeneous. The Hals want rock-climbing walls and exquisite dining facilities to supplement top-notch academic programs. The Francises, increasingly, are opting out of walking the tightrope between their obligations and the receding shore of promised success. Billy Willson "show[ed]" Kansas State "a fair pair of heels" (46–47) after earning a 4.0 his first semester of general education courses, writing on social media, "You're spending thousands of dollars to learn information you won't ever even use just to get a piece of paper."[55] Critics validly pointed out the absurdity of an engineering student's complaint about learning the quadratic formula, but they tended, too, to ignore or mischaracterize his statements. The president of KSU's faculty senate, Andrew Bennett, argued that a beginning student lacks the credibility and experience to criticize the general education curriculum.[56] Rather than address Willson's concerns about higher education's costs, however, Bennett dismissed those concerns as uninformed. Perhaps, but maybe we should be more attentive to what students like Willson (and those not as privileged) say. Indeed, if we have adopted the "customer service" model of higher education, and the customer is always right, maybe we should increase the options on the menu.

Instead, however, most solutions to problems in higher education advocate again and again programs that "offer free community college for high school students with a B average and create clear transfer pathways from community colleges to four-year institutions" or that "encourage high-achieving, low-income students to enroll at selective colleges and universities and provide the academic support, peer mentoring, financial support, and cultural capital that they especially need to be successful."[57] Such programs are shortsighted in seeing a bachelor's degree as the only worthy goal and in only imagining "high-achieving, low income students" to be worth the trouble, despite their recognition that they need to have systems in place "to intervene early" "when students are about to go off track."[58] Our institutions recognize class as an obstacle to success only for "good students" who have triumphed over their circumstances. They neglect students whose early education, health, (un)employment, incarceration, and so on, have prevented them from being "college-ready," even when they are encouraged to attend nevertheless.

When college is presented as an investment in one's financial success, can we blame students if they are skeptical that higher education will enrich the soul? Broadening their minds will not help many of them take care of their families or pay off the very loans they take out to afford schooling. Again, most colleges and universities sell themselves in this manner because they want well-prepared students, but many new traditional students, as collateral damage, fall victim to a discourse intended for their more privileged peers; they set out on ventures they cannot complete, when what they really want is a future they can afford to be a part of.

Increasing access to four-year liberal arts or research colleges and universities is failing the economically disadvantaged. Our "hyper-credentialed life experiences and ideologies are blinding us to alternative pathways to the middle class."[59] We should destigmatize "tracking" in high schools and quit peddling the fiction that everyone *should* go to a four-year institution to obtain a degree in order to lead a good life. It is irresponsible to insist, "four years good, two years bad." Until we can guarantee equity in primary and secondary education, expanding access to four-year institutions is doomed to fail. Patrick Garry writes, "In 2012, while the unemployment rate was over 8 percent and millions more had dropped out of the labor force…nearly half of employers reported difficulty in filling job openings" and "half of these employers said the reason was a lack of technical competencies or hard skills."[60] If we better utilized our community colleges, "the under-appreciated crown jewels of America's feeble attempts at equal opportunity," to provide people with "world-class technical skills,"[61] many of those hurt by the economic downturn might have made it through more easily. Such an education would better prepare those entering a changing economy predicated upon "skilled services."

The American middle class can be rebuilt, and inequality reduced, by encouraging more first-generation students and those otherwise under-prepared to obtain a marketable trade, rather than selling them the dream of entry into the societal elite via a series of expensive degrees. It is counterproductive to expect Francis to be Hal. Francis literally cannot be Hal. He does not have the upbringing or social network to achieve such a high station, but this is not to say Francis cannot lead a comfortable life. Rather than require our new traditional students, many of whom have been robbed by less than ideal educational systems based on the zip code they were born in, to conform to a narrow ideal, we should provide them with options. Tracking students for technical school will not deny them the American dream but will help them attain a realizable version of it. Maybe then Francis, after fulfilling his apprenticeship, could save some money and run his own tavern like Mistress Quickly. He could purchase a home and send his sons and daughters to a good grammar school. Thus, like John Adams, his study of "practical subjects would give his…children room 'to study painting, poetry, musick, architecture, statuary, tapestry, and porcelaine.'"[62] One of them could master the language Hal so prizes, become the next Shakespeare, and teach our inner Hals to have more empathy for Francises everywhere.

Notes

1. Patrick Garry, "Education as the Key to Opportunity and Upward Mobility," *RenewAmerica.com*, March 20, 2015: http://www.renewamerica.com/analysis/garry/150320. Accessed December 29, 2016.
2. Michael Greenstone, Adam Looney, Jeremy Patashnik, and Muxin Yu, *Thirteen Economic Facts About Social Mobility and the Role of Education*, (Washington, DC: The Brookings Institution, 2013): https://www.brookings.edu/research/thirteen-economic-facts-about-social-mobility-and-the-role-of-education/. Accessed December 29, 2016.
3. David A. Bergeron and Carmel Martin, "Strengthening Our Economy Through College for All" (Washington, DC: Center for American Progress, 2015): https://www.americanprogress.org/issues/education/reports/2015/02/19/105522/strengthening-our-economy-through-college-for-all/. Accessed January 4, 2017.
4. Robert Schwartz and Nancy Hoffman, "Pathways to Upward Mobility," *National Affairs* 37 (2015): http://www.nationalaffairs.com/publications/detail/pathways-to-upward-mobility. Accessed January 14, 2017.
5. Greenstone et al., "Thirteen Economic Facts."
6. Jake New, "Debt-Averse Teens," *Inside Higher Ed*, November 18, 2014: https://www.insidehighered.com/news/2014/11/18/study-teenagers-want-go-college-are-particularly-averse-student-debt. Accessed December 29, 2016.
7. Floyd Norris, "Fewer U.S. Graduates Opt for College After High School," *The New York Times*, April 25, 2014: https://www.nytimes.com/2014/04/26/business/fewer-us-high-school-graduates-opt-for-college.html. Accessed December 29, 2016.
8. Anya Kamenetz and Cory Turner, "The High School Graduation Rate Reaches a Record High—Again," *National Public Radio*, October 17, 2016: http://www.npr.org/sections/ed/2016/10/17/498246451/the-high-school-graduation-reaches-a-record-high-again. Accessed August 2, 2017.

9. Doug Lederman, "Downward Spiral on Enrollments," *Inside Higher Ed*, December 16, 2015: https://www.insidehighered.com/news/2015/12/16/decline-postsecondary-enrollments-continues-and-speeds. Accessed January 12, 2017.
10. Norris, "Fewer U.S. Graduates Opt for College."
11. Wilson Peden, "Upward Mobility Through Higher Education: Can We Get Back on Track?" (Washington, DC: Association of American Colleges and Universities, 2015): https://www.aacu.org/leap/liberal-education-nation-blog/upward-mobility-through-higher-education-can-we-get-back-track. Accessed January 14, 2017.
12. Garry, "Education as the Key to Opportunity."
13. Andrew Kreighbaum, "Report: Students at HBCUs Have Burdensome Debt," *Inside Higher Ed*, December 15, 2016: https://www.insidehighered.com/quicktakes/2016/12/15/report-students-hbcus-have-burdensome-debt. Accessed December 29, 2016.
14. Robert Reich, "Why College Isn't (and Shouldn't Have to Be) for Everyone," *Bill Moyers*, March 26, 2015: http://billmoyers.com/2015/03/26/college-isnt-shouldnt-everyone/. For a definition of "good jobs," see n. 16. Accessed December 29, 2016.
15. Ibid.
16. Anthony P. Carnevale, Jeff Strohl, Ban Cheah, and Neil Ridley, *Good Jobs That Pay Without a BA* (Washington, DC: Georgetown University Center on Education and the Workforce): https://goodjobsdata.org/wp-content/uploads/2017/05/Good-Jobs-wo-BA-final.pdf. The authors of this study "chose $35,000 ($17 per hour for a full-time job) as the minimum earnings for those under age 45, and $45,000 ($22 per hour for a full-time job) for workers age 45 and older." See p. 2, Fig. 2. Accessed August 2, 2017.
17. Ibid.
18. Anthony P. Carnevale, Martin Van Der Werf, Michael C. Quinn, Jeff Strohl, and Dmitri Repnikov, *Our Separate & Unequal Public Colleges: How Public Colleges Reinforce White Racial Privilege and Marginalize Black and Latino Students* (Washington, DC: Georgetown University Center on Education and the Workforce): https://1gyhoq479ufd3yna29x7ubjnwpengine.netdna-ssl.com/wp-content/uploads/SAUStates_FR.pdf. Accessed December 10, 2018.
19. United States Department of Labor, "Fastest Growing Occupations," *Occupational Outlook Handbook* (Washington, DC: Bureau of Labor Statistics, 2018): https://www.bls.gov/ooh/fastest-growing.htm. Accessed August 2, 2017.
20. John Guillory, concerning the adoption of the general education curriculum, writes, "In a university system that was constantly restratifying,

universities and colleges that offered some curricular option for studying traditional culture were able to maintain a higher status than those that failed to offer this option." See John Guillory, "Who's Afraid of Marcel Proust? The Failure of General Education in the American University," *The Humanities and the Dynamics of Inclusion Since World War II*, ed. David A. Hollinger (Baltimore: Johns Hopkins University Press, 2006), 35. I should note here that Guillory's description of the contradiction between general education's inherent elitism with its proclaimed democratizing purpose—that all students must be culturally educated—is related to my argument about recruitment strategies. Education that leads directly to a trade is not as prestigious as one that sells itself as concerned with instilling traditional culture. Students, understandably, want to attend a "good school," hence they are often attracted to those that emphasize general education, although their own end goals might be employability and job security.

21. Terry Eagleton, *William Shakespeare* (Oxford: Blackwell, 1986), ix–x, quoted in William Shakespeare, *Hamlet*, ed. Ann Thompson and Neil Taylor (London: Arden Shakespeare, 2006), 26.
22. Harvard University, "About Harvard": https://www.harvard.edu/about-harvard. Accessed November 12, 2017; University of South Carolina, "About University of South Carolina": http://www.sc.edu/about/index.php. Accessed November 12, 2017; South Carolina State University, "About": https://www.scsu.edu/aboutscstate.aspx. Accessed November 12, 2017. The school websites of an Ivy League private research university, a public research university, and a public HBCU all highlight the leadership of their graduates, despite the wide-ranging differences in their student populations.
23. Guillory's "Proust" as well as his "The System of Graduate Education," *PMLA* 115, no. 5 (October 2000): 1154–63 convincingly describe the development of general education. Colleges and universities, after World War II, focused not so much on training a cultural elite for democratic rule but were in the business of "credentialing" the influx of non-elite students to meet the demands of the changing economy. We are at a similar juncture, and the dynamics of the economy require a less cumbersome system of credentialing. The typical four-year college's general education distribution requirements are often a stumbling block to the new traditional student academically and financially.
24. William Shakespeare, *King Henry IV, Part 1*, ed. David Scott Kastan (New York: Bloomsbury, 2002). All subsequent quotations from the play will be cited parenthetically.
25. Paul Dean, "Shakespeare's Historical Imagination," *Renaissance Studies* 10, no. 1 (1997), 35, quoted in David Ruiter, "Harry's (in) human

face," in *Spiritual Shakespeares*, ed. Ewan Fernie (New York: Routledge, 2005), 51.

26. Jonathan Goldberg, *Sodometries: Renaissance Texts, Modern Sexualities* (Stanford: Stanford University Press, 1992), 160, 161.
27. Kastan, ed., *1 Henry IV* intro, 5.
28. This quotation and ones immediately following come from the university's homepage: https://sc.edu. Accessed November 12, 2017.
29. thatswhatyouget2, "I Will Not Be a…," YouTube video, 00:22, posted November 24, 2010: https://www.youtube.com/watch?v=x-3lgt3dmSDs. Accessed January 14, 2017.
30. Amherst College, "The Amherst Story": https://www.amherst.edu/amherst-story. Accessed November 6, 2017.
31. Clemson University: www.clemson.edu. Accessed January 13, 2017.
32. E. M. W. Tillyard, *Shakespeare's History Plays* (London: Chatto & Windus, 1944; reprinted Penguin, 1962), quoted in William Shakespeare, *1 Henry IV*, ed. Gordon McMullan (New York: W.W. Norton, 2003), 253. Tillyard is excerpted in the critical back matter.
33. Derek Cohen, "History and Nation in *Richard II* and *Henry IV*," *Studies in English Literature, 1500–1900* 42, no. 2 (2002), 303. Tillyard writes of Hal, "Shakespeare makes him…the *cortegiano*, the fully developed man, contrasted with Hotspur, the provincial" (quoted in McMullan, *1 Henry IV*, 253).
34. Jose Antonio Bowen, "Helping Students Embrace Discomfort," *Inside Higher Ed*, December 7, 2016: https://www.insidehighered.com/views/2016/12/07/educating-students-ambiguity-and-discomfort-essay?utm_content=buffer4e15a&utm_medium=social&utm_source=twitter&utm_campaign=IHEbuffer. Accessed December 29, 2016.
35. Julianne Chiaet, "Novel Finding: Reading Literary Fiction Improves Empathy," *Scientific American,* October 4, 2013: https://www.scientificamerican.com/article/novel-finding-reading-literary-fiction-improves-empathy/. Accessed December 29, 2016.
36. This is by no means to suggest that the privileged are only interested in propagating their privilege. As we know, privilege, once revealed, can allow us to help those suffering from lack of it. I am positing the negative possibility of benefiting from privilege, namely to further exercise it.
37. Gillian B. White, "In D.C., White Families Are on Average 81 Times Richer Than Black Ones," *The Atlantic*, November 26, 2016: https://www.theatlantic.com/business/archive/2016/11/racial-wealth-gap-dc/508631/. Accessed December 29, 2016.
38. David Leonhardt, "California's Upward-Mobility Machine," *The New York Times*, September 16, 2015: https://www.nytimes.com/2015/

09/17/upshot/californias-university-system-an-upward-mobility-machine.html. Accessed January 12, 2017.

39. Neal McCluskey, "Many Factors at Play in Minority Access to Higher Education" Washington, DC: Cato Institute (2015): https://www.cato.org/publications/testimony/many-factors-play-minority-access-higher-education. Accessed January 12, 2017.
40. David Wescott, "Is This Economist Too Far Ahead of His Time?" *The Chronicle of Higher Education*, October 16, 2016: http://www.chronicle.com/article/Is-This-Economist-Too-Far/238050. Accessed December 9, 2016.
41. Kastan, ed., *1 Henry IV*, 206, n. 4.
42. William Shakespeare, *King Henry IV Part 2*, ed. James C. Bulman (New York: Bloomsbury Arden Shakespeare, 2016).
43. Kastan, ed., *1 Henry IV*, 206, n. 5–6.
44. Kastan, ed., *1 Henry IV*, 206, n. 11.
45. Kastan, ed., *1 Henry IV*, 206, n. 4.
46. Ruiter, "Harry's (in)human face," 59.
47. Guillory, "Proust," 35.
48. Erik Sherman, "Wealthy Kids 8 Times More Likely to Graduate College Than Poor," *Forbes*, February 5, 2015: http://www.forbes.com/sites/eriksherman/2015/02/05/wealthy-college-kids-8-times-more-likely-to-graduate-than-poor/#38d790fd5727. Accessed January 12, 2017.
49. Joshua Kim, "How to Scale the Liberal Arts," *Inside Higher Ed*, January 9, 2017: https://www.insidehighered.com/blogs/technology-and-learning/how-scale-liberal-arts. Accessed January 12, 2017.
50. Joe Pinsker, "Rich Kids Study English," *The Atlantic*, July 6, 2015: http://www.theatlantic.com/business/archive/2015/07/college-major-rich-families-liberal-arts/397439/. Accessed January 12, 2017.
51. As I mentioned above, Hal portrays himself as in control of his destiny, despite the myriad constraints placed upon him. He casts his "reformation" as choosing to accept his place as Prince of Wales when he is good and ready to do so. Hal is also eager to make others pawns, as he does in this scene with Francis and Falstaff, and will continue to do so as King Harry with Fluellen and Williams.
52. Kastan, ed., *1 Henry IV*, 209, n. 49.
53. Henry IV, Worcester, and Hotspur often distance themselves from their questionable deeds or portray themselves as lacking agency. In *Henry V*, King Harry declines to stay Bardolph's execution for stealing from a church while pushing a dubious claim to the French throne and resuming an unnecessary war.

54. Emily Badger, "How Poverty Taxes the Brain," *CityLab*, August 29, 2013: https://www.citylab.com/life/2013/08/how-poverty-taxes-brain/6716/. Accessed January 12, 2017.
55. Scott Jaschik, "Giving the Finger to K-State and General Education," *Inside Higher Ed*, December 21, 2016: https://www.insidehighered.com/news/2016/12/21/freshman-announces-hes-dropping-out-kansas-state-and-sets-debate-general-education. Accessed January 12, 2017.
56. Ibid.
57. "Higher Education: The Engine Driving Upward Mobility," *Ellucian*, September 29, 2015: https://blog.ellucian.com/Blog/Higher-education--the-engine-driving-upward-mobility/. Accessed December 29, 2016.
58. Ibid.
59. Michael J. Petrilli, "Kid, I'm Sorry, but You're Just Not College Material," *Slate*, March 18, 2014: http://www.slate.com/articles/life/education/2014/03/college_isn_t_for_everyone_let_s_stop_pretending_it_is.html. Accessed December 29, 2016.
60. Garry, "Education as the Key to Opportunity."
61. Reich, "Why College Isn't for Everyone."
62. Pinsker, "Rich Kids."

Place and Privilege in Shakespeare Scholarship and Pedagogy

Marisa R. Cull

Place is everywhere in Shakespeare—an enduring fascination of the playwright himself and of critics who have studied his work. When I speak of "place" here, I am primarily speaking of geographic place, but so too in this word is the echo of Shakespeare's other most frequent use of the term, to refer to one's familial, political, or social stature. Indeed, characters in Shakespeare often connect their geographic place with the "place" they hold in the esteem of others. When, in the third act of *Cymbeline*, the disguised Imogen comes upon the home of her still-unknown neighbors, living in rural Wales, their longtime guardian Belarius begs that she not "measure our good minds / By this rude place we live in" (3.6.62–63).[1] The moment is poignant: while Belarius has been a kind and loving presence in the lives of Guiderius and Arviragus, he remains insecure about the circumstances in which he has raised them, periodically lamenting their rural lodgings, "this hard life" (4.4.27) that has kept them "still hot summer's tanlings and / The shrinking slaves of winter" (4.4.29–30). For Belarius, geographical isolation has meant "want of breeding" (4.4.26), a lack of education and decorum, a crisis that is temporarily mediated in the play by the arrival of Imogen, who attempts to teach her brothers more gentle manners.

M. R. Cull (✉)
Randolph-Macon College, Ashland, VA, USA

S. O'Dair and T. Francisco (eds.), *Shakespeare and the 99%*,
https://doi.org/10.1007/978-3-030-03883-0_11

Of course Shakespeare is not always so derisive of rural circumstances; his plays abound with celebrations of country life, and, indeed, much has been written on Shakespeare's own "rural" background as a child in Stratford. In *As You Like It*, readers are treated to abundant praise for the unencumbered circumstances of the pastoral, and in some of Duke Senior's most memorable panegyric, we see a contrast to Belarius's assumptions about how geography corresponds with "civilization." For the duke, rural life is civilizing in and of itself: "And this our life exempt from public haunt / Finds tongues in trees, books in the running brooks, / Sermons in stones, and good in everything" (2.1.15–17). What we need to know, Duke Senior suggests, can be found in the untouched offerings of nature, more wisdom herein than any human civilization has offered. More than this, though, is Duke Senior's view of what nature protects against: "Are not these woods," he asks, "More free from peril than the envious court?" (2.1.3–4). Away from the pressures of court life, from the geographic "center," the duke reasons, he is freer to think, to explore, to play—and this offers its own brand of civilization. Of course in Duke Senior's rural paradise, begirt around as he is by his fellow exiled courtiers, no one is suddenly inclined, like the "wild" Guiderius is, to chop off the head of an intruder; indeed, what Duke Senior seems to take most pleasure in about his circumstances is the newness of it all (one wonders what Belarius might have said to him about raising—alone, for many years—two willful young boys in a cave), and he is blissfully unaware of the economic realities of some of his fellow forest-dwellers, who worry over shearing sheep for "churlish" masters (2.4.72). Yet like *Cymbeline*, and like so many of Shakespeare's plays, *As You Like It* explores the harmonies and disharmonies between one's physical place and one's social or cultural place.

For academics, such explorations are surely familiar on a personal level. In a job market defined by scarcity, almost all entirely forego questions of geography when applying for positions, many live and work far from the places they identify as geographic "homes" (the regions in which, for example, they were born and raised, or with which they identify themselves most strongly), and many, in obtaining positions, negotiate distances not just from extended families, but from partners and even children. Still others, who work in adjunct or otherwise part-time positions, have their sense of geographic place complicated by work they do at multiple institutions—in different cities, small towns, and sometimes even in different states. On academic blogs and forums geographic place is a topic of periodic, and often fraught, discussion: what might I do to increase my contacts in an area to which I hope to relocate? Should I take a good job in a location I hate? How can I convince a search committee I'm "game" for staying in a far-flung, deeply isolated location? These questions can feel even more complex when an academic's geographic locations have been, for many years prior to obtaining permanent employment, transient: undergraduate education in one place, perhaps, graduate education in one or more, and, more frequently in recent years, a postdoctoral fellowship somewhere entirely new. In each spot, then, the task is to find one's bearings: to learn the location itself and one's "place" within it, and, perhaps most vexingly, to learn how the realities of institutional place will affect how one relates to the academic community at large. Just as for Shakespeare's characters, it is a necessary confrontation, a negotiation of the harmonies and disharmonies that so often come from where one has fallen on the map.

But the question of just how to confront such matters is complicated. In what little research there is considering the question of geography and academic careers, those complications emerge repeatedly. In 1974, Michael M. Gruneberg, Richard Startup, and Patrick Tapsfield published one of the first sociological studies of faculty life as it relates to place, focusing—in a turn that surely would have delighted Shakespeare—on a Welsh university college near Swansea (less isolated today, to be sure, than in the 1970s). Their work revealed the sometimes contradictory attitudes faculty have toward their geographic location: survey respondents reported, for example, that while they had positive feelings about the town itself, they were inclined to think negatively when they compared their location with institutions in other parts of Britain. They reported "isolation from adequate library facilities and from other colleagues in the same discipline"; one respondent indicated feeling as though the college was "the end of the line," geographically speaking, and that "One will always be an outsider in Wales to some extent."[2] Yet those who had grown up or attended school in Wales felt less isolation, reporting more job satisfaction. Far more recently, in a 2005 study focusing on retention for mid-career faculty, Caroll Ann Trotman and Betsy E. Brown noted the ways in which a campus's location can be an asset, but their study focused exclusively on faculty employed at the sixteen institutions in the University of North Carolina system—many of which have an enviable geographic position—and did not report on how faculty in different disciplines correlated their satisfaction to their location.[3]

Pamela L. Eddy and Jeni Hart's 2012 "Faculty in the Hinterlands: Cultural Anticipation and Cultural Reality" focused on academics in "small, geographically remote institutions," exploring how such faculty adapt in particular to their professional lives, but this, too, was limited by discipline, considering only faculty working in the field of higher education studies (i.e., student affairs administration and college student personnel).[4] And in 2015, R. H. Stupnisky, M. B. Weaver Hightower, and Y. Kartoshkina considered the various influences on "new faculty success," noting—frustratingly, for anyone who has ever participated in the MLA job market in particular—that for job candidates, "strong consideration of job location is recommended."[5] Other studies are reminders, too, of how faculty might experience location differently from one another: R. M. Bennefield has demonstrated the ways in which faculty of color are likely to feel more isolated in rural locations—not only isolated from colleagues, but also isolated from communities of color more broadly. One scholar interviewed as part of Bennefield's reporting, Dr. Louis Chude-Sokei, working in African, Caribbean, and African American literature and culture, noted that rural or otherwise geographically isolated locations really only work for faculty of color who "are married and have families" or who "just dig in and do the work" without focusing on the culture surrounding the institution.[6]

For these reasons and more, questions of place can feel murky, unanswerable, too subject to matters of personal preference, of discipline, of the job market's vagaries, of demographics. And aren't we, anyway, living in a time during which geography should matter less? After all, when Imogen leaves Lud's Town in *Cymbeline* to travel to Milford Haven, she undertakes a days-long, dangerous, and exposed journey. A modern academic looking to get from London to Milford Haven could do so via car in about six hours, or—were they willing to take a bit longer to do the changes required—via train. Many twenty-first-century faculty travel (when they have the funding to do so) more frequently and with more comfort than perhaps is readily acknowledged as compared to their predecessors. When faculty gather, for example, at the annual meeting of the Shakespeare Association of America each year, they may be reminded of the good fortune they enjoy in being able to reconnect with old friends and colleagues. There are, too, the vibrant intellectual communities formed in online spaces—in Facebook groups, on Twitter, through robust mailing lists and web workshops. The Internet has also provided resources that once would have remained inaccessible to many of us—select performances from the Globe are now live-streamed, editions of rare playbooks are now digitized. All these are, as Doreen Massey puts it, "the relations that bind communities, whether they be local societies or worldwide organizations"[7]; this is how the social becomes the spatial, even when one is far from others or from one's most cherished "home." And so, here is another complication to considering issues of space: this century's relative connectedness can, in many ways, make it easier to overcome the real and imagined challenges of geographic place.

Beyond this relative connectedness, however, there is also this specific community's relative privilege. As *Shakespeare and the 99%* aims to show, categories of privilege abound within this corner of academia, and considering issues of place and privilege in Shakespeare studies demands first an acknowledgment of the advantage Shakespeareans share within the academy and within the field of English studies as teachers and scholars of an author who still has—at least at present—such profound status that his work is still required reading at nearly every high school in the United States. The long arm of Shakespeare's influence has, in some ways, "closed the gap" in terms of geographic difference, if only because there is a history in this country of organizations whose mission is to bring Shakespeare to rural or underserved populations: The Oregon Shakespeare Festival (founded 1935), which now enjoys worldwide recognition, began as a tribute to the Chautauqua movement, a late nineteenth-century adult-education program that sought to bring art and culture to underserved, primarily rural, areas.[8] Montana Shakespeare in the Parks, too, makes it a goal to serve the most rural parts of its own and surrounding states[9]; the Utah Shakespeare Festival's Shakespeare-in-the-Schools program operates throughout small communities in Utah, Nevada, Arizona, and Wyoming, and Colorado.[10] Perhaps most famously, the National Endowment of the Arts launched in 2003 its "Shakespeare in American Communities" program (partnering with the programs named above and many more); the goal was to perform Shakespeare's work in all fifty states (plus D.C. and the U.S. Virgin Islands), particularly in communities where such access is limited.[11] If you are a teacher of Shakespeare and such an opportunity has not come your way, the trend suggests it very well might. But even if it doesn't—we would do well to remember that there are likely no Samuel Beckett scholars in rural Oklahoma holding their breath for the NEA to mount a multi-million dollar effort to bring the theater of the absurd to their home turf.

Yet acknowledging this cultural privilege—and, indeed, acknowledging increased connectedness, or variable matters of geographical "taste," be we Belariuses or Duke Seniors—does not mediate the many and quite profound ways that the metaphorical landscape of Shakespeare studies is overlaid with the geographical landscapes in which we live and work. In this essay I am interested in that metaphorical/geographical dynamic, particularly at U.S. institutions and particularly in our lives as scholars and teachers. In the rooms of conferences, in the pages of disciplinary journals and scholarly monographs, and—perhaps most importantly—in the syllabi and lesson plans of classrooms, place is an untold story, a freedom and constraint with which all faculty wrestle, and one that does, as I hope to suggest here, shape the present and future of the field. In thinking about place, I hope to keep in play Shakespeare's dual sense of the word, considering how physical location correlates with social/cultural—or, in this case, professional—position.

* * *

I want to begin by considering how place inflects the world of research and scholarship in Shakespeare studies. To consider research and scholarship first is not, to be sure, a reflection of how this work is prioritized in the daily lives of faculty: after all, for many members of the "99 percent" to whom this collection's title partly refers, professional success within one's institution may be largely defined by teaching and service, with research and scholarship taking (a sometimes distant) third place. Yet what nearly all faculty in the field of Shakespeare studies share is a doctoral education either that explicitly emphasizes research and scholarship as the primary means of preparation for faculty life, or that implicitly suggests (through the mentorship of faculty employed at doctoral-granting institutions) that faculty life is largely defined and measured by such work. As Eddy and Hart point out in their study of the "Faculty in the Hinterlands," this is the great divide between how faculty "culturally anticipate" the work of their professional lives and how they actually live them out: many work at institutions that are "markedly different and pointedly lower on the Carnegie classification scale" than those from which they graduated, with heavier teaching loads, more pressing service demands, and—the point with which I am most concerned here—considerably less access to resources that might best inform their research interests.[12]

That Eddy and Hart focus their study on faculty working in the field of higher education studies, rather than, say, Shakespeare studies, should be a pointed reminder that this disconnect is present in all fields, not just this one. But considering the broader trends in literary studies provides meaningful insight into how geography can inflect our work in more pointed ways. A decade ago, in the 2007 issue of *Profession*, Jane Gallop opened her essay on the prominence of "historicization" in literary studies by recounting an exchange she'd had with a job candidate, who described the struggle to get published: "it is impossible," she'd said, "to get published without archival work."[13] Gallop's essay, finally, is less interested in this candidate's specific claim than she is in challenging literary studies' increasingly historicist approach to reading and understanding texts: what has happened, she asks, to close reading, to all those disciplinary conventions that were largely responsible for legitimizing English departments in the academic firmament? Have all English professors turned into cultural historians rather than literary scholars? As a scholar whose research has been heavily influenced by the historicist turn Gallop laments, I admit to being unconvinced, or at least more willing to see the way cultural history and close reading support, rather than undermine, each other. And yet I am again and again drawn to that job candidate's remark for a slightly different reason, and particularly in light of Eddy and Hart's work on the cultural anticipation of graduate training and the cultural reality of faculty jobs. Has Shakespeare studies, as a field, created a "cultural anticipation" for work that is heavily dependent on archival materials when many of its scholars will go on to the cultural reality of locations where such materials are largely inaccessible? In embracing the full potential of the Shakespeare archive—the records of playing companies in London, the properties lists, the architectural drawings of playhouses, the intricate, often perplexing vagaries of page to stage—has Shakespeare studies made it more difficult for colleagues without access to such archives to participate in the scholarly conversation?

Consider, for example, a graduate student who undertakes a project in the field of book history, a rich and exciting subset of Shakespeare scholarship that has, in recent years especially, garnered high-profile attention in our scholarly community (those who attended the 2016 Shakespeare Association of America conference in New Orleans might particularly remember the meeting's plenary session—"Forensic Shakespeare"—which took the field of book history to almost dizzying heights, with DNA analysis of folio pages). That student may find herself encouraged to such a project by graduate faculty who have similar interests, or who track the field's newest and most visible scholarship. That student may or may not live within easy reach of archival collections such as those found at the Folger Shakespeare Library in Washington, DC, or the Huntington Library in San Marino, California. And yet most assuredly, by virtue of attending a doctoral-granting institution, that student will have access to many items in these collections and more with university-supported access to databases such as Early English Books Online. That student also may find research funding and grant opportunities that make it possible, at some point during her program of study, to travel to archives to further this research, to survey collections that the still-expanding reach of electronic databases has not even begun to touch. That student may be embarking upon an exciting, field-changing scholarly project that is wholly informed and supported by material that is not available in any corner of the world—no matter how fast the Internet and its devoted digital scholars, working to expand electronic collections, upload new material.

That student may also find herself, at the close of her doctoral education, fortunate enough to find a rare tenure-track position. But the realities of the current job market suggest that her position will place her—at least for her first job, should she wish someday to try her luck twice—at an institution quite unlikely to grant access to databases like Early English Books Online. There may be some small comfort in the fact that a major professional organization—in this case, the Renaissance Society of America—grants access to EEBO for members (who pay, at the time of this writing, an income-adjusted annual fee ranging between 35.70 and 147.90 USD for membership). But this can only be a truly small comfort, as in October 2015, scholars found out how tenuous such access was, when ProQuest canceled RSA's access to EEBO without warning (membership was restored—within a day—after scholars on Twitter protested vehemently), citing concerns over the profit-damaging possibility of providing access to a database through professional organizations, as opposed to the more lucrative contracts in play from institutional libraries.[14] For a junior professor who relies on such access to inform her research—to, perhaps, begin preliminary work in a digital archive that may well need to be continued in an actual one—such volatility is obviously disquieting, and it is matched by parallel concerns that also make other types of research difficult. Geographic isolation from cities with major research libraries, for example, makes interlibrary services run far slower (and often, far more expensively); moreover, for colleges with smaller-scale library budgets, EEBO is very likely only one on a long list of databases not supported, and our scholar may find herself without access to recent issues of disciplinary journals that would help to inform her research. She may also, as many faculty do, labor under a travel budget of less than one-thousand dollars (if she has one at all)—and if she is in a geographically isolated location, such a budget is unlikely to support travel to archives or major research libraries, particularly for the length of time she might need to complete the work her home institution simply cannot support.

Such frustrations will be familiar to many, even to those who are living within easy driving distance to major archival collections: for as the above scenario points out, the actual, physical archive is only one component of how scholarship is executed. It may be tempting, in the face of this geographic disparity, to hang up the mantle of material/cultural history and focus on work that requires Gallop's preferred "close reading" of the text (so long as we can forget what we are now widely taught to know about the instability of the Shakespeare text). It may be similarly tempting to consider whether we ought to be warning graduate students early on about the transferability of their scholarly projects, projects that may meet with real, intractable difficulties at different institutions. And yet the solutions are not so simple. As Ann E. Austin puts it, "each discipline uniquely defines and legitimates research questions, research methods"[15]; in Shakespeare studies, more than ever, archival work confers legitimacy. To compete in an oversaturated marketplace, graduate students and early career faculty may feel that they can hardly ignore the trends of the discipline, especially not if their faculty advisors are invested in archive-dependent work. If one's perception of the scholarly landscape—informed, in part, by what is given precedence at conferences, what is published in disciplinary journals in the field—is that it is highly conditioned by the necessity of regular access to *place-specific* tools for conducting research, then one's corresponding perspective of geographic circumstance will necessarily be fraught.

The reality is, then, that the field is shaped at least in part by questions of place, with work in certain areas of scholarly interest largely executed and published by scholars with certain types of place-specific access. What this means for individuals without access is, of course, a rising correlation between the relative isolation of their geographic place and the relative limitations of their professional place within the firmament of Shakespeare studies. Such personal circumstances may be ameliorated in ways both scholarly (applying for short- or long-term fellowships at major research libraries, if one's home institution can support a faculty member's absence) and surreptitious (appealing to colleagues at other institutions for library access codes). More important, however, is the collective response of the community to the realities and challenges of place. Those faculty who mentor graduate students—who help to create and direct their programs of study—should be especially familiar with the limitations geography might place on their students' research in future years. Those faculty who review and rank grant and fellowship applications should take seriously how geographic isolation may have shaped—or, indeed—stalled the progress a scholar may have made in early career years had they been based elsewhere.[16] Journal editors, too—who are tasked with, according to Jana Argersinger and Michael Cornett, seeking out "emerging trends in scholarship," "whole new areas of research," and "provocative new work" presented at disciplinary conferences[17]—might also consider the nuances of place in their calculations about what work is valuable and worthy of wider dissemination among the scholarly community.

Considering what scholarship has value, what scholarship has worth—this, of course, requires the most drastic, community-wide effort to be more expansive in thought, more welcoming in practice. The community's solution to differences of geographic place should not merely be efforts to anticipate and accommodate slower progress toward the production of scholarship that requires place-specific access. Indeed, the community must consider the ways it marginalizes other types of scholarship—the scholarship of pedagogy, for example, or of performance studies, or of public service (all considered in the next section of this essay)—by making them less visible in our conference and publication spaces. The reality of academic life in certain geographic spaces will shape a scholar's research agenda, and the community at large should encourage, embrace, and celebrate the ways in which these different agendas and outcomes add texture to a landscape that, at present, is at risk of becoming strikingly uniform.

This work must be done at all levels of the profession, but particularly in graduate schools and on hiring committees, where the most unrealistic of young scholars' "cultural anticipations" about academic life take shape, ultimately inflecting their sense of satisfaction with their literal, geographic place and their sense of self-worth within the more vexing, indistinct professional "place" within the community. As a body of scholars with a shared devotion to Shakespeare studies, we might minimize geographic and professional marginalization by acknowledging and taking seriously how place affects current faculty and how it will affect future faculty in terms of research type and productivity.

* * *

Of course, for much of the 99 percent—and, indeed, sometimes for the 1 percent, too—concerns regarding research productivity are often subsumed by the more immediate, expansive responsibilities of teaching and service at our home institutions. One's relationship to such responsibilities is conditioned largely by institutional culture, by written (and more often than not, unwritten) expectations about how thoroughly faculty should engage with students and with institutional governance. These matters, too, involve place; faculty at rural colleges, for example, report increased expectations on their physical presence on campus, even as they recognize the benefits of what is often a shorter commute to campus and a feeling of safety on that campus.[18] Learning spaces themselves are also sites of geographical diversity, which can condition students' experiences as well as those of faculty; in a recent study focusing specifically on the composition classroom, Johnathon Mauk has argued that "academic space" is particularly vexing for first-generation and commuter college students, who struggle to find a location for themselves—a struggle that often exists right alongside that of their instructors, who may or may not have permanent offices or adequate classroom spaces.[19]

But unlike the geographical challenges that press on scholarly pursuits, it can be tempting to assume that the nuances of place matter less in the Shakespeare classroom itself, where the text is the shared starting "place." Yet this is a dangerous temptation: faculty experiences here, too, are deeply textured by place, whether by the locations from which their students hail or by the technology they have available in classrooms. Moreover—and it is to this phenomenon to which I wish to devote most time here—the very principles that undergird the teaching of Shakespeare can make place a central concern for faculty. The *way* Shakespeare is taught, of course, is subject to trends, to movements within the field that shape the collective sense of what students should (and can) know when they complete work in a Shakespeare course. One such movement that bears particular relation to the topic of place is a renewed and revised emphasis on performance studies as a means of communicating the nuance of Shakespeare to students.

In 2009, the *English Journal*—published by the National Council of Teachers of English and devoted primarily to pedagogical scholarship for those teaching at the middle and high school level—devoted its September issue to "revolutionary approaches to teaching Shakespeare." Its contents are impressive, inspirational—and not just for middle and high school teachers, but for any teacher/scholar who thinks seriously about the theory and practice of working with students on Shakespeare. The issue's guest editor, Michael LoMonico, who works as the Senior Consultant on National Education for the Folger Shakespeare Library, articulates clearly what is a running theme of the issue's contents:

> The best way to get students to like Shakespeare is by getting them to perform Shakespeare. Performing Shakespeare does not mean having students sit at their desks reading aloud, or having students stand in front of the room reading aloud, or the teacher acting out scenes for the class. It also doesn't mean memorizing a sonnet or soliloquy and reciting it privately for the teacher. It means engaging students with words in such a way that requires them to make informed decisions about the text and then speaking those lines and interacting with their classmates. It might also mean working with a group of their classmates to edit a scene, create a director's prompt book for it, figure out what sort of minimal costumes and props they need, and perform it in a classroom or schoolwide festival.[20]

To learn Shakespeare via performance is not, of course, a new idea, and faculty at institutions of higher education have long contemplated the "overemphasis on the printed page" in the Shakespeare classroom, proposing performance projects of varying detail in the pages of journals like *College English*.[21] But certainly over the last two decades, with organizations like the Folger Shakespeare Library spearheading national outreach programs for these "on your feet" methods of teaching Shakespeare's work, performance-based study of Shakespeare has become increasingly prominent, a frequent topic of conversation among faculty who experiment with these methods in their classrooms and the subject of several book-length studies, including the RSC's recent *Transforming the Teaching of Shakespeare* and the MLA's *Teaching Shakespeare Through Performance*.

So much appeals about the pedagogical ideas proposed in performance-based teaching of Shakespeare, not the least of which is how very adaptable and engaging it is, not just to any level of student (especially for those students who see themselves—in an increasingly visual world—as "visual learners"), but to any *location*. In their performance-based study guides for individual plays, The American Shakespeare Center advocates for an "Elizabethan Classroom," noting that even the most basic classroom space—at the minimum, one needs a room and some chairs—can be transformed into an approximation of an Elizabethan stage, so long as students are educated as to the "geography of the space."[22] Here, the front of the classroom becomes "upstage," gaps in between a rectangular configuration of desks can be used as "stage right door" and "stage left door." What the ASC and the Folger advocate is that no special tools—no special spaces—are required for performance-based study of Shakespeare: when students are on their feet, working actively with even small sections of the Shakespeare text, the results can be incredibly rewarding. That such methods have been adopted so widely—whether in the form of regular class activities or more independent, culminating end-of-semester projects—is testament to their effectiveness.

What happens, though, when your geographic place makes it possible to supplement such pedagogical methods with professionally-staged productions of Shakespeare's work, or, in some cases, with education programs staffed by professional (or semi-professional) actors and directors? Writing in 1962 about his own performance studies work in the classroom, Lawrence McNamee notes that this "surrogate theater," while effective in the classroom environment, is but a pale comparison to the "living theater," to "the effect, the catharsis" we feel while in the *actual* theatrical space.[23] In my own work as a faculty member at Randolph-Macon College—located in the small town of Ashland, Virginia—work with the "living theater" has been a near-constant supplement to my own pedagogy, owing to the institution's geographic proximity to both the Folger Theatre in Washington, DC (approximately ninety miles away) and The American Shakespeare Center in Staunton, Virginia (approximately 100 miles away). Neither, of course, is directly in my backyard, and trips to both require planning and funding—sometimes provided by my home institution, sometimes supplemented by students. But the comparatively affordable cost of group sales tickets, the relatively manageable distance, and the offering of matinee performances make these performances an attainable goal for me in most academic years, and the effect on my own teaching and on my students' experiences has been profound. In part this is due to what comes most naturally out of watching any performance of Shakespeare's work: following shows, students are eager to discuss director and actor choices, to compare their own expectations to what they actually experienced as audience members, to explain what they enjoyed and what disappointed them.

But an additional privilege of these particular theatrical spaces is their intersection with what is undoubtedly another worthy preoccupation of Shakespeare studies in recent years: the material realities of the early modern playing space. The Folger Theatre is cast in the Elizabethan style, while the American Shakespeare Center's playing space, The Blackfriars Playhouse, recreates Shakespeare's playhouse home of the same name. At the Blackfriars in particular, replicating early modern staging conditions in performance is a priority, with minimal sets, shared lighting for the audience and the players, role doubling, and music (performed by the actors) before the performances. In my own courses, having such a space within geographical reach allows for more immediate engagement with these material realities; indeed, in a recent course, students spent a full week at the American Shakespeare Center as participants in a "Little Academe"—during which time they saw performances and rehearsals for the Actors' Renaissance season (modeled on principles of actual early modern rehearsal practice), learned from ASC actors and educators, and participated in their own performance exercises on the Blackfriars stage. To have spaces like this within reach of my institution has made it easier for me to keep students informed about the interplay between page and stage, a focus that is more important than ever in scholarly studies about Shakespeare's work.

Privilege in terms of this kind of access varies widely. For one colleague, Niamh O'Leary, working in a mid-size urban environment at Xavier University, there may not be an Elizabethan or Jacobean-style playing space, but there is a dedicated Shakespeare company nearby (Cincinnati Shakespeare), which has "allowed [her] Shakespeare syllabus to be dictated in part by the plays in [the company's] current season."[24] While funding limitations prevent her from making required group outings to all these shows, the proximity nevertheless informs her teaching regularly:

> I have found viewing the productions has enhanced my ability to teach the plays, as I can incorporate my recollections to help students consider alternative interpretations of a scene. I've also used their publicity photos, which they publish in albums on their Facebook page, to discuss characters and scenes with students. And I've been fortunate to get a grant that has allowed me, one semester, to bring the actors into my classroom regularly to work with students.[25]

Contrast this with another colleague, Rachel E. Clark, working at Wartburg College in Waverly, Iowa. Her college is roughly three and a half hours (by vehicle) from the nearest major city that mounts productions, and because of funding constraints, she might only expect to attend such a production over the course of a single day, a near-prohibitively difficult schedule for travel with student groups, though she does take such trips whenever possible.[26] There are, of course, other options for exposing students to professional performances of Shakespeare's work—films, recorded performances of stage productions—but this is still an important way in which landscape matters. Geographical place can have real, lasting effects on the planning and execution of courses, and how students receive the content within them. This is especially the case when a disciplinary trend—in this case, toward performance-as-pedagogy—will be variably executed depending on one's proximity to live, professional performances.

For those faculty who feel the pull toward performance-based pedagogy in comparatively rural locations, the work of making live performance part of the pedagogical experience—whether that involves more expansive travel, the organizing of professional "tour stops" on one's campus, or, perhaps in the most cost-effective way, the planning, organizing, and execution of amateur productions using one's own students and/or members of the wider community—can become its own demanding brand of institutional and community service. To make such efforts as a faculty member can be deeply rewarding on a personal level; it can also be, for some faculty, rewarding on a professional level, too, particularly if one's institution has heeded Ernest Boyer's call for a more expansive definition of what qualifies as scholarly work.[27] Moreover, such service can and does translate into scholarship of its own: consider, for example, the work of David Jolliffe, who has published widely on his experiences living and working in rural Arkansas, work that has expanded into literacy initiatives in the surrounding communities. This is powerful, important scholarship (though sadly and infrequently spotlighted within the profession now); it reveals the various ways in which texts are "transacted" to students.[28] But it also work that is shaped by location, work that may begin in the classroom space but that extends into various other "spaces" of one's professional and personal life. To participate in a broader professional movement that foregrounds the live performance of Shakespeare's work, particularly as a pedagogical strategy, is to feel the very real freedom and constraint of one's geographic place.

* * *

What, finally, is to be gained by acknowledging these complexities in the field, by acknowledging the sometimes painful divide between a shared sense of place as Shakespeare scholars and a widely divergent sense of place as professionals living and working in different geographic locations? I began this essay by considering Shakespeare's most oft-used definitions of "place"—our physical location, but also our social position within our communities. As we have seen, those definitions can intertwine uncomfortably in the Shakespeare community, with geographic place shaping the way scholars plan and execute their work, work that comes to define their professional status within a system that is often disturbingly heedless of and unmindful about circumstances of location.

But there is one more way in which this term should speak to us in the context of Shakespeare's work, and that, of course, is in the context of performance. When, in the final scene of *A Midsummer Night's Dream*, Theseus prepares to "hear that play" for which Bottom and company have so comically prepared, he instructs the ladies who accompany him to "take [their] places" for the show—an echo, of course, of a phrase still in wide use in the theater today. To "take one's place" in the theater means to assume your mark on the stage—to literally position yourself in the right "place"—but it also means to take on your *role*, to become the character you are playing. In this meaning, in some ways, is the coalescence of the geographic and the social. When faculty members arrive at what is to become their "home" institutions, they not only take a new geographical place; they also take a new social place within the institution and within the field of Shakespeare studies more generally. As I have suggested, the latter is tightly, inextricably interwoven with the former, and a major part of academic life. Because of this, faculty will always be enacting their roles, as Shakespeare's actors were, with the space of their particular stage as a crucial, unavoidable context.

To say that one's social place within the field is determined solely by one's geographical place is, to be sure, overly simplistic. So, too, are the artificial, largely U.S. borders with which I have mapped my considerations in this small critical arena. But even in the limited confines of this chapter—indeed, of this book overall—it remains important to say that as a group, the academic Shakespeare community will be problematically remiss if it fails to acknowledge the way circumstances of location condition circumstances of productivity and of pedagogy—and, indeed, of status and reputation. As a community of scholars invested in advancing the field of Shakespeare and early modern drama, we share in an intellectual space. But in order for that intellectual space to be as open and as welcoming to new scholars and teachers as it should be, for it to be as expansive as it needs to be, we should not shy away from discussing these circumstances and asking the difficult questions about how they have shaped and how they continue to shape our field as a whole. Shakespeare's characters felt keenly the way place and privilege intersect, and so too should we, particularly if we are committed to a scholarly community that takes seriously the experiences of the 99 percent. To borrow a phrase from Belarius: all of "our good minds" deserve it, no matter where we have landed on the map.

Notes

1. *Cymbeline*, 3.3.62–63. All quotations from Shakespeare's plays are taken from Stephen Greenblatt, et al., ed., *The Norton Shakespeare* (New York: W. W. Norton, 2015). They will hereafter be cited parenthetically.
2. Michael Gruneberg, Richard Startup, and Patrick Tapsfield, "The Effect of Geographical Factors on the Job Satisfaction of University Teachers," *The Vocational Aspect of Education* 26, no. 63 (1974): 25–29, esp. 25, 28.
3. Caroll Ann Trotman and Betsy E. Brown, "Faculty Recruitment and Retention: Concerns of Early and Mid-Career Faculty," *TIAA-CREF Research Dialogue* 86 (2005): 1–10.
4. Pamela L. Eddy and Jeni Hart, "Faculty in the Hinterlands: Cultural Anticipation and Cultural Reality," *Higher Education* 63 (2012): 751–769.
5. R. H. Stupnisky, M. B. Weaver Hightower, and Y. Kartoshkina, "Exploring and Testing the Predictors of New Faculty Success: A Mixed Methods Study," *Studies in Higher Education* 40, no. 2 (2015): 368–390, esp. 387.
6. R. M. Bennefield, "Tales from the Boondocks," *Black Issues in Higher Education* 16 (1999): 24–29.
7. Doreen Massey, "Politics and Space/Time," in *Place and Politics of Identity*, ed. Michael Keith and Steve Pile (New York: Routledge, 1993), 141–161. See especially page 151.
8. Oregon Shakespeare Festival, "Our History": https://www.osfashland.org/en/about/our-history.aspx. Accessed April 28, 2018.
9. Montana Shakespeare in the Parks, "Mission and History": https://www.shakespeareintheparks.org/about/overview. Accessed December 10, 2018.
10. Utah Shakespeare Festival, "The Tour": http://www.bard.org/tour/. Accessed April 28, 2018.
11. See www.shakespeareinamericancommunities.org for more information, or visit https://www.arts.gov/national/shakespeare/about for an executive summary of the program. Accessed December 10, 2018.
12. Eddy and Hart, 751–752.
13. Jane Gallop, "The Historicization of Literary Studies and the Fate of Close Reading," *Profession* (2007): 181–186, esp. 181.
14. Ellen Wexler, "Subscription Scare Fuels Worries over Who Controls Data That Scholars Need," *The Chronicle of Higher Education*, October 30,

2015: https://www.chronicle.com/article/Subscription-Scare-Fuels/234003. Accessed December 10, 2018.

15. Ann E. Austin, "Preparing the Next Generation of Faculty: Graduate School as Socialization to the Academic Career," *Journal of Higher Education* 73, no. 1 (2002): 94–122, esp. 97. Austin also asks us to consider how our disciplines promote work relationships between scholars (for example, whether cross-institutional collaboration is prominent). Because most graduate students in literary studies work independently, there is not often a substantive model for collaborative work in our field; such a model might promote cooperation between faculty with more and less archival access.
16. Certainly our home institutions, too, should be as attentive as possible to this; evidence from all types of institutions suggests that a more productive faculty (in research terms) offers more benefit to students and "exerts a great influence on perceived faculty quality and academic reputation." See J. Fredericks Volkwein and Kyle V. Sweitzer, "Institutional Prestige and Reputation Among Research Universities and Liberal Arts Colleges," *Research in Higher Education* 47, no. 2 (2006): 129–148, esp. 132–134.
17. Jana Argersinger and Michael Cornett, "Everyone's Argus: The Journal Editor in the Academy," *Profession* (2009): 105–111, esp. 107.
18. In addition to Eddy and Hart's "Faculty in the Hinterlands" and Bennefield's "Tales from the Boondocks," see also Susan Ambrose, Therese Huston, and Marie Norman, "A Qualitative Method for Assessing Faculty Satisfaction," *Research in Higher Education* 46, no. 7 (2005): 803–827. Their findings show, predictably, that faculty experiences of rural life in academia are mixed.
19. Johnathon Mauk, "Location, Location, Location: The Real (E)states of Being, Writing, and Thinking in Composition," *College English* 65, no. 4 (2003): 368–388.
20. Michael LoMonico, "Shakespearean Ruminations and Innovations," *English Journal* 99, no. 1 (2009): 21–28, esp. 24.
21. See, for example, Morris Eaves, "The Real Thing: A Plan for Producing Shakespeare in the Classroom," *College English* 31, no. 5 (1970): 463–472.
22. Cass Morris, *The American Shakespeare Study Guide: The Basics* (Staunton: The American Shakespeare Center, 2009). See especially page 6.
23. Lawrence McNamee, "New Horizons in the Teaching of Shakespeare," *College English* 23, no. 7 (1962): 583–585, esp. 585.
24. Niamh O'Leary, E-mail Message to Author, February 2, 2016.
25. Ibid.
26. Rachel E. Clark, E-mail Message to Author, January 21, 2016.
27. Ernest Boyer, *Scholarship Reconsidered: Priorities of the Professoriate* (New York: Jossey-Bass, 1990).
28. See, for example, his "Shakespeare and Cultural Capital Tension: Advancing Literacy in Rural Arkansas," *Community Literacy Journal* (2012): 77–88.

Who Did Kill Shakespeare?

Sharon O'Dair

In 1937, Harvard University Press published Huntington Brown's edition of Thomas Healey's *The Discovery of a New World* (1609), a translation of Bishop Joseph Hall's Latin satire, *Mundus Alter Et Idem*, which had been published four years earlier (ca. 1605).[1] Neither the publication of Healey's *Discovery* nor of Hall's own *Mundus* was authorized by Hall, and, Richard McCabe explains, "none of Hall's works caused him so much embarrassment as [the *Mundus*]: one of its most attentive and critical readers was that redoubtable enemy of episcopacy, John Milton," who skewered Hall and the satiric *Mundus* some three decades later.[2]

Brown's is just the third edition of this first piece of Antarctic fiction, and it contains a foreword by retired United States Navy Rear Admiral, Richard E. Byrd. Odd to think Harvard University Press might have pegged *The Discovery* a possible best seller, marketing being the main reason, one would think today, to include a foreword containing the words of the famous aviator and explorer, who then was between his

My title alludes to Patrick Brantlinger, "Who Killed Shakespeare? An Apologia for English Departments," *College English* 61, no. 6 (1999): 681–691, which also appears in his *Who Killed Shakespeare? What's Happened to English Since the Radical 60's* (New York: Routledge, 2001), 13–30.

S. O'Dair (✉)
University of Alabama, Tuscaloosa, AL, USA

S. O'Dair and T. Francisco (eds.), *Shakespeare and the 99%*,
https://doi.org/10.1007/978-3-030-03883-0_12

second and third expeditions to the Austral continent. More likely is that Byrd's penning of the foreword is the happy result of Brown's having dedicated the edition to him; perhaps they were friends. The foreword reproduces a letter addressed to "My dear Brown," thanking him for the "honor you have done me in the dedication of this fascinating volume" and offering the "hope that this book will receive the wide attention it deserves."[3] Today, one might chuckle at this—an edition! Of a translation! Receiving the wide attention it deserves!—but Byrd's foreword reminds us that norms (and indeed structures) do change in our profession, a point that provides the basis for this essay and, I would wager, most of the essays in this collection.

Norms change, too, for explorers. While today's explorers may brave unfettered wind and sun to cross a snow- and ice-laden continent, they are now called adventurers—or extreme sports enthusiasts—and they endure harsh and grueling conditions not to explore uninhabited and unknown topographies—nunataks, dry valleys, deep crevasses—but to support a charity, while attempting, say, to become the first person to use a bike in getting to the pole. Or more charitably, to recreate successfully the trips of doomed ancestors, as David Grann describes those of Henry Worsley, also for charity.[4] Unlike the exploits of Worsley, those of the extreme sports enthusiasts are available to all, via a cruise, perhaps, or under the guidance of a company called Jagged Globe that will fly one directly "to 89 degrees south [and] straight on to the Antarctic plateau for a relatively straight-forward ski across the final 60 nautical miles to the Pole." Straightforward the ski may be, and take only five days instead of fifty, but it "will still give … a real taste of Antarctic exploration and the commitment and hostile environment will be real."[5]

Really? The real—small *r*, never mind capital *R*—is problematic. The real (or the factual) became a problem for Bishop Hall, too. McCabe claims that Hall cleverly "anticipated the achievements of modern science-fiction by basing his imaginary voyage squarely upon universally received scientific and cartographical opinions." Five maps adorn the *Mundus Alter* (but not the 1609 Englished version) and in them "fact and fantasy jostle in the same perplexing combinations as they do in the most scholarly productions of Mercator and Ortelius." Even more clever was Hall's recognition—McCabe calls it "a masterstroke of invention"—that the assumed existence of Terra Australis offered massive "satiric potential,"[6] which, given my purposes here, is well represented by these words in Brown's edition:

> *It hath ever offended me to look upon the geographical maps and find this:* Terra Australis, nondum Cognita. The unknown Southern continent. *What good spirit but would grieve at this? If they know it for a Continent, and for a Southern continent, why then do they call it unknown? But if it be unknown, why do all the geographers describe it after one form and site? Idle men that they are, that can say, this it is, and yet we know it not: How long shall we continue to be ignorant in that which we profess to have knowledge of?*[7]

Satire, that jostling of fact and fantasy, is what got Bishop Hall into trouble with John Milton during the Smectymnuan debate. Not one to let slip an opening, Milton pounced on Hall, jeering that in his focus on the real, on "*the sinnes of Christendome,*" Hall fails to achieve gravitas, offering neither "reproofe nor better teaching" to those who err.[8] Rather, Hall "ramble[s] over the huge topography of his own vain thoughts," bringing "us … nothing but a meer tankard drollery … *rip[ping] up the saddest vices with a laughing countenance.*" In this he is "very foolish," and far, very far, from "that grave and noble invention which the greatest and sublimest wits in sundry ages, *Plato* in *Critias*, and our two famous countreymen, the one in his *Utopia*, the other in his *new Atlantis* chose … to display [in] the largenesse of their spirits by teaching this our world better and exacter things, then were yet known, or us'd."[9]

In pointing out that science is about the real, "about getting it right (for the time being)," Gordon Teskey aims in a review of work in early modern studies not only to be witty and precise but also to underscore art's and criticism's far different aim, which is to take sides in a "mental fight," a fight that has "no positive it to get right." Art is about "taking sides" and so, too, is criticism "but not without forgetting there is another side, which we should be thankful for because it makes us better by contest."[10] I do not know Milton's writings well enough to know if he would side with Teskey, but I do know, thanks to the editorial work of Don Wolfe, that Milton was less complimentary to More and Bacon in *Areopagitica*, composed some two years later, in lines that condemn the escapism of speculative utopias: we do not want "to sequester out of the world into Atlantic and Utopian polities, which never can be drawn into use, will not mend our condition; but to ordain wisely as in this world of evil, in the midst whereof God hath placed us unavoidably."[11]

Since any number of readers might imitate Milton to pounce and jeer at what follows in this essay, may I say that I do have a moral purpose in presenting what follows, in presenting these main themes. First, disciplinary identity and disciplinary authority are linked, and their fates are linked in a reinforcing manner—when the former is smudged, the latter is weakened, and when latter is weakened, the former is susceptible to yet more smudging. And second, while such smudging and weakening were necessary, crucial, forty years ago, their ill effects have been visible for some time and their continuation threatens the viability of literary criticism, especially of the study of early literature, and thus the livelihoods of current and future practitioners. Stanley Fish once said that being a literary critic is "Nice work if you can get it."[12] The problem, as Fish knows, and has known for more than twenty years, is whether you can.

* * *

Some years ago, winter break found me in Hawai'i on the south shore of Maui. Hawaiians adore their beaches and protect their access to them. Legally, hotels, resorts, and even homeowners must maintain public access to beaches that front their properties. In Wailea, an upscale community, access includes not just sandy cuts to a number of beaches, but a paved mile-long walking path, beautifully maintained, with plantings of indigenous flora and stunning views of the Pacific Ocean—and of the Fairmont Kea Lani, the Four Seasons Maui, and multi-million dollar condominiums. Sunset was nearing, and my traveling companion and I strolled on this path, populating it with others anticipating the sunset. By chance I looked away from the flora and sea and the dropping sun and noticed a middle-aged, upper middle-class woman approaching us, her two pre-pubescent children and middle-aged husband in single-file tow. As she neared me, within say, a yard or maybe two, she stopped. "Oh!!," she cried, stepping back some six inches. I looked at her and followed her eyes, which settled on the edge of the path, near the flora, across from the Four Seasons Maui, maybe a foot from me.

And then she cried, louder still, "A rat!" Mashing up Hamlet, I thought, "a rat, a very palpable rat!"[13] Not mashing up *The Tempest*, I thought, "the very rats have quit it."[14] The rat, I saw, was small; subsequently I discovered it was a Polynesian rat. Turning her head to face her children and middle-aged husband—who, like an impossible train, had stopped dead in their tracks, each one some yard or so behind the other—the mother said, with some insistence, "No, it's not, is it?" She turned again, toward me, and smiled. Then she said definitively, to her children, her husband, and me, too: "It's not a rat. It's a cute, furry Hawaiian creature." She was enlisting me, but unsuccessfully, because when her husband passed me, I said to him, *sotto voce,* "called a rat." At this the husband chortled, and his wife, again turning her head, asked, "what did she say?" Faintly, I heard the husband repeat the words I had just spoken.

Anyone reading these lines is an accomplished, likely a professional reader, and each knows what the middle-aged, upper middle-class woman was doing when she faced down the Polynesian rat across from the Four Seasons Maui. She was protecting her children from fear, attempting to maintain their innocence. She was also in denial and thus modeling denial for her children, refusing to face facts staring her right in the face, that even the Four Seasons Maui has rats, paradise has rats, species wreaking havoc, in this case an invasive one, piggybacking on human activity. And she did so in a move well known to literary critics and citizens alike, and very well exercised in our recent history, proclaiming the rat to be other than what it is: "It's a cute, furry Hawaiian creature."

For decades now, critics have insisted that literature is not elitist, difficult writing, not literature with a capital L, and certainly not the best that has been thought and said. Nor is literary criticism its own sort of difficult writing that trumpets its own style, mimicking, sometimes approaching, the art it analyzes. Rather, literature is democratic, multicultural writing (or visuals, increasingly in today's classrooms, visuals); it's literature with a capital L, yes, but also genre fiction, movies, TV, fan fiction, video games, Facebook, and YouTube; it's open source peer review, memoir, history, philosophy, anthropology, linguistics, cognitive science, and the scientized (or in some naysayers' view, the neoliberal) digital humanities. And literary criticism assesses those many and varied cultural products in any style, because any form of communication is as worthy as another. The point is not to produce what Teskey calls "criticism as art," a writing that crackles "with bias, or topspin, and … splendid assurance"[15] but rather the empowerment of all and an end to oppression and exploitation, in short, social justice.

I want to call a rat a rat, to defend literature and literary criticism, even though each is elitist and constituted through the production and reception of difficult writing. Like many others in their different ways—Stanley Fish, Jane Gallop, Marjorie Garber, Gordon Teskey, Heather Love, Rita Felski, Caroline Levine, and Joseph North—I want to save those activities, the production and reception of difficult writing. I want my colleagues to stop doing cultural studies, stop pretending to be historians, stop aspiring to be scientists, and most importantly, as

Teskey pleads, stop running away from art. Time has come to confess, as Bishop Hall would have it, that we are "ignorant in that which we profess to have knowledge of"—poverty, ecology, scientific method—and to write all of these innovations "into the history of stopping," as William Warner and Clifford Siskin would have us do with cultural studies. Time has come to "reclaim what made our enterprise valuable in the first place."[16]

But it does not take a mammalian scientist or, rather, a professional reader of texts, to point to the rub, or aporia, in that directive: Enterprise? Valuable? In the first place? For whom? Warner and Siskin think the enterprise valuable because it "mediat[es] society's relation to the dominant technologies for reading and writing."[17] Fish, Gallop, and Garber think it valuable because it enables close, difficult reading; Teskey thinks it valuable because it enables spectacular, difficult writing, criticism as art. Many others think it valuable because of the ethical effects it generates. Despite methodological innovations of great pitch and moment, literary criticism demands today what it demanded in 1970, what Heather Love calls "the 'theological exercise' of close, sustained textual analysis [and] the intimacy of ethical pedagogy mediated … through a sustained encounter with an exemplary literary text."[18] More recently, Levine and North, in different ways, have argued that the literary is valuable because it in fact offers a significant way to benefit leftist politics, which has stalled in the current moment. Levine writes, not always convincingly, about a new kind of formalism, one that acknowledges and analyzes the power of form not only in literature but in society as well. Insisting that literary critics can analyze non-literary forms, too, and thus "rethink the historical workings of political power and the relations between power and aesthetics," Levine doesn't stop until she sees actual socio-political benefit: "For those who care passionately about unjust arrangements of power … formalism offers a promising way forward" to establish as yet undefined but just arrangements of power.[19] But value, whether literary or socio-political, is not transparent, and, as Fish articulated in 1995, the public—the people and their representatives in government—rarely find compelling our own justifications for our practices. This is true whether they are political or interventionist, like Levine's or North's, which hold that critics can forward a left political agenda; or whether they are quasi-theological, abstracted from exigencies of social life—such as Fish's that "[l]iterary interpretation, like virtue, is its own reward"[20] or Garber's that literature's value lies in its "inexhaustibility, and by its ultimate refusal to be applied or used, even for moral good."[21] Such justifications, whether they underscore the morality or the amorality of what literary critics do, tend to be counterproductive.

Yet the counterproductive is mostly what is offered. Fish again touts the counterproductive, in 2008's *Save the World on Your Own Time*, even as he abandons his earlier idea that public relations can counter attacks on the humanities and the university in general, and even as he identifies a justification for what literary critics do, a usefulness that might well satisfy the public: the "improvement of a particular skill," that of writing, "which is something the world really needs and something an academic with the appropriate training can actually do. But he or she won't ever get around to doing it if the class is given over to multiculturalism or racial injustice or globalization or reproductive rights or third-world novels or any of the other "topics," which, as worthy of study as they might be, take up all the air space and energy in the room and leave the students full of banal opinions but without the ability to use prepositions or write a clean English sentence."[22] The teaching of writing: "*something the world really needs and something an academic with the appropriate training can actually do.*" The emphasis is mine. Fish, of course, refuses to justify academic work this way since "[a]n unconcern with any usefulness to the world is the key to its distinctiveness."[23] Even in 2008, however, such a stance seemed perverse to me, or perhaps more pertinently, seemed to be a luxury.

For professors laboring in institutions of little or no prestige, which is to say, for almost all professors, uselessness will not do, not given the economic and political situations in which they find themselves in the second decade of the twenty-first century. For those who love difficult reading and difficult writing, and who love teaching both even in underendowed, tuition-dependent institutions, where pay raises sometimes recede into memory, where objectives and outcomes weigh in syllabi more than the works of Shakespeare or Milton, where students often are not ready for college, justification cannot be a refusal to justify. Justification must be the useful, what is valuable to the public—the people, and their representatives in government. If it is not, then professors will suffer at the hands not only of state legislatures but of federal ones, and of Arne Duncan and Barack Obama, too, much less Betsy DeVos and Donald Trump. In President Obama's speech on the state of the union in 2012, higher education was singled out, put "on notice," and "for the first time" told that "the government [very well may] punish colleges that fail … to control tuition or that d[o] not provide good value."[24] That establishing "good value" is difficult and strikingly problematic does not render the attempt unnecessary. Kate McLuskie and Kate Rumbold point out that in the United Kingdom, "the value attached to particular content [e.g. Shakespeare, literary study, university education] that was viewed as beyond the market ha[s] been replaced by a value assigned to participants' and the audiences' engagement with culture." In words that apply, I think, even more closely to the United States, McLuskie and Rumbold warn that those who "continue to insist on the value of … content as 'an end it itself'" will find that their "arguments have little purchase on the current scale for value."[25]

Gallop thinks close reading is a valuable skill and in justifying it, she does not follow Fish's lead, separating a concern for disciplinary distinctiveness from either the utility of the discipline outside of or its survival within institutions of higher learning.[26] And neither do I. I want to defend literature and literary criticism, close reading and spectacular writing, and the teaching of both, not because all of this is like virtue or is all so prettily useless. Rather I want to defend literature and literary criticism because the democratization and politicization described above—what sociologist Michèle Lamont calls "the disciplinary broadening and diversification of criteria of evaluation"[27] in which English has persisted for at least two generations—has not achieved what it claimed it would achieve, not for students and not for faculty, which is to say a grand egalitarianism, initiated and inspired by critique. Instead, one sees devalued degrees, student debt, and the deprofessionalizing of (almost all of) the professoriate. Joseph North, in his recent *Literary Criticism: A Concise Political History*, minces no words, arguing convincingly to me that the turn to scholarship, to the now hegemonic "historicist/contextualist paradigm," was not the progressive victory its adherents claim it to be. "In fact," North insists, "it is better to say the opposite is true: in its most salient aspects, the turn to the current paradigm in the late 1970s and early 1980s was symptomatic of the wider retreat of the left in the neoliberal period and was thus a small part of the more general victory of the right."[28]

The broadening and politicizing of the discipline or, as I have put it, the smudging of the discipline, has not strengthened the discipline, or clarified its identity, or resulted in a more just society. The discipline has little public face or standing—the public increasingly views us skeptically and we now face a legitimation crisis. We, the professors, are afraid to judge and the discipline has become, as one respondent in Lamont's ethnography puts it—and this respondent is herself an English professor—a "sort of no-man's land or an open field where everybody can be kind of a media expert."[29] Rita Felski puts the problem somewhat differently but still accurately, arguing that the field is one in which almost anyone can be an expert in politicized critique, which has become so predictable as to be easy, easy for professors to produce and easy for students to learn. "Something, somewhere—a text, an author, a reader, a genre, a discourse, a discipline—is always already guilty of some crime," according to Felski.[30] What should give one pause is this: Felski's criticism of current methodology resembles all too closely Richard Levin's critique of New Criticism, made in 1979, that the method had devolved into an easy and largely pointless but still competitive game—"My Theme Can Lick Your Theme."[31] A mere one year after Levin's critique, Stephen Greenblatt published *Renaissance Self-Fashioning*, and a politically enthusiastic historicist revolution in methodology was underway, one that ended up slighting, if not suppressing, the literary: the politicization of the field "has diminished or disabled our appreciation of works of art."[32] The slighting of, the suppression of, the literary, of the aesthetic, has allowed others, both inside and outside the academy, inside and outside the discipline, to do so, too, resulting in mockery and deprofessionalization and, increasingly, precarity and poverty.[33]

As is obvious, given my discussion so far, I am not the first to put forward some version of this anxiety, this fear; nor will I be the last. Like North, I think "the discipline's present situation … is troubling enough … that we need to work out how to do things differently in future."[34] North wants his argument to be heard particularly by graduate students, so that they know "what may be at stake when their supervisors encourage them, under the sign either of 'scholarship' or 'politics', to produce yet another historicist/contextualist paper, article, dissertation. If they resist doing this, and are then somewhat confused by the speed with which the rhetoric of the market ('job market') arrives to enforce the norm, then perhaps at least they will be better equipped to understand why."[35]

North does not go far enough, however, for these graduate students at elite PhD programs are indeed subject to the "job market" North derides, and even if they understand North's point, they likely will also be socialized not to care about it.[36] My perhaps scandalous aim here is to motivate not just graduate students at elite PhD programs but also the literary critical non-elite, people already employed, they who are the majority of professors in this country, to separate themselves from the assessments of the elite, assessments that dominate discourse about our field, but that cannot save the non-elite. Elites cannot save non-elites because they do not know what it means to work in an institution with open admissions, underprepared students, heavy service loads, low salaries, or multiple and non-literary programs within an English department. This is true, too, because elites, in their discussions of method, value, and what is going to save us (including those by Levine and North, with whose critiques of historicist hegemony in the field I largely concur) reveal again and again blind spots that leave them open to the charge of hypocrisy or just plain silliness. In a recent issue of *PMLA*, partly devoted to discussion—or rather, critique—of Levine's work.

Langdon Hammer puts the matter as follows: "The idea of doing political work in the world by imagining 'thoughtful relations among forms' is a disciplinary fantasy of empowerment that reflects the continuing crisis conditions of our profession and the resulting demand for literary scholarship to do more than it is commonly supposed to."[37] Which is to say, as Michael W. Clune does, that "the formalism practiced by literary critics has no extraliterary significance. This isn't a bug, it's a feature." The exultant praise *Forms* has received "shows that many critics want to engage the wider world of knowledge and action without being shamed or ignored."[38]

But this blind spot—that critics repeatedly ask literary criticism to do more than its remit allows, in order to create a more just society—is not new; it has characterized the field for at least thirty years and the result has been, in fact, being shamed and ignored. Nor is it the blind spot that matters most to that political desire, if I may be so bold as to say. What matters most, and what disables such programs or manifestos is that they do not see that justice must begin at home, in academia. Or at least, they fail to explain why academia is exempt from its egalitarian prescriptions for other social institutions. Levine says "a hierarchy will always afford inequality" and that she is offering a method of analyzing forms that is going to result in (or afford?) political progress, a redistribution of wealth, and a reduction in inequality. Yet Levine works at Cornell University; she is part of an academia that is steeply and durably hierarchical, and hence by her own definition a form that affords inequality. And in addition affords the reproduction of privilege—a fact that is demonstrated by her own life: she is the daughter of a professor, a prominent historian, who talked and argued with her from an early age about literature. Touting the pedagogical benefits of "the seminar room," an expensive and exclusionary educational setting she describes at a number of elite colleges and universities, Levine apparently is unaware that most professors and most students in American higher education today will never "sit around a long table and observe one another."[39] One might gamble that the children of the nanny and housekeeper Levine thanks by name in her acknowledgments will never so sit (or possibly have never so sat), even though these women allowed her not to do housework or look after her own children so she could write.[40] It cannot be surprising that the public and their representatives disregard or even mock attempts like these to intervene in the making of social policy, particularly regarding inequality, when the academy is among society's most hierarchical and unequal institutions. As I shall point out below, a handful of elite institutions continue to produce the majority of professors in this country, regardless of discipline, while resources are extraordinarily unequal across institutions, faculty, and students. In other words, it is quite clear that the study of forms has not afforded Levine the ability to acknowledge, much less critique or dismantle, the hierarchy of the form in which she works, and grew up, academia.

* * *

In *Academically Adrift*—a controversial study of undergraduate education in the United States—Richard Arum and Josipa Roksa argue that "[l]imited learning in the U.S. higher education system cannot be defined as a crisis because institutional and system-level organizational survival is not being threatened in any significant way." Not one of the many stakeholders—not parents, not students, not faculty, not administrators, not governments—is "primarily interested in undergraduate student academic growth, although many are interested in student retention and persistence."[41] I find it difficult to disagree, and the compelling implication is that, with some shaking out, colleges and universities will survive and English departments, too. What may be in crisis, however, what may not survive, is the study of literature and especially the study of early literature. Or perhaps each will survive only in the institutions of the elite.

At this point, I should define what I mean by elites in the profession. In previous work, I defined elites as those holding a tenured or tenure-track position that affords them—and affords them because of the labor of others—the opportunity to pursue research and writing. In an article about the role of service in our profession, I focused on the discipline's two-tiered system of professional employment and urged readers to consider that graduate students, adjuncts, and lecturers serve "*not only students and the institution but the research professoriate as well.*"[42] But many, if not most, of the tenured or to-be-tenured—those who teach in small liberal arts colleges, those who teach in regional state universities—share much with graduate students and contingent faculty. I want to suggest that rather than just teaching load, what defines elites are working conditions overall, including opportunities for voice and influence, via publication or appointments to professional governing bodies, for example. Working conditions include the composition of departments, too, whether a department houses literary critics exclusively or nearly so, or whether it houses a variety of sub- and even outright different disciples, such as linguistics or film production, or English education.

For the purposes of this essay, elites—the academic 1 percent—are colleagues who hold degrees from the top twenty or so PhD programs who also teach in them or teach in prestigious liberal arts colleges and research universities. Elites are those who dominate discussion about the state of the profession, including within our professional organizations, those whose views circulate as complete assessments, even when their views are, as Katie Hogan insists, obviously "incomplete."[43] Already, I have exemplified this problem in the above discussion about the value of literary study, but here I would like to offer an example focused on Shakespeare, by considering the question of "The Vanishing Shakespeare." I refer to the report published in 2007, by the American Council of Trustees and Alumni (ACTA), which documented that the nation's most prestigious colleges and universities had slowly eliminated requirements in Shakespeare as part of the major in English.[44] On behalf of all Shakespeareans and literary critics more widely, Shakespeareans at these institutions countered this allegation, but did so indirectly, avoiding the potentially uncomfortable question of requirements, even though as scholars all know and as John Guillory explained over twenty-five years ago, "the history of the literary curriculum has always been characterized by a tendency to modernize the syllabus at the expense of older works."[45] In any case, those defending us against ACTA focused instead on the easier argument regarding the number of students who take Shakespeare. As Walter Cohen summarizes Wendy Wall's memo to ACTA, "requiring English majors to take Shakespeare is like my insisting that my kids eat pizza and ice cream. It's going to happen anyway."[46]

One might wonder about this analogy: should kids eat more pizza and ice cream? This may depend on the quality of the pizza and the ice cream, or maybe on the quality of the kids. But my point is rather that ACTA's beef and data from Northwestern or Cornell turning it into Tofutti are irrelevant to the status of Shakespeare in this country, in higher education, and, most importantly to most Shakespeareans, in one's professional life. I do not have current figures about the percentage of English majors at the University of Alabama who take Shakespeare, though it is an easy bet to say it is not Northwestern's 99 percent or Cornell's 90 percent. This, however, I do know: When, circa 1991, Shakespeare was a requirement for the English major, the English department at the University of Alabama offered three sections of Shakespeare each semester, sometimes four, capped at thirty-five students each. Since then, after eliminating the requirement, Alabama has offered two such sections per semester, but the undergraduate student body has more than doubled, from about 17,000 to about 38,000. Of course, eliminating a requirement in the major for Shakespeare makes it easier to eliminate or reduce the presence of Shakespeare in lower-division courses; subsequently, Alabama eliminated literature from its two-semester sequence of first-year composition. At the University of Alabama, unequivocally, Shakespeare's works are taught less now, to fewer undergraduates, than they were in 1991.

This fact troubles the notion that no one in the discipline thinks Shakespeare should be taught less often. At the University of Alabama, in the early nineties, enough faculty, and in particular the very people ACTA accuses of doing so, cutting-edge theorists and multiculturalists, were persuaded that a requirement in Shakespeare was unnecessary and indeed intellectually, socially, and politically retrograde; and that even if Shakespeare's works were not retrograde, a requirement was unnecessary since students would clamor to take the course, to eat the pizza and the ice cream. Obviously, similar persuasion obtained at Northwestern and Cornell, and elsewhere throughout the country, but at Northwestern and Cornell the literary critics had much better reason to assume undergraduate majors would take courses in Shakespeare, even if not required to do so. They had—and still have—cover; the kids eat the pizza ... and the ice cream. Notwithstanding this, whether at Alabama, Northwestern, or Cornell, the professoriate did think Shakespeare should be taught less and it did not care if that turned out to be the case. Which it did, at least at Alabama, and I would suggest that Alabama's experience is normative, not Northwestern's or Cornell's.

Woe to Shakespeare when the literary critics were in charge of departments. But today, as I have already pointed out, the discipline is different, an entity called "English Studies"; it is not homogenous and (tenure-line) literary critics constitute barely a majority, and sometimes are a minority, of faculty in many English departments. These literary critics share power with linguists, folklorists, compositionists of multiple stripes, media specialists, including digital humanists, English education specialists, and creative writers. And save for the latter, these are colleagues who have no necessary love of literature and especially no necessary love of early literature. In institutions where a course in Shakespeare is required today, such as those where the certification of secondary school teachers is a principal duty—institutions of no interest either to ACTA or our elite apologists, I might add, which is a significant point[47]—these colleagues will join colleagues in modern and contemporary literature to eliminate requirements in early literature, perhaps especially Shakespeare, still the symbol of the once-potent Western canon. Those colleagues who happily use the APA style sheet or run empirical studies on human subjects or turn texts into data sets want more students in their classes and more colleagues like them in the department. Increasingly, they get both.

Early in *Troilus and Cressida*, with war stalemated, despite seven years of battle, the Greeks ponder the future and what has led them to this pass. Ulysses atomizes the problem as a failure of the whole to heed the requirements of rank and hierarchy, of degree, a failure exemplified by Achilles. A famous speech, this, and a long one, and in it Ulysses analogizes order in the heavens to order in human affairs, and disorder above to disorder below, apostrophizing thus:

> O, when degree is shaked,
> Which is the ladder to all high designs,
> Then enterprise is sick! How could communities,
> Degrees in schools and brotherhoods in cities,
> Peaceful commerce from dividable shores,
> The primogeneity and due of birth,
> Prerogative of age, crowns, scepters, laurels,
> But by degree, stand in authentic place?
> Take but degree away, untune that string,
> And hark what discord follows. Each thing meets
> In mere oppugnancy.[48]

Hierarchy, or the crumbling of it or the reordering of it, was a problem for Shakespeare and it is a problem for academia and the social order today. Despite—or precisely because of—centuries of democratization, of the expansion of rights to more and more classes of people, the persistence of hierarchy rankles. Because it persists. Shakespeare's Ulysses no doubt would say it persists because it is necessary, or natural. Economist Thomas Piketty and historian Walter Scheidel might agree: their respective studies document that equality only occurs—or nearly occurs—from a violent reordering of the social order, a violent destruction of capital, at which point, hierarchy re-emerges, only with a perhaps slightly different cast of characters at the top.[49]

Since the late 1960s and the early 1970s, elites in academia have promoted egalitarianism thoroughly and continuously, but, as with their response to "The Vanishing Shakespeare," this egalitarianism is problematic. Some might call it disingenuous or even phony, for it is an egalitarianism pursued within an established and persistent hierarchy. Members of previously excluded groups of people have been admitted to elite institutions—as graduate students and as faculty—but the number and ranking of those institutions has changed almost not at all. This was not unanticipated: almost twenty years ago, Guillory argued that equality does not follow easily from democratization, which brings with it "intensified effects of competition and stratification."[50] Furthermore, as has been argued and demonstrated repeatedly, including by Guillory in the same article, the prestige hierarchy of the graduate schools is crucial to one's ability to secure a professorship. Perhaps most recently Aaron Clauset et al. show that across the three disciplines they studied—computer science, business, and history—"faculty hiring follows a common and steeply hierarchical structure that reflects profound social inequality" and indeed puts paid to the notion that people enter these institutions and depart from them to assistant professorships based on intellectual merit alone.[51] Indeed, so steep and so durable are these hierarchies "that individual faculty placement may be predictable from doctoral prestige alone, without directly modeling the characteristics or preferences of individuals or institutions."[52] In a popular discussion of the research published in *Slate* magazine, Clauset, writing with journalist Joel Warner, puts the matter bluntly: "Just 18 elite universities produce half of all computer science professors, 16 schools produce half of all business professors, and eight schools account for half of all history professors."[53]

Unlike Levine who recently has discovered the power of social forms—or what I would call social structures, including norms and roles—I have long considered and analyzed that power in theory, in Shakespeare's plays, and in society. Like Levine, I think two generations of literary critics overplayed their hands when they failed to imagine or analyze the positive effects of social structure, just as they overplayed their hands when they slighted, or suppressed, the literary. So as I conclude this essay, I do not call on colleagues to imagine they can easily upend structures that are in place, but as I suggested in opening this essay, norms and roles can change—and can be changed—in our profession. Essays in this volume—by Denise Albanese, by Katherine Boutry, by Fayaz Kabani, by Doug Eskew, by Daniel Bender—repeatedly call for us to recognize this, arguing that professional experience in non-elite institutions spurs one to break out of the ideological and methodological norms learned in graduate school. Which might be to say that the writers of these essays recognize, as do I, that like elites in politics, finance, religion, and sports, our intellectual elites have led us to a place that does not benefit the non-elite, whose professional lives are circumscribed by conditions, already enumerated above, that do not affect the elite, those who taught us and those whom we admire.

Rather than submit to degree—perhaps better yet, rather than submit to superior degrees—I suggest that professors of early literature teaching at non-elite colleges and universities continue to think about ways to rescue themselves and their students from the perhaps unintended effects of forty years of democratization in access to higher education. Because that democratization has not affected the status hierarchy of institutions of higher education, it has funneled resources and power upward, leaving more and more of the professoriate in precarity or near-poverty, while putting many if not most students and families into financial duress to afford the most prestigious educations they can in this deeply problematic economy. Regarding syllabi—what English departments teach—it is true, for example, that the canon frequently changes, and must, but it does not follow that such change should require the replacement of the oldest by the newest text. Nor does it mean that Shakespeare can or should stand alone as "The Renaissance" or as "Early Literature"; as Cohen observes, "the synecdochic approach to the cultural past" is obviously not good for students—or citizens—today.[54] The non-elite professoriate can, and in my view should, insist to their colleagues that the skills of close reading and elegant—or at least more or less correct—writing are valuable in the marketplace, and not just the marketplace of ideas; and that these skills, *pace* Fish, can be taught and evaluated by us, by literary critics, by professors of early literature. And in so doing, non-elite professors of early literature and Shakespeare can—and in my view should—acknowledge and indeed embrace the demise or end of the carbon-intensive and wasteful research culture. Guillory argued in the mid-1990s that the professional desire to teach graduate students, which is to say the professional desire to do research, is "phantasmic," unachievable unless "the number of graduate students … increase[d] geometrically."[55] Few heeded Guillory then, just as few heeded Margery Sabin a few years later, who called on "those who would defend the teaching of literature [to] rouse themselves to exert a responsible counter influence to [the field's] anti-literary proposals."[56] Is the time now for professors to renounce the "pyramid scheme" that grounds the research culture?[57] Is it time now to embrace the teaching of undergraduate students? In my view, the answers are "yes" and "yes": teaching is where institutional and organizational resources and rewards should lie, as indeed increasingly they are.

The non-elite professoriate can use its numbers and strengths to warn elites in our field that what is happening below will happen eventually at the top. Already elite PhD-granting institutions sport fewer faculty in early literatures than they did thirty years ago, are training fewer graduate students, and rumors whisper that the quality of those graduate students is sinking. And why should it be otherwise when the elite PhD programs and the Modern Language Association seem to think PhD education is actually (and ironically) advanced training for careers in business, media, and administration? If the literature professoriate, both elite and non-elite, is serious about justifying the humanities, saving the study of literature in English, and effecting social change, the way forward, I believe, is to advocate for a literary pedagogy that provides instruction in the valuable skill of writing. Like Levine's seminar, such a "faculty-intensive" classroom devoted to literature and writing is expensive,[58] but unlike "the seminar room," such a classroom does not require a long, wooden table in a lovely, paneled room. The "faculty-intensive" writing classroom is one that, as Fish observes, can justify the public's investments in higher education by offering a valuable skill to students. And thereby it can improve the working conditions of non-elite faculty everywhere. In addition—and I agree with North here—such a classroom can "enrich the culture directly by cultivating new modes of subjectivity, new capacities for experience—using works of literature as a means."[59] It can, in other words, help realize some of the political desire critics have chased since the 1970s and continue to chase today. The literature classroom that hones students' writing is a classroom of cultivation open to everyone; it might also be a source, when those students grow up and enter society, of desired social change.

Notes

1. Joseph Hall, *The Discovery of a New World* [*Mundus Alter Et Idem*], trans. Thomas Healy, ed. Huntington Brown (Cambridge: Harvard University Press, 1937).
2. Richard A. McCabe, *Joseph Hall: A Study in Satire and Meditation* (Oxford: Clarendon Press, 1982), 73.
3. Brown, *Discovery*, vii, viii.
4. David Grann, "The White Darkness: A Solitary Journey Across Antarctica," *The New Yorker*, February 12 and 19, 2018, 48–75. A solo attempt to cross the continent ended in Worsley's death, at age 55.
5. "South Pole—The Last Degree," Jagged Globe Explorations: https://www.jagged-globe.co.uk/ski/i/last+degree.html. Accessed March 1, 2018.
6. McCabe, *Hall*, 85.
7. Ibid., 12.
8. John Milton, *Complete Prose Works of John Milton*, vols. 1 and 2, ed. Don M. Wolfe (New Haven: Yale University Press, 1953), 1: 882.
9. Ibid., 1: 881.
10. Gordon Teskey, "Recent Studies in the English Renaissance," *Studies in English Literature, 1500–1900* 50, no. 1 (2010): 244.
11. Milton, *Prose*, 2: 526.
12. Stanley Fish, *Professional Correctness: Literary Studies and Political Change* (New York: Harvard University Press, 1995), 114.
13. See William Shakespeare, *Hamlet*, ed. Ann Thompson and Neil Taylor (London: Arden, 2006), 5.2.262.
14. William Shakespeare, *The Tempest*, ed. Virginia Mason Vaughan and Alden T. Vaughan (London: Arden, 2011), 1.2.146–148.
15. Teskey, "Studies," 247.
16. William B. Warner and Clifford Siskin, "Stopping Cultural Studies," *Profession* (2008): 95, 105.
17. Ibid., 106.
18. Heather Love, "Close but Not Deep: Literary Ethics and the Descriptive Turn," *New Literary History* 41, no. 2 (2010): 374.
19. Caroline Levine, *Forms: Whole, Rhythm, Hierarchy, Network* (Princeton: Princeton University Press, 2015), xii, xiii.

20. Fish, *Professional*, 110.
21. Marjorie Garber, *The Use and Abuse of Literature* (New York: Pantheon Books, 2011), 30.
22. Stanley Fish, *Save the World on Your Own Time* (New York: Oxford University Press, 2008), 44–45.
23. Ibid., 56.
24. Barack Obama, "State of the Union Address," Washington, DC, January 24, 2012: https://obamawhitehouse.archives.gov/the-press-office/2012/01/24/remarks-president-state-union-address. Accessed March 1, 2018.
25. Kate McLuskie and Kate Rumbold, *Cultural Value in Twenty-First-Century England* (Manchester: Manchester University Press, 2014), 7.
26. Jane Gallop, "The Historicization of Literary Studies and the Fate of Close Reading," *Profession* (2007): 181–186.
27. Michèle Lamont, *How Professors Think: Inside the Curious World of Academic Judgment* (Cambridge: Harvard University Press, 2009), 73.
28. Joseph North, *Literary Criticism: A Concise Political History* (Cambridge: Harvard University Press, 2017), 3.
29. Lamont, *Think*, 74.
30. Rita Felski, *The Limits of Critique* (Chicago: University of Chicago Press, 2015), 39, 118, 149.
31. Richard Levin, *New Readings vs. Old Plays: Recent Trends in the Reinterpretation of English Renaissance Drama* (Chicago: University of Chicago Press, 1979), 28.
32. Felski, *Limits*, 114.
33. Creating a discipline open to mockery is serious: in 1997, Carol Christ, at the time the provost of the University of California, Berkeley (and currently Chancellor of that campus), warned in *Profession* that if a department chair wants to obtain funds for faculty lines, he or she should ensure the department is not the one on campus "whose name need only be mentioned to make people laugh" ("Retaining Faculty Lines," *Profession* [1997]: 55). Two years later, in *The New York Review of Books*, Andrew Delbanco cites the line to add that Christ "does not name the offender—but everyone knows that if you want to locate the laughingstock on your local campus these days, your best bet is to stop by the English department" ("The Decline and Fall of Literature," *The New York Review of Books*, November 4, 1999: http://www.nybooks.com/articles/1999/11/04/the-decline-and-fall-of-literature/. Accessed April 30, 2018.
34. North, *History*, xi.
35. Ibid.
36. Nor does North emphasize the structural and political incentives for graduate programs to over-produce PhDs. See my "Superserviceable

Subordinates, Universal Access, and Prestige-Driven Research," in *Over Ten Million Served: Gendered Service in Language and Literature Workplaces*, ed. Michelle A. Massé and Katie J. Hogan (Albany: SUNY Press, 2010). Two demands, contradictory though they are, fuel our current situation: universal access to higher education and prestige- or status-driven research. Both require cheap labor.
37. Langdon Hammer, "Fantastic Forms," *PMLA* 132, no. 5 (2017): 1204. Daniel Bender makes a similar point in his essay in this volume.
38. Michael W. Clune, "Formalism as the Fear of Ideas," *PMLA* 132, no. 5 (2017): 1197.
39. Levine, *Forms*, 45, 47. I taught many seminars without a table or a seminar room.
40. Ibid., xvi.
41. Richard Arum and Josipa Roksa, *Academically Adrift: Limited Learning on College Campuses* (Chicago: University of Chicago Press, 2010), 124, 125.
42. O'Dair, "Superserviceable," 39.
43. Katie Hogan, "Superserviceable Feminism," *The Minnesota Review*, n.s. 63–64 (2005): 108.
44. American Council of Trustees and Alumni, *The Vanishing Shakespeare,* comp. Anne D. Neal and Charles Mitchell (Washington, DC: ACTA, 2007).
45. John Guillory, *Cultural Capital: The Problem of Literary Canon Formation* (Chicago: University of Chicago Press, 1993), 15.
46. Walter Cohen, "Dehistoricizing Shakespearean Value," (paper presented at the annual meeting of the Shakespeare Association of America, Washington, DC, 2009), 1–2.
47. The Common Core notwithstanding, when the secondary schools follow the colleges and universities to eliminate the requirement in Shakespeare, the professional game truly will be up. At many non-elite colleges and universities, students in Education provide significant numbers to classes in Shakespeare.
48. William Shakespeare, *Troilus and Cressida*, ed. David Bevington (New York: Bloomsbury, 2015), 1.3.101–111.
49. See Thomas Piketty, *Capital in the Twenty-First Century*, trans. Arthur Goldhammer (Cambridge: Harvard University Press, 2014) and Walter Scheidel, *The Great Leveler: Violence and the History of Inequality from the Stone Age to the Twenty-First Century* (Princeton: Princeton University Press, 2017).
50. John Guillory, "The System of Graduate Education," *PMLA* 115, no. 5 (2000): 1155. See also my *Class, Critics, and Shakespeare: Bottom Lines on the Culture Wars* (Ann Arbor: University of Michigan Press, 2000).
51. Aaron Clauset, Samuel Arbesman, and Daniel B. Larremore, "Systematic inequality and hierarchy in faculty hiring networks," *Science Advances* 1,

no. 1 (2015): 1. The authors write, "Despite the confounded nature of merit and social status within measurable prestige, the observed hierarchies are sufficiently steep that attributing their structure to differences in merit alone seems implausible" (6). Although English is not one of the disciplines cited here, it is a safe bet that English, too, is subject to this prestige hierarchy and at a rate akin to History's.

52. Ibid., 3.
53. Joel Warner and Aaron Clauset, "The Academy's Dirty Secret," *Slate*, February 23, 2015: http://www.slate.com/articles/life/education/2015/02/university_hiring_if_you_didn_t_get_your_ph_d_at_an_elite_university_good.html. Accessed April 25 and 27, 2018.
54. Cohen, "Dehistoricizing," 10.
55. John Guillory, "Preprofessionalism: What Graduate Students Want," *Profession* (1996): 98.
56. Margery Sabin, "The Debate: Seductions and Betrayals in Literary Studies," rev. of *Professional Correctness*, by Stanley Fish, *The Rise and Fall of English*, by Robert Scholes, and *The Academic Postmodern and the Rule of Literature*, by David Simpson, *Raritan* 19, no. 1 (1999): 127.
57. Guillory, "Preprofessionalism," 97.
58. Levine, *Forms*, 47.
59. North, *History*, 6.

Afterword: Shakespeare, the Swing Voter

Craig Dionne

> I am a little shy where to begin; for the interest of the story is sadly in the way of poetry. It is safer, therefore, to read the play backwards
> —Ralph Waldo Emerson, on reading Shakespeare.[1]

Shakespeare, a Reagan Democrat? A Clinton conservative? The guy who voted for Obama, and then Trump? A Democrat who didn't vote for Kennedy because he's Catholic? We could probably go back even further with more examples. To call Shakespeare a swing voter is not as ludicrous as it sounds. There is a long history of Shakespeare's own particular ambivalence in representing ethical controversies and different perspectives. A. P. Rossiter was one of the first modern critics to describe the radical ambivalence in Shakespeare's works. His theory of Shakespeare's plays working as an extreme ironic detachment is often discussed as an idealistic overvaluation of his drama, offering a poor man's version of Keats' idea of negative capability.[2] Shakespeare, we are told, was able to identify with two opposing moral perspectives at the same time, a philosophical juggling of plates if not an ethical three-card

C. Dionne (✉)
Eastern Michigan University, Ypsilanti, MI, USA

S. O'Dair and T. Francisco (eds.), *Shakespeare and the 99%*,
https://doi.org/10.1007/978-3-030-03883-0_13

monte. “Shakespeare’s intuitive way of thinking […] is dynamic,” Rossiter explains, “alterative, not tied to its age. It has that extra degree of freedom which is given only by what I call a constant ‘Doubleness’: a thoroughly English empiricism which recognizes the coextancy and juxtaposition of opposites, without submitting to urges…to obliterate or annihilate the one in the theoretic interests of the other” (62).

To be able to identify with others, to speak for them, but perhaps not *with* them. “Dramatic irony causes an exact juxtaposition of opposites in the mind of the audience,” Rossiter explains, “the effect is some kind of detached sardonic amusement.”[3] To identify with both Petruchio’s chauvinism *and* Katherine’s desperation, or with Shylock’s dejection *and* Gratiano’s bristling anti-Semitism, is to be a vehicle for a significant form of disengagement, to be a royalist *and* a plebeian skeptic, to vote for both camps in a way that encourages a liberal openness perhaps at one with today’s marketplace of exchange, but not in a way that necessarily unhinges the structures of power. Others have made similar claims, including Stephen Greenblatt, whose description of Shakespeare’s identity erased by his radical self-abnegating empathy for others echoes Rossiter’s argument.[4]

Rossiter’s lectures at Cambridge on Shakespeare’s history plays were given in the early 1950s, and so it’s important to think about the context in which this idealization of radical ambiguity circulated during the beginning of the Cold War and the beginning of the global economic system we define now as neoliberalism. Indeed, I would suggest that Rossiter’s definition of the bard’s aesthetic should be read as describing Shakespeare’s historical importance to the twentieth-century Western academy, not necessarily the description of the plays as such. If we are describing the way Shakespeare’s work is being used, and not his aesthetic, then perhaps we are describing more how his texts can be wrapped around any hidden agenda or local identity.[5] Rossiter is defining the grid through which his plays will be read in the postwar university. I would describe this as the hegemonic appropriative gesture that defines traditional humanist uses of Shakespeare’s work, a practice grounded in early modern humanism’s use of classical works to justify legal precedent and court politics.

Does Shakespeare’s ironic undecidability structure a similar detachment in the reader? This is an important question, one that Shakespeareans rarely ask given the matter-of-fact business of advancing historicist and/or presentist responses to the deeper philosophical pulls of his art. But let’s be honest, Shakespeare’s own class politics is the elephant in the room, if I may use a cliché that has its own irony these days. When Richard III in Act 3 affects a piety to win the hearts of the Alderman for his coronation, we may feel certain Shakespeare is advancing the Tudor stereotype of Richard as a deceitful tyrant manipulating the simple commoners. Here is a scene that pulls the veil on our present political moment: a Machiavellian populism. But what about *Coriolanus*? In this notorious Roman tragedy, we experience a decidedly different image of the commoners, a fickle mob led too easily by the scheming Tribunes. Shakespeare's view of the 99 percent is an interesting question. In the following, I want to discuss more how Shakespeare functions as the poet of a neoliberalism whose plays can help further both conservative and progressive agendas. The two-eyed bard has a long history in American culture. Teaching his plays in the twenty-first century to poor and working-class students challenges us to think how his own aesthetic ambivalence fits in the neoliberal university.

In response to the question, do we want to use his plays to teach the 99 percent, the essays in this collection answer with a resounding "Yes" It is refreshing to read essays that argue there is nothing one would rather do than use Shakespeare's plays to fight against neoliberalism, to struggle against divisions in class, race, and gender in this country in the wake of the Occupy Wall Street movement. It is still worth asking whether or not we're helped or hindered by Shakespeare's own cultural pluralism. Rossiter's description of Shakespeare's double-eyed nature might be a good place to start when asking, as Mara Amster, Denise Albanese, and Doug Eskew do in this collection, what it is exactly we're asking students to identify with when challenged with Shakespeare's complex characters and plots. Rossiter at times reads like a formalist when describing Shakespeare's tendency to not take sides in ethical debates. Like the new critics, Rossiter praises Shakespeare for his hedging equivocations, which he describes as mature.[6] Isn't this how the formalists naturalized a reactionary middle-class quietism? Mature, restrained….circumspect. Rossiter avers that a lack of appropriate sympathy can lead *not* to an ethical connection to the Other, but to a "detached sardonic amusement." In our narratives about Shakespeare's place in the new university, and the way we use him to teach reading and writing to the 99 percent, one might begin by thinking of the way this poet of Otherness fits in the broader context of twenty-first century political literacy and how a poet known for ethical ventriloquism is employed to promote a neoliberal agenda.[7]

Humanism has always read the past with a purpose; it was always a pragmatic exercise in justifying present concerns. When used to accommodate the American cult of individual self-reliance and growth, we recall Ralph Waldo Emerson's praise of Shakespeare as a kind of open commonplace book, a compendium of oddly collected perceptions and viewpoints that can be transposed and made to support one's own individualized perspective. Often ignored as vulgarized popular forms of Shakespeareana, commonplace Shakespeare belongs to the project of American self-development, as his work replaces the classics in the humanist arsenal of reading for practical wisdom. Reading Shakespeare in this way is complicit with other cultural practices that reify social interaction in modern society.[8] If the fractured, collated textual logic I speak of here sounds like the postmodern effect separating the constituent parts of everyday perception into disconnected and autonomous wholes—to make the everyday parts of daily life speak in the way that Marx famously described the commodity's dislocated status—then this is because Shakespeare's role in contemporary American literary humanism has always been one of compromise, modification, and revision, of assimilating raw bits of culture and weaving them into new wholes. Emerson famously defined the importance of Shakespeare's writing as a sacred icon of wordly wisdom: "he is like some saint whose history is to be rendered into all languages," he explained, "into verse and prose, into songs and pictures, and cut up into proverbs; so that the occasion which gave the saint's meaning the form of a conversation, or of a prayer, or of a code of laws, *is immaterial, compared with the universality of its application*. So it fares with the wise Shakespeare and his book of life. He wrote the airs for all our modern music: he wrote the text of modern life; the text of manners: he drew the man of England and Europe; the father of the man in America." Shakespeare's book of life is, in a fashion, the father to the man, if the history of his legacy in commonplace literacy proves anything. Emerson himself acknowledged in his private notebooks that Shakespeare in this country is "the only modern writer who has the honor of a Concordance" —"pulverized into proverbs"—he complained—even though his own advice on how to read his plays for their "flattering painting of Nature" could be said to epitomize the very practice he declaimed. "I must say that in reading the plays," he writes, "I am a little shy where to begin; for the interest of the story is sadly in the way of poetry. It is safer, therefore, to read the play backwards."[9]

Which layer of Shakespeare's vestments do we intend to use to promote our own particular perspective? We might ask how this both-sides-of-the-coin perspective empowers the new corporate university. Does it lead to a radical destabilization of all moral systems (this is maybe how a poststructuralist might spin this, right)? If so, how might this wildly reflective changeable taffeta of art be appropriated by Western culture as a vehicle to promote divergent perspectives but in a way that does not reflect on the limits of Shakespeare's own ironic distance?

A partial answer to the question is suggested in my title. Swinging Shakespeare in this way might look like Carol and Ken Adelman's "Movers and Shakespeare" Executive Training course in Arlington, Virginia, which uses Shakespeare to help business and government managers run a more effective office. They promise to teach future CEO's how to "build a winning team with *Henry V*":

> Today's executives face sometimes daunting challenges, but they're nothing compared to what King Henry was going through 600 years ago. He built a strong and diverse team, created a smart plan, and then motivated his 6000-person company to execute. Ethical Training: Doing Right to Do Well is a case study drawn from the history books, with insight from Shakespeare (and a few U.S. Air Force generals).[10]

The Adelmans also teach diversity using *The Merchant of Venice*. "Develop workplace and customer empathy" they explain, and "Improve productivity, competitiveness, and profits." "It may surprise you," say the Adelmans while echoing Emerson's impression of Shakespseare's multivalence, but "Shakespeare's heroes come in all flavors and colors. This is especially true in the 'Merchant of Venice,' where diverse characters are in the center of the action. Each faces prejudice, yet none acts like a victim."[11] The Adelmans' own conservative politics makes them perhaps too easy a target for such analysis. We can compare the Adelmans' use of Shakespeare to teach ethics in the workplace with Ralph Cohen's special "Program for Professionals" business workshop at the American Shakespeare Center, which boasts of using lessons from his works to "enhance written and oral presentation skills….Explore leadership styles. Adapt to multiple challenges…Examine case studies in leadership."[12] If we needed an example of how Shakespeare's work is used to advance the naked embrace of corporate culture, we need look no further.

This language makes us wince, but I would suggest that from an outsider's perspective to those unfamiliar with the discourse of literary scholarship or academic literary politics, these uses of Shakespeare to enlighten workshop participants to ethics and diversity might appear indistinguishable from our own appropriation of his work. At the very least, it begs the question I raise at the beginning of this essay about how the bard's notorious two-eyed aesthetics leaves itself vulnerable to many kinds of interpretive choices.[13]

Movers and Shakespeares and *Programs for Professionals* are examples of how the 1 percent reads Shakespeare, a crude parody of academic multiculturalism. If it feels like a dark mirror to our own interpretive gestures, it's because even when we are historicizing the discourses and social practices in his work we are still doing it from a context that makes those topics relevant to us today. I think it is nonetheless important to ask how different this model is from teaching the 99 percent. For Cohen and the Adelmans, Shakespeare is made a utility to a system that has been determined, in the words of Bill Readings, by the moral vacuity of the corporate university in ruins, where "thought is non-productive labor, and hence does not show up as such on balance sheets except as waste."[14] These business workshops are doing the yeoman's service of making Shakespeare recognizable to the balance sheet. They introduce Shakespeare to an otherwise a-literate managerial class (and we should applaud them for it!). But the very terms of their appropriation—turning to Shakespeare to exploit the fat purses of corporations always in need of finding innovative programs to build confidence among their bureaucratic meritocracy smacks of "if you can't beat them…" At the very least, this approach ignores the more critical insights of his art. Like Emerson, these appropriations make Shakespeare a poet of grandiloquence and an emblem book of virtue. It flattens the plays by ignoring the more subversive and emancipatory portrayal of power as merely an emblem of leadership.

Shakespeare for the 99 percent dares, rather, to listen to what Shakespeare has to proffer: he lets us question Hal's manipulation of others, to see the pain of Falstaff's humiliation, he lets us hear Portia's breezy racism and feel the hurt of Shylock's enforced conversion. To make these passages about profit, or efficiency, is to miss the point: Shakespeare may be modeling how discrimination aids in the social mobility of the elite class, but his own imaginative generosity, as some have called it, allows us to see how this hateful bias works.[15] To advance an unbridled neoliberalism through Shakespeare by using his plays as a vehicle to enhanced communication or business leadership is to ignore the dark truth of this unfettered market system.

We no longer live in a time where the question of Shakespeare's polyvalence or two-eyed aesthetic compels us when considering the importance of his work. While this question did mark a period of New Historicism, as I note above, today it seems the question of Shakespeare's pluralism can strike some of us as superfluous, perhaps already answered.[16] The cultural studies model we have inherited from the last decades of the twentieth century, especially the legacy of New Historicism in Shakespeare and early modern literature, staked its claim against the conservative quietism of traditional formalist appreciation. To this degree, neoliberalism was made evident—called out as such—through the very theoretical discourses that marked our historicist readings of the past. These were not just readings of Tudor Absolutist power in *Midsummer Night's Dream* or philosophical musings about the colonial cast of Iago's control of Othello, but also critiques of the corporate hegemony and Reagan's endorsement of fascism in Central America.[17] We should not forget this. When New Historicism is canonized as the editorial matrix of our field via a succession of ever-larger editions from W. W. Norton & Company, Inc. and lucrative publication deals are made to scholars whose works marked this very era, it's hard to remember the political intent of New Historicism's beginnings. But I want to suggest that there is a far darker neoliberal logic at work behind the disappearance of the question of Shakespeare's place in the humanist curriculum. Many of us advance what we feel is emancipatory reading practices regardless of the text taught. In so doing, we may be assuming that students have already learned how to read for the cultural politics of the work, how to trace the implied political grain of the text's aesthetic. As one of my colleagues suggested in a profound moment of revelation, "with cultural studies as a practice, it doesn't matter what text we teach. We can teach anything, right?"

What the professor of cultural studies might call textual pluralism, the neoliberal administrator might call outcome-based curriculum. In the last fifteen years at Eastern Michigan University, where I teach, there has been a shift to an outcome-based General Education curriculum that allows students to select from a range of courses to fulfill their humanities requirements. Students must select any two courses from a list of Humanities courses that is quite extensive. It invites students to choose Shakespeare among a list of electives: Lit 210 Intro to Shakespeare *or* Phil 224 Ethics and Food, *or* Phil 228 Global Ethics, *or* WGST 226 Gender, Sexuality, and Religion, *or* CHL 137 Harry Potter: Literary Allusion, Children's Literature and Popular Culture, and so on.

If you want a visual map of life in the trenches at a working-class comprehensive university, I can think of no better example of what this warfare looks like. Here is a bird's eye view of the Maginot lines of the trenches themselves. Even though such an arrangement of "knowledge in the disciplines" (as we call this rubric at EMU's Gen Ed selections) sounds a lot like Bill Readings' original solution at surviving in the ruins of the university by "loosening disciplinary structures," marking "disciplinarity as a permanent question," what we get is something of the reverse.[18] Readings' antidote to working in the corporate university in an era of ruthless capitalism was to build into the play of thought a grounded historical reflection that questions disciplinary boundaries. He called this "dereferentialisation…that opens up new spaces and breaks down existing structures of defense against thought."[19] But the outcome-based educational model employed at my school, if this were its original intention, ends up reconstituting these boundaries by forcing programs to work against each other (rather than together) to advance their intellectual tools of inquiry as a special commodity no other program can offer.

This is the true invisible hand of neoliberalism at work in the new university's managerial control of faculty. There is a rationalist principle of freedom that masks a deeper economic incentive. While faculty are told they have the freedom to decide what classes will compose the "knowledge of their discipline," the university has covertly delimited the authority of the faculty to the question of disciplinary knowledge alone rather than larger concerns of the academic health of the university. The most detrimental effect of the new curriculum, aside from the fact that this forces something of a reifying exchange value to the experience offered in all these humanities classes (think Marx's parsing through what makes coats, books, shovels universally equivalent), is that the university employs a corporate accounting scheme to pay each program differently based on its Full Time Equivalent (FTE) teaching loads, making the enrollment numbers in each of its Gen Ed courses a kind of meat market for recruitment. What determines a successful class is the enrollment: anything below your department's break-even point as the FTE is charmingly called (our English department's FTE is 23: an "aggregated average" enrollment) and the class is canceled. This is the nefarious accounting language that defines the health of each academic discipline. If incoming freshmen do not choose to take your program's Gen Ed courses, then your FTE numbers go down, and if your FTE's go down, your department is allotted less money and fewer resources (less for supplies, less travel money for conferences, and even fewer teaching lines for tenure and non-tenure sections per term). Effectively, the outcome-based curriculum forces departments to compete for students, as it turns the experience of education from the students' perspective into a tour through a shopping mall.

Outcome-based programs like this force departments to compete with each other in order to survive. You don't *get* to teach your course online. You *have* to teach it online. Sexy titles? Departments invent new courses to sell the sizzle. It's about marketing your class so that it can fill. And this can get ugly when trying to think of new ways to attract students. (I was told by a well-minded colleague to title my summer Shakespeare course "Witches and Monsters in Shakespeare" and truth be told, I am considering it.) It also creates anxious turf fights in which programs are forced to police the academic boundaries of their discipline: Is that class in Theater on "Interpretive Reading" encroaching on *our* domain in literary criticism? And they might rightfully ask, is that class on "Hollywood Narrative" teaching *our* film class? All of this rancor and competitive tension is behind the scenes but spills out in predictable ways on college-level committees whose task it is to read proposals for these classes. The silliest part? The student, the consumer, decides what classes are important, not the faculty. This wouldn't be a problem if public and land-grant universities were flush with enrollments, but this is not the case due to declining enrollments across the board. I assume this is a familiar story to all who teach in the trenches at public universities.

The story about how we got here offers its own lesson in *overdetermination*, and mapping it out can feel like following a Rube Goldberg comic depicting the Renaissance trivium being stretched on the rack by Rich Uncle Pennybags in the game of Monopoly. The overall decline in tax revenues in state coffers forces legislatures to pay colleges less out of its annual budgets, forcing schools to increase tuition to make up the slack, which in turn makes higher education a debtor's prison for generations of working families. As Sharon O'Dair and Timothy Francisco observe in the introduction of this collection, the end result is a perfect storm of impending economic catastrophe, as universities employ more and more draconian corporate strategies to cope with the declining resources. Teaching is finally just calculated as a fixed cost or one abstracted service among many that figure the college degree as a commodity. Administrators in the new university simply account for teaching costs as one of many abstracted numbers that can be streamlined in different ways, as described by Jeffrey Di Leo: it is "decision-making based on getting the maximum amount of 'labor' from the academic working-class—with the lowest level of cost and risk."[20]

How else to lower production cost? It's a teeter-totter logic: increase enrollments per course, increase teaching loads, lower salaries. Or simply hire cheaper labor (adjuncts and grad students instead of tenure-track faculty). The p word (profit) is nary whispered in discussions of semester schedules, but it hangs in the air like a sour smell. Sadly, it's a perfectly rationalized economic plummet to the bottom. Who genuinely profits from this system? Citizens bank. Wells Fargo. Students are necessarily factored into this equation as consumers of loans. Professors can sometimes feel like hustlers in an elaborate confidence trick. Students, to make it through this maze, often take the easiest route based purely on a sense of survival. Who can blame them? And where, in this tempest, is Shakespeare? The essays in this book respond with a much-needed frame. Against Emerson's general confusion about where to begin, the essays in this volume know exactly what time it is and offer a healthy reminder of why we've chosen this career in the first place. DiLeo has argued powerfully that overturning the neoliberal university may be futile, so the best strategy is to trouble it from within.[21] Perhaps Di Leo's description of neoliberalism suffers from the "winner loses" logic Fredric Jameson famously ascribed to Michel Foucault: "Insofar as the theorist wins…by constructing an increasingly closed and terrifying machine, to that very degree he loses, since the critical capacity of his work is thereby paralyzed, and the impulses of negation and revolt, not to speak of those of social transformation, are increasingly perceived as vain and trivial in the face of the model itself."[22] More than just troubling it from within, these essays work against the Emersonian proviso to read Shakespeare backward by considering immaterial the historical and political contexts of his writing. We may appear to appropriate this swing-voting poet in the same way as the Movers and Shakespeares but when we resist the consumer-oriented process that makes the bard a feel-good tourism, a mere commonplace for emblems of virtue or hackneyed verities, we are pulling the veil on the very system that means to take advantage of students. The essays here in *Shakespeare and the 99%* work to *restore* the political context to Shakespeare's empathetic investments, especially those scenes of education that help us account for the continuing legacy of humanist literacy and its role in providing social mobility through reading the literatures of the past. Reading—and paying—Shakespeare *forward.*

Notes

1. Ralph Waldo Emerson, *Journals and Miscellaneous Notebooks*, vol. 10, ed. Merton M. Sealts (Cambridge: Belknap Press of Harvard University Press, 1971), 23, 31.
2. Keats describes this: "when a man is capable of being in uncertainties, mysteries, doubts, without any irritable reaching after fact and reason—Coleridge, for instance, would let go by a fine isolated verisimilitude caught from the Penetralium of mystery, from being incapable of remaining content with half-knowledge. This pursued through volumes would perhaps take us no further than this, that with a great poet the sense of Beauty overcomes every other consideration, or rather obliterates all consideration." John Keats, *The Complete Poetical Works and Letters of John Keats*, Cambridge Edition, ed. Horace E. Scudder (Houghton: Mifflin and Company, 1899), 277.
3. A. P. Rossiter, *Angel with Horns: Fifteen Lectures on Shakespeare* (New York: Longman, 1957), 51.
4. See Stephen Greenblatt, *Renaissance Self-Fashioning: From More to Shakespeare* (University of Chicago Press, 1980). It is too easy to see the fetish of ambivalence a preoccupation of the early twentieth century formalists alone, since even historicism attends to Shakespeare's double voice as a given by defining it as a symptom of social pressures and historical contexts. Thus, Joel Altman's *The Tudor Play of Mind: Rhetorical Inquiry and the Development of Elizabethan Drama* (Berkeley: University of California Press, 1978), sees this double vision as an instance of grammar school rhetorical training; Annabel Patterson, *Censorship and Interpretation: The Conditions of Reading and Writing in Elizabethan England* (Madison: University of Wisconsin, 1984), sees the self-erasure of ambivalence as trace of the pressures of censorship, while Stephen Mullaney's *The Place of the Stage: License, Play and Power in Renaissance England* (Ann Arbor: University of Michigan Press, 1988), describes the dislocated suburbs, "the liberties," structuring the ironic doubleness to the early modern drama.
5. In parsing through the way Shakespeare's ambiguity is retooled to work as a commodity for different interests, see Michael Bristol's theory of the "supply side of culture" in his *Big-Time Shakespeare* (New York: Routledge, 1996), 28–58.
6. Rossiter fetishizes ambiguity as the very definition of art, which is to say, he makes uncertainty the baseline definition of *all* art: if it does not loll in a resplendent doubt, it's just propaganda, or worse, evangelical twaddle.
7. Shakespeare's notorious canonization as a poet "for all time" goes back to Ben Jonson's praise for his works in the 1623 Folio, if not in Robert Greene's withering complaint in his *Groats-Worth of Wit* (1592) of the

Upstart Crow who is Jack of all parts ("absolute *Johonnes factotum*"). Greene's prescient aside introduces Shakespeare on the stage of history by declaring that his real identity is hidden underneath a veneer of fictional roles (a "Player's hide"). Renascence Editions: http://www.luminarium.org/renascence-editions/greene1.html. Accessed December 10, 2018.

8. See Marjorie Garber's *Profiling Shakespeare* (New York: Routledge, 2008), and my "Commonplace Literacy and the Colonial Scene: The Case of the Carriacou's Shakespeare Mas," in *Native Shakespeares: Indigenous Appropriations on a Global Stage*, ed. Craig Dionne and Parmita Kapadia (New York: Routledge, 2016).
9. Emerson, *Journals and Miscellaneous Notebooks*, 23, 31.
10. Movers and Shakespeares, "Team Builders": https://www.moversandshakespeares.com/team-building-page. Accessed December 10, 2018.
11. Ibid., "Diversity Training": https://www.moversandshakespeares.com/diversity-training-page. Accessed December 10, 2018.
12. American Shakespeare Center. "Leadership Training": https://americanshakespearecenter.com/education/leadership-training/. Accessed December 10, 2018.
13. See Marjorie Garber's description of the Adelmans' background in government and business (Carol was in public health and Kenneth was Director of Arms Control for Ronald Reagan), *Shakespeare and Modern Culture* (New York: Anchor Press, 2009), 194–196. We should feel lucky *Movers and Shakespeares* is not using Machiavelli to teach "How to Treat Colleagues," or Spenser's *Faerie Queene* on "How to Make Your Company Global." It's easy to joke, but it is hard not to read between the lines of the Adelmans' advertising that future business leaders are reading Shakespeare to discover the best ways to betray friends and hang insolent employees from trees, how to marshal the penniless troops ("food for powder") to forge imperial dynasties.
14. Bill Readings, "Dwelling in the Ruins," *University of Toronto Quarterly* 66, no. 4 (1997): 589.
15. The term is Greenblatt's in "Shakespeare's Leap," *The New York Times*, September 12, 2004: https://www.nytimes.com/2004/09/12/magazine/shakespeares-leap.html?mtrref=www.google.com&gwh=EFB5E3536B765AE0CD006FC3EF143612&gwt=pay. Accessed December 10, 2018.
16. Shakespeare's "aesthetic distancing" of even his own disillusion—that his own religious doubt is framed with poetic ambivalence—teases at the continuing question of his politics in terms of religious reform. John Cox's idea of "skeptical faith," in *Seeming Knowledge: Shakespeare and Skeptical Faith* (Waco: Baylor University Press, 2007) attempts to square this circle by

framing the question of Shakespeare's doubt within a religious discourse, a strong trend in the last twenty years to read Shakespeare as Catholic and all his mysteries as recusancy. Much of the current historicist readings attempt to frame Shakespeare's skepticism in classical antecedents or through his reading of Montaigne, or trace this ambivalence through sixteenth-century contradictions in political and economic forces: Stephen Greenblatt's "Shakespeare and the Exorcists," in *Shakespearean Negotiations: The Circulation of Social Energy in Renaissance England* (Berkeley: University of California Press, 1988), discusses Shakespeare's distancing gestures in the context of Reformation critiques of Catholic ritual, while Jonathan Dollimore's *Radical Tragedy: Religion, Ideology and Power in the Drama of Shakespeare and His Contemporaries* (Chicago: University of Chicago Press, 1984); and Richard Halpern's *The Poetics of Primitive Accumulation: English Renaissance Culture and the Genealogy of Capital* (Cornell, NY: Cornell University Press, 1991) place the idea of decentered subjectivity in the neo-Marxist contexts of Althusserian critiques of power and "primitive accumulation" respectively. Hugh Grady's *Shakespeare, Machiavelli, and Montaigne* argues forcefully that there is a trajectory in Shakespeare's work from political critique to doubt.

17. Respectively: Louis Adrian Montrose, "'Shaping Fantasies': Figurations of Gender and Power in Elizabethan Culture," *Representations* 2 (1983): 61–94, and Stephen Greenblatt, "Improvisation and Power," in *Literature and Society*, ed. Edward W. Said (Baltimore: Johns Hopkins University Press, 1980), 57–99.
18. Bill Readings, "Dwelling in the Ruins," 583–592.
19. Ibid., 592.
20. Jeffrey Di Leo, "Is Higher Education Working Class? The Politics of Labor in Neoliberal Academe," *Rhizomes: Cultural Studies in Emerging Knowledge*, no. 27: https://doi.org/10.20415/rhiz/034. Accessed Decemeber 10, 2018.
21. Jeffrey Di Leo, *Corporate Humanities in Higher Education: Moving Beyond the Neoliberal Academy* (New York: Palgrave Macmillan, 2013).
22. Fredric Jameson, *Postmodernism, or, the Cultural Logic of Late Capitalism* (Durham: Duke University Press, 1991): http://xroads.virginia.edu/~drbr/jameson/jameson.html. Accessed December 10, 2018.

Bibliography

99%: The Occupy Wall Street Collaborative Film. 97 min. New York: Gigantic Pictures, 2013.

Abate, Corinne S. "Neither a Tamer Nor a Shrew Be: A Defense of Petruchio and Katherine." In *Privacy, Domesticity, and Women in Early Modern England*, edited by Corinne S. Abate, 31–45. Burlington, VT: Ashgate, 2003.

Abu-Lughod, Janet L. *Before European Hegemony: The World System A.D. 1250–1350*. Oxford: Oxford University Press, 1991.

Adams, Elizabeth, and Howard Adams, eds. *A Century of Commitment: Frostburg State University 1898–1998*. Frostburg, MD: FSU Foundation, 1997.

Ahmed, Sara. *The Cultural Politics of Emotion*. 2nd ed. London: Routledge, 2014.

Albanese, Denise. *Extramural Shakespeare*. New York: Palgrave Macmillan, 2010.

"Allegany County, Maryland Educational Data." TownCharts, 2016: http://www.towncharts.com/Maryland/Education/Allegany-County-MD-Education-data.html.

Altman, Joel. *The Tudor Play of Mind: Rhetorical Inquiry and the Development of Elizabethan Drama*. Berkeley: University of California Press, 1978.

American Council of Trustees and Alumni. *The Vanishing Shakespeare*. Compiled by Anne D. Neal and Charles Mitchell. Washington, DC: ACTA, 2007.

Amin, Samir. *Eurocentrism*. New York: New York University Press, 1989.

Anievas, Alexander, and Kerem Nişancıoğlu. *How the West Came to Rule: The Geopolitical Origins of Capitalism*. London: Pluto Press, 2018.

Aronowitz, Stanley. "The Winter of Our Discontent." *Situations* 4, no. 2 (2012): 37–76.

S. O'Dair and T. Francisco (eds.), *Shakespeare and the 99%*,
https://doi.org/10.1007/978-3-030-03883-0

Aristotle, *The Politics*. Book 3. The Internet Classics Archive, edited by Daniel C. Stevenson. Web Atomics, 1994–2000: http://classics.mit.edu/Aristotle/politics.3.three.html.

Arum, Richard, and Josipa Roksa. *Academically Adrift: Limited Learning on College Campuses*. Chicago: University of Chicago Press, 2010.

Ascham, Roger. *The Schoolmaster*, edited by Lawrence V. Ryan. Ithaca: Cornell University Press, 1967.

Austin, Ann E. "Preparing the Next Generation of Faculty: Graduate School as Socialization to the Academic Career." *Journal of Higher Education* 73, no. 1 (2002): 94–122.

Badger, Emily. "How Poverty Taxes the Brain." *CityLab*, August 29, 2013: https://www.citylab.com/life/2013/08/how-poverty-taxes-brain/6716/.

Baldwin, T.W. *Shakespeare's Small Latine and Lesse Greeke*. 2 Vols. Urbana: University of Illinois, 1944.

Barber, C.L. *Shakespeare's Festive Comedy: A Study of Dramatic Form and Its Relations to Social Custom*. Princeton: Princeton University Press, 1959.

Barabak, Mark Z. "Voters in This Democratic Part of Colorado Backed Trump. After 100 Days, They Have No Regrets." *Los Angeles Times*, April 27, 2017: http://fw.to/oouxFNH.

Barthes, Roland. "From Work to Text." In *The Rustle of Language*, by Roland Barthes and translated by Richard Howard, 56–64. New York: Hill and Wang, 1986.

Bate, Jonathan. *Shakespeare and Ovid*. Oxford: The Clarendon Press, 1993.

Belsey, Catherine. *Critical Practice*. London: Routledge, 1980.

———. *The Subject of Tragedy: Identity and Difference in Renaissance Drama*. London: Routledge, 1985.

Bender, Daniel. "Native Pastoral in the English Renaissance: The 1549 Petition and Kett's Rebellion." In *Conversational Exchanges in Early Modern England*, edited by Kristen Abbott Bennett, 1–18. Newcastle upon Tyne: Cambridge Scholars Publishing, 2015.

Benjamin, Jessica. *The Bonds of Love: Psychoanalysis, Feminism, and the Problem of Domination*. New York: Pantheon Books, 1988.

Bennefield, R.M. "Tales from the Boondocks." *Black Issues in Higher Education* 16 (1999): 24–29.

Bergeron, David A., and Carmel Martin. "Strengthening Our Economy Through College for All." Washington, DC: Center for American Progress, 2015: https://www.americanprogress.org/issues/education/reports/2015/02/19/105522/strengthening-our-economy-through-college-for-all/.

Berlant, Lauren. *Cruel Optimism*. Durham: Duke University Press, 2011.

Bernstein, William J. *A Splendid Exchange: How Trade Shaped the World*. New York: Grove Press, 2008.

Best, Stephen, and Sharon Marcus. "Surface Reading: An Introduction." *Representations* 108, no. 1 (2009): 1–21.

Bevington, David, ed. *The Complete Works of Shakespeare*. 5th ed. New York: Longman, 2003.

Bloom, Paul. *Against Empathy: The Case for Rational Compassion*. New York: Ecco, 2016.

Boden, Margaret A. *The Creative Mind: Myths and Mechanisms*. London and New York: Routledge, 2005.

Bourdieu, Pierre. *Outline of a Theory of Practice*, translated by Richard Nice. Cambridge: Cambridge University Press, 1977.

———. *Distinction: A Social Critique of the Judgement of Taste*, translated by Richard Nice. Cambridge: Harvard University Press, 1984.

Bourdieu, Pierre, and Jean-Claude Passeron. *Reproduction in Education, Society and Culture*, translated by Richard Nice. London: Sage, 1977.

Bowen, Jose Antonio. "Helping Students Embrace Discomfort." *Inside Higher Ed*, December 7, 2016: https://www.insidehighered.com/views/2016/12/07/educating-students-ambiguity-and-discomfort-essay?utm_content=buffer4e15a&utm_medium=social&utm_source=twitter&utm_campaign=IHEbuffer.

Boyer, Ernest. *Scholarship Reconsidered: Priorities of the Professoriate*. New York: Jossey-Bass, 1990.

Boose, Lynda E. "*The Taming of the Shrew*, Good Husbandry, and Enclosure." In *Shakespeare Reread: The Texts in New Contexts*, edited by Russ McDonald, 193–225. Ithaca: Cornell University Press, 1994.

Booth, Stephen. "The Function of Criticism at the Present Time and All Others." *Shakespeare Quarterly* 41, no. 2 (1990): 262–268.

Brantlinger, Patrick. "Who Killed Shakespeare? An Apologia for English Departments." *College English* 61, no. 6 (1999): 681–690.

———. *Who Killed Shakespeare? What's Happened to English Since the Radical 60's*. New York: Routledge, 2001.

Brathwait, Richrd. *The English Gentlewoman, Drawne Out to the Full Body*. London: B. Alsop and T. Fauucet, 1631.

Brecht, Bertolt. "Alienation-Effects in Chinese Acting." In *Brecht on Theatre: The Development of an Aesthetic* (13th ed.), by Bertolt Brecht and edited by Steve Giles, Marc Silberman, and Tom Kuhn; translated by John Willett, 91–99. New York: Hill and Wang, 1992.

Bristol, Michael. *Shakespeare's America, America's Shakespeare*. London: Routledge, 1990.

———. *Big-Time Shakespeare*. New York: Routledge, 1996.

Brown, Carolyn E. "Katherine of *The Taming of the Shrew*: 'A Second Grissel'." *Texas Studies in Literature and Language* 37, no. 3 (1995): 285–313.

Brown, Paul "'This Thing of Darkness I Acknowledge Mine': *The Tempest* and the Discourse of Colonialism." In *Political Shakespeare: New Essays in Cultural Materialism*, edited by Jonathan Dollimore and Alan Sinfield, 48–71. Ithaca: Cornell University Press, 1985.

Brooks, Dennis. "'To Show Scorn Her Own Image': The Varieties of Education in *The Taming of the Shrew*." *Rocky Mountain Review of Language and Literature* 48, no. 1 (1994): 7–32.

Brownlee, Jamie. "Elite Power and Educational Reform: An Historiographical Analysis of Canada and the United States." *Paedogogica Historica: International Journal of the History of Education* 49, no. 2 (2012): 194–216.

Burnett, Mark Thornton. *Shakespeare and World Cinema*. Cambridge: Cambridge University Press, 2013.

Burton, Tara Isabella. "What a Lesser-Known Shakespeare Play Can Tell Us About Harvey Weinstein." *Vox*, November 15, 2017: https://www.vox.com/culture/2017/11/15/16644938/shakespeare-measure-for-measure-weinstein-sexual-harassment-play-theater.

Bushnell, Rebecca. *A Culture of Teaching: Early Modern Humanism in Theory and Practice*. Ithaca: Cornell University Press, 1996.

Caesar, Julius. *The Gallic Wars*. The Internet Classics Archive, edited by Daniel C. Stevenson. Web Atomics, 1994–2000: http://classics.mit.edu/Caesar/gallic.6.6.html.

Carnevale, Anthony P., Jeff Strohl, Ban Cheah, and Neil Ridley. "Good Jobs That Pay Without a BA." Washington, DC: Georgetown University Center on Education and the Workforce, 2017.

Carrell, Jennifer Lee. "How the Bard Won the West." *Smithsonian* 29, no. 5 (1998): 89–107.

Castiglione, Baldessar. *The Book of the Courtier*, translated by Charles Singleton. New York: Anchor Books, 1959.

Chakrabarty, Dipesh. *Provincializing Europe: Postcolonial Thought and Historical Difference*. Princeton: Princeton University Press, 2009.

Chiaet, Juliann. "Novel Finding: Reading Literary Fiction Improves Empathy." *Scientific American*, October 4, 2013: https://www.scientificamerican.com/article/novel-finding-reading-literary-fiction-improves-empathy/.

Christ, Carol. "Retaining Faculty Lines." *Profession* (1997): 54–60.

Cicero. *Defense of Lucius Flaccus*. University of Chicago: Perseus Projects Texts, 2018: http: perseus.uchicago.edu/perseus-cgi/Flac14.16.

Clauset, Aaron, Samuel Arbesman, and Daniel B. Larremore. "Systematic Inequality and Hierarchy in Faculty Hiring Networks." *Science Advances* 1, no. 1 (2015): 1–6.

Clune, Michael W. "Formalism as the Fear of Ideas." *PMLA* 132, no. 5 (2017): 1194–1199.

Cohen, Derek. "History and Nation in *Richard II* and *Henry IV*." *Studies in English Literature, 1500–1900* 42, no. 2 (2002): 293–315.

Cohen, Walter. "Dehistoricizing Shakespearean Value." Paper Presented at the Annual Meeting of the Shakespeare Association of America, Washington, DC, 2009.

Coley, Chrissy. "Higher Education: The Engine Driving Upward Mobility." *Ellucian*, September 29, 2015: https://wwwblog.ellucian.com/Blog/Higher-education--the-engine-driving-upward-mobility/.

Corum, Richard. "'The Catastrophe Is a Nuptial': *Love's Labour's Lost*, Tactics, Everyday Life." In *Renaissance Culture and the Everyday*, edited by Patricia Fumerton and Simon Hunt, 271–298. Philadelphia: University of Pennsylvania, 1999.

Cornett, Michael. "Everyone's Argus." *The Journal Editor in the Academy. Profession* (2009): 105–111.

Cottom, Tressie Macmillan. *Lower Ed: The Troubling Rise of For-Profit Colleges in the New Economy*. New York: The New Press, 2017.

Cousins, A.D. "Humanism, Female Education, and Myth: Erasmus, Vives, and More's 'To Candidus'." *Journal of the History of Ideas* 65, no. 2 (2004): 213–230.

Coward, Rosalind, and John Ellis. *Language and Materialism: Developments in Semiology and the Theory of the Subject*. London: Routledge and Kegan Paul, 1977.

Cox, John. *Seeming Knowledge: Shakespeare and Skeptical Faith*. Waco: Baylor University Press, 2007.

Cox-Jensen, Freyja. *Reading the Roman Republic in Early Modern England*. Leiden: Brill, 2012.

Csikszentmihalyi, Mihaly. *Flow: The Psychology of Optimal Experience*. New York: Harper & Row, 2009.

Davis, Mike. *Planet of Slums*. New York: Verso, 2006.

Dean, Paul. "Shakespeare's Historical Imagination." *Renaissance Studies* 10, no. 1 (1997): 27–40.

de Beauvoir, Simone. *The Second Sex*, translated by Constance Borde and Sheila Malovaney-Chevallier. New York: Vintage Books, 2009.

Deena Prichep. "Beware of Those College Brochures That Tout Diversity in Campus Life." *MPRNews*, December 29, 2013: https://www.mprnews.org/story/2013/12/30/education/beware-of-those-college-brochures-that-tout-diversity-in-campus-life.

Delbanco, Andrew. "The Decline and Fall of Literature." *The New York Review of Books*, November 4, 1999: http://www.nybooks.com/articles/1999/11/04/the-decline-and-fall-of-literature.

Deleuze, Gilles, and Felix Guattari. *A Thousand Plateaus: Capitalism and Schizophrenia*, translated by Brian Massumi. Minneapolis: University of Minnesota Press, 1987.

de Tocqueville, Alexis. *Democracy in America*. 2 vols., edited by Phillips Bradley. New York: Vintage Classics, 1990.

Di Leo, Jeffrey R. *Corporate Humanities in Higher Education: Moving Beyond the Neoliberal Academy*. New York: Palgrave Macmillan, 2013.

———. "Is Higher Education Working Class? The Politics of Labor in Neoliberal Academe." *Rhizomes: Cultural Studies in Emerging Knowledge*, no. 27 (2014): https://doi.org/10.20415/rhiz/034.

Dionne, Craig. "Commonplace Literacy and the Colonial Scene: The Case of the Carriacou's Shakespeare Mas." In *Native Shakespeares: Indigenous Appropriations on a Global Stage*, edited by Craig Dionne and Parmita Kapadia, 37–57. New York: Routledge, 2016.

Dollimore, Jonathan. *Radical Tragedy: Religion, Ideology and Power in the Drama of Shakespeare and His Contemporaries*. Chicago: University of Chicago Press, 1984.

Dollimore, Jonathan, and Alan Sinfield, eds. *Political Shakespeare: New Essays in Cultural Materialism*. Ithaca: Cornell University Press, 1985.

Drakakis, John, ed. *Alternative Shakespeares*. London: Methuen, 1985.

Eagleton, Terry. *William Shakespeare*. Oxford: Blackwell, 1986.

Earle, Ethan. *A Brief History of Occupy Wall Street*. New York: Rosa Luxemburg Stiftung, 2012.

Eaves, Morris. "The Real Thing: A Plan for Producing Shakespeare in the Classroom." *College English* 31, no. 5 (1970): 463–472.

Eddy, Pamela E., and Jeni Hart. "Faculty in the Hinterlands: Cultural Anticipation and Cultural Reality." *Higher Education* 63 (2012): 751–769.

Eggert, Katherine. "Nostalgia and the Not Yet Late Queen: Refusing Female Rule in *Henry V*." *ELH* 61, no. 3 (1994): 523–550.

Elliott, Euel. "How Occupy Wall Street Led to the Rise of Donald Trump." *Fortune*, March 2016: http://fortune.com/2016/03/23/occupy-wall-street-donald-trump-rise/.

Emerson, Ralph Waldo. *Journals and Miscellaneous Notebooks*, vol. 10, edited by Merton M. Sealts. Cambridge: Belknap Press of Harvard University Press, 1960.

Enterline, Lynn. "Rhetoric, Discipline, and the Theatricality of Everyday Life in Elizabethan Grammar Schools." In *From Performance to Print in Shakespeare's England*, edited by Peter Holland and Stephen Orgel, 173–190. Basingstoke: Palgrave Macmillan, 2006.

———. *Shakespeare's Schoolroom: Rhetoric, Discipline, Emotion*. Philadelphia: University of Pennsylvania Press, 2012.

Erasmus, Desiderius. *Ciceronianus, or, the Best Way of Speaking* (1535), translated by Izora Scott. New York: Columbia Teacher's College, 1908.

Evans, G.B. *The Riverside Shakespeare*. Boston: Houghton Mifflin, 1974.

Faust, Drew Gilpin. "Why Campus Inclusion Matters." *The Atlantic*, August 24, 2016: https://www.theatlantic.com/video/index/497252/why-campus-inclusion-matters/.

Favreau, Jon, et al. "A Government Eclipse." *Pod Save America*, February 9, 2018: https://crooked.com/podcast/government-eclipse-live-denver/.

Felski, Rita. *The Limits of Critique*. Chicago: University of Chicago Press, 2015.

Ferguson, Niall. *The Ascent of Money: A Financial History of the World*. London: Penguin, 2008.

Fine, Sarah. "'A Slow Revolution': Toward a Theory of Intellectual Playfulness in High School Classrooms." *Harvard Educational Review* 84, no. 1 (April 2014): 1–23.

Finke, Laurie. "Knowledge as Bait: Feminism, Voice, and the Pedagogical Unconscious." *College English* 55, no. 1 (1993): 7–27.

Fish, Stanley. *Professional Correctness: Literary Studies and Political Change*. New York: Clarendon Press, 1995.

———. *Save the World on Your Own Time*. New York: Oxford University Press, 2008.

Fitter, Chris. *Radical Shakespeare: Politics and Stagecraft in the Early Career*. New York: Routledge, 2013.

Forker, Charles R., ed. *King Richard II*. London: Bloomsbury, 2002.

Frankl, Victor. *Man's Search for Meaning*. London: Rider, 2012.

French, R.W. "Shakespeare and the Common Reader." *College English* 38, no. 1 (1976): 86–87.

Fritz, Savannah. "We Can't Wait Another Year." *The Harvard Crimson*, March 23, 2017: https://www.thecrimson.com/article/2017/3/23/fritz-we-cant-wait/;.

Gallop, Jane. "The Historicization of Literary Studies and the Fate of Close Reading." *Profession* (2007): 181–186.

Garber, Marjorie. *Profiling Shakespeare*. New York: Routledge, 2008.

———. *The Use and Abuse of Literature*. New York: Pantheon Books, 2011.

Garry, Patrick. "Education as the Key to Opportunity and Upward Mobility." *RenewAmerica.com*, March 20, 2015: http://www.renewamerica.com/analysis/garry/150320.

Georg, Lukács. *History and Class Consciousness: Studies in Marxist Dialectics*, translated by Rodney Livingstone. Cambridge: MIT Press, 1971.

Gibson, Joan. "Educating for Silence: Renaissance Women and Language Arts." *Hypatia* 4, no. 1 (1989): 9–27.

Goldberg, Jonathan. *Sodometries: Renaissance Texts, Modern Sexualities*. Stanford: Stanford University Press, 1992.

Goody, Jack. *Renaissances: The One or the Many?* Cambridge: Cambridge University Press, 2010.

Grann, David. "The White Darkness: A Solitary Journey Across Antarctica." *The New Yorker*, February 12 and 19, 2018: 48–75.

Greenblatt Named University Professor of the Humanities. *The Harvard Gazette*, September 21, 2000: https://news.harvard.edu/gazette/story/2000/09/greenblatt-named-university-professor-of-the-humanities/.

Greenblatt, Stephen. "Improvisation and Power." In *Literature and Society*, edited by Edward Said, 57–99. Baltimore: Johns Hopkins University Press, 1980a.

———. *Renaissance Self-Fashioning: From More to Shakespeare*. Chicago: University of Chicago Press, 1980b.

———. Introduction. "The Forms of Power and the Power of Forms in the Renaissance." *Genre* 15, nos. 1–2 (1982): 1–6.

———. *Shakespearean Negotiations: The Circulation of Social Energy in Renaissance England*. Berkeley: University of California Press, 1988.

———. "Shakespeare's Leap." *The New York Times*, September 12, 2004: https://www.nytimes.com/2004/09/12/magazine/shakespeares-leap.html?mtrref=www.google.com&gwh=EFB5E3536B765AE0CD006F-C3EF143612&gwt=pay.

Greene, Thomas M. *The Light in Troy: Imitation and Discovery in Renaissance Poetry*. New Haven: Yale University Press, 1982.

Greenstone, Michael, Adam Looney, Jeremy Patashnik, and Muxin Yu. *Thirteen Economic Facts About Social Mobility and the Role of Education*. Washington, DC: The Brookings Institution, 2013.

Guillory, John. *Cultural Capital: The Problem of Literary Canon Formation*. Chicago: University of Chicago Press, 1993.

———. "Preprofessionalism: What Graduate Students Want." *Profession* (1996): 91–99.

———. "The System of Graduate Education." *PMLA* 115, no. 5 (October, 2000): 1154–1163.

———. "Who's Afraid of Marcel Proust? The Failure of General Education in the American University." In *The Humanities and the Dynamics of Inclusion Since World War II*, edited by David A. Hollinger, 25–49. Baltimore: Johns Hopkins University Press, 2006.

Halpern, Richard. *The Poetics of Primitive Accumulation: English Renaissance Culture and the Genealogy of Capital*. Ithaca: Cornell University Press, 1991.

Hall, Joseph. *The Discovery of a New World* [Mundus Alter Et Idem], translated by Thomas Healy and edited by Huntingdon Brown. Cambridge: Harvard University Press, 1937.

Hammer, Langdon. "Fantastic Forms." *PMLA* 132, no. 5 (2017): 1200–1205.

Hampton, Timothy. *Writing from History: The Rhetoric of Exemplarity in Renaissance Literature*. Ithaca: Cornell University Press, 1990.

Harpham, Geoffrey Galt. "From Eternity to Here: Shrinkage in American Thinking About Higher Education." *Representations* 116, no. 1 (2011): 42–61.

Harvey, Katherine A. *The Best-Dressed Miners: Life and Labor in the Maryland Coal Region, 1835–1910*. Ithaca: Cornell University Press, 1969.

Hebdige, Dick. *Subculture: The Meaning of Style*. Padstow, England: TJ International, 1979.

Hobson, John M. *The Eastern Origins of Western Civilisation*. Cambridge: Cambridge University Press, 2004.

Hogan, Katie. "Superserviceable Feminism." *The Minnesota Review* n.s. 63–64 (2005): 95–111.

Holstun, James. "Utopia Pre-empted: Kett's Rebellion, Commoning, and the Hysterical Sublime." *Historical Materialism* 16, no. 3 (2008): 3–53.

Hoxby, Caroline, and Christopher Avery. "The Missing 'One-Offs': The Hidden Supply of High Achieving, Low-Income Students." *Brookings Papers on Economic Activity*. Washington, DC: The Brookings Institute, 2013.

Howard, Jean E., and Paul Strohm. "The Imaginary Commons." *Journal of Medieval and Early Modern Studies*. 37, no. 3 (2007): 549–557.

Howard, Jean E., and Phyllis Rackin. *Engendering a Nation: A Feminist Account of Shakespeare's English Histories*. London: Routledge, 1997.

Humfreville, J. Lee. *Twenty Years Among Our Hostile Indians*. 1903. Reprint, Mechanicsburg, PA: Stackpole Books, 2002.

Hutcheon, Elizabeth. "Imitating Women: Rhetoric, Gender, and Humanist Pedagogy in English Renaissance Drama." PhD dissertation, University of Chicago, 2011.

Hyman, Jeremy S., and Lynn F. Jacobs. "Why Does Diversity Matter at College Anyway?" *US News and World Report*, August 12, 2009: https://www.usnews.com/education/blogs/professors-guide/2009/08/12/why-does-diversity-matter-at-college-anyway.

Ingraham, Christopher. "The Richest 1 Percent Now Owns More of the Country's Wealth Than at Any Time in the Past 50 Years." *The Washington Post*, December 6, 2017: https://www.washingtonpost.com/news/wonk/wp/2017/12/06/the-richest-1-percent-now-owns-more-of-the-countrys-wealth-than-at-any-time-in-the-past-50-years/?noredirect=on&utm_term=.8d564ab9966b.

Institute for Humane Studies at George Mason University, Arlington VA: https://theihs.org/.

Isenberg, Nancy. *White Trash: The 400-Year Untold History of Class in America*. New York: Viking, 2016.

James, M.E. "Obedience and Dissent in Henrician England: The Lincolnshire Rebellion in 1536." *Past and Present* 48 (August 1970): 78.

Jameson, Fredric. *The Political Unconscious: Narrative as a Socially Symbolic Act*. Ithaca: Cornell University Press, 1982.

———. *Postmodernism, or, the Cultural Logic of Late Capitalism*. Durham: Duke University Press, 1991.

Jaschik, Scott. "Giving the Finger to K-State and General Education." *Inside Higher Ed*, December 21, 2016: https://www.insidehighered.com/news/2016/12/21/freshman-announces-hes-dropping-out-kansas-state-and-sets-debate-general-education.

Jardine, Lisa. "Cultural Confusion and Shakespeare's Learned Heroines: 'These Are Old Paradoxes'." *Shakespeare Quarterly* 38, no. 1 (1987): 1–18.

———. "Women Humanists: Education for What?" In *Feminism and Renaissance Studies*, edited by Lorna Hutson, 48–81. Oxford: Oxford University Press, 1999.

Kamenetz, Anya, and Cory Turner. "The High School Graduation Rate Reaches a Record High—Again." *National Public Radio*, October 17, 2016: http://www.npr.org/sections/ed/2016/10/17/498246451/the-high-school-graduation-reaches-a-record-high-again.

Karras, Ruth Mazo. "Women's Labors: Reproduction and Sex Work in Medieval Europe." *Journal of Women's History* 15, no. 4 (2004): 153–158.

Kaufmann, Walter. *The Future of Humanities: Teaching Art, Religion, Philosophy, Literature and History*. New Brunswick: Transaction Publishers, 1995.

Keats, John. *The Complete Poetical Works and Letters of John Keats*, Cambridge Edition, edited by Horace E. Scudder. Houghton: Mifflin and Company, 1899.

Kelleher, Dorothy. "Jaquenetta's Baby's Father: Recovering Paternity in *Love's Labour's Lost*." In *Love's Labour's Lost*, edited by F. Hardison Londré, 304–312. New York: Routledge.

Kim, Joshua. "How to Scale the Liberal Arts." *Inside Higher Ed*, January 9, 2017: https://www.insidehighered.com/blogs/technology-and-learning/how-scale-liberal-arts.

Kincheloe, Joe L. "Critical Pedagogy in the Twenty-First Century." In *Critical Pedagogy: Where Are We Now?*, edited by Peter McLaren and Joe L. Kincheloe, 9–42. New York: Peter Lang, 2007.

Klein, Ezra. "Who Are the 99 Percent?" *The Washington Post*, October 4, 2011: https://www.washingtonpost.com/blogs/ezra-klein/post/who-are-the-99-percent/2011/08/25/gIQAt87jKL_blog.html?noredirect=on&utm_term=.c6f78308729d.

Klein, Naomi. *This Changes Everything: Capitalism vs. the Climate*. New York: Alfred Knopf, 2014.

Koon, Helene Wickham. *How Shakespeare Won the West: Players and Performances in America's Gold Rush, 1849–1865*. Jefferson, NC: McFarland & Co., 1989.

Kreighbaum, Andrew. "Report: Students at HBCUs Have Burdensome Debt." *Inside Higher Ed*, December 15, 2016: https://www.insidehighered.com/quicktakes/2016/12/15/report-students-hbcus-have-burdensome-debt.

Kroeger, Teresa, Tanyell Cooke, and Elise Gould. *The Class of 2016: The Labor Market Is Still Far from Ideal for Young Graduates*. Washington, DC: Economic Policy Institute, 2016.

Lamont, Michèle. *How Professors Think: Inside the Curious World of Academic Judgment*. Cambridge: Harvard University Press, 2009.

Lederman, Doug. "Downward Spiral on Enrollments." *Inside Higher Ed*, December 16, 2015: https://www.insidehighered.com/news/2015/12/16/decline-postsecondary-enrollments-continues-and-speeds.

Leonhardt, David. "California's Upward-Mobility Machine." *The New York Times*, September 16, 2015: https://www.nytimes.com/2015/09/17/upshot/californias-university-system-an-upward-mobility-machine.html.

———. "Princeton—Yes, Princeton—Takes on the Class Divide." *The New York Times*, May 30, 2017: https://www.nytimes.com/2017/05/30/opinion/princeton-takes-on-class-divide.html.

Levine, Caroline. *Forms: Whole, Rhythm, Hierarchy, Network*. Princeton: Princeton University Press, 2015.

Levine, Lawrence W. *Highbrow / Lowbrow: The Emergence of Cultural Hierarchy in America*. Cambridge: Harvard University Press, 1988.

Levin, Carole, and John Watkins. *Shakespeare's Foreign Worlds: National and Transnational Identities in the Elizabethan Age*. Ithaca: Cornell University Press, 2009.

Levin, Richard. *New Readings vs. Old Plays: Recent Trends in the Reinterpretation of English Renaissance Drama*. Chicago: University of Chicago Press, 1979.

Lois, George. *Damn Good Advice (for People with Talent!)*. London: Phaidon Press, 2012.

LoMonico, Michael. "Shakespearean Ruminations and Innovations." *English Journal* 99, no. 1 (2009): 21–28.

Lorde, Audre. "The Master's Tools Will Never Dismantle the Master's House." In *This Bridge Called My Back: Writings by Radical Women of Color*, edited by Cherríe Moraga and Gloria Anzaldúa, 94–101. New York: Kitchen Table Press, 1983.

Love, Heather. "Close but Not Deep: Literary Ethics and the Descriptive Turn." *New Literary History* 41, no. 2 (2010): 371–391.

Lyotard, Jean-François. *The Postmodern Condition: A Report on Knowledge*, translated by Geoff Bennington and Brian Massumi. St. Paul: University of Minnesota Press, 1984.

Magnusson, Lynn. "Scoff Power in *Love's Labour's Lost* and the Inns of Court: Language in Context." *Shakespeare Survey* 57 (2004): 196–208.

Maguire, Laurie E. "'Household Kates': Chez Petruchio, Percy, and Plantagenet." In *Gloriana's Face: Women, Public and Private, in the English Renaissance*, edited by S.P. Cerasano and Marion Wynne-Davies, 129–166. Detroit: Wayne State University Press, 1992.

Marcus, Jon, and Holly K. Hacker. "The Rich-Poor Divide on America's College Campuses Is Getting Wider, Faster." *The Hechinger Report*, December 17, 2015: http://hechingerreport.org/the-socioeconomic-divide-on-americas-college-campuses-is-getting-wider-fast/.

Martin, Jonathan. "Freire vs. Marx: The Tension Between Liberating Pedagogy and Student Alienation." *Discourse of Sociological Practice* 6, no. 2 (2004): 27–32.

Mason, Robert. *A Mirror for Merchants*. London: T Creede, 1609.

Massey, Doreen. "Politics and Space/Time." In *Place and Politics of Identity*, edited by Michael Keith and Steven Pile, 141–161. New York: Routledge, 1993.

Massumi, Brian. "The Future Birth of the Affective Fact: The Ontology of Threat." In *The Affect Theory Reader*, edited by Melisa Gregg and Gregory J. Seigworth, 52–70. Durham: Duke University Press, 2010.

Mauk, Johnathan. "Location, Location, Location: The Real (E)states of Being, Writing, and Thinking in Composition." *College English* 65, no. 4 (2003): 368–388.

Mazzola, Elizabeth. "Schooling Shrews and Grooming Queens in the Tudor Classroom." *Critical Survey* 22, no. 1 (2010): 2–25.

McCabe, Richard A. *Joseph Hall: A Study in Satire and Meditation*. Oxford: Clarendon Press, 1982.

McCluskey, Neal. "Many Factors at Play in Minority Access to Higher Education." Washington, DC: Cato Institute, 2015: https://www.cato.org/publications/testimony/many-factors-play-minority-access-higher-education.

McLuskie, Kate, and Kate Rumbold. *Cultural Value in Twenty-First-Century England*. Manchester: Manchester University Press, 2014.

McManaway, James G. "Shakespeare in the United States." *PMLA* 79, no. 5 (1964): 513–518.

McNamee, Lawrence. "New Horizons in the Teaching of Shakespeare." *College English* 23, no. 7 (1962): 583–585.

Michaels, Walter Benn. *The Trouble with Diversity: How We Learned to Love Identity and Ignore Inequality*. New York: Metropolitan Books, 2006.

———. "Dude, Where's My Job?" *PMLA* 127, no. 4 (2012): 1006–1009.

Milkman, Ruth, Stephanie Luce, and Penny Lewis. "Changing the Subject: A Bottom-Up Account of Occupy Wall Street in New York City." New York: The Murphy Institute, 2013.

Milton, John. *Complete Prose Works of John Milton*, Vols. 1 and 2, edited by Don M. Wolfe. New Haven: Yale University Press, 1953.

Montaigne, Michel. *The Essayes*, translated by John Florio. London: Grant Richards, 1908.

Montrose, Louis Adrian. "'Shaping Fantasies': Figurations of Gender and Power in Elizabethan Culture." *Representations* 2 (1983): 61–94.

Morison, Richard. *Remedy for Sedition* reprinted in *Humanist Scholarship and Public Order: Two Tracts Against the Pilgrimage of Grace by Sir Richard Morison with Historical Annotations and Related Contemporary Documents*, edited by David Berkowitz. Washington, DC: Folger Shakespeare Library, 1984.

Morris, Cass. *The American Shakespeare Study Guide: The Basics.* Staunton: The American Shakespeare Center, 2009.

Moore, Jason W. *Capitalism in the Web of Life: Ecology and the Accumulation of Capital.* London: Verso, 2015.

Morstein-Marx, Robert. *Mass Oratory and Political Power in the Late Roman Republic.* Cambridge: Cambridge University Press, 2004.

Mowat, Barbara A. "The Founders and the Bard." *The Yale Review* 97, no. 4 (2009): 1–18.

Mulcaster, Richard. *Positions.* London, 1581.

Mullaney, Stephen. *The Place of the Stage: License, Play and Power in Renaissance England.* Ann Arbor: University of Michigan Press, 1988.

New, Jake. "Debt-Averse Teens." *Inside Higher Ed*, November 18, 2014: https://www.insidehighered.com/news/2014/11/18/study-teenagers-want-go-college-are-particularly-averse-student-debt.

Newfield, Christopher. *Unmaking the Public University: The Forty-Year Assault on the Middle Class.* Cambridge: Harvard University Press, 2011.

Newman, Karen. *Fashioning Femininity and English Renaissance Drama.* Chicago: The University of Chicago Press, 1991.

Norris, Floyd. "Fewer U.S. Graduates Opt for College After High School." *The New York Times*, April 25, 2014: https://www.nytimes.com/2014/04/26/business/fewer-us-high-school-graduates-opt-for-college.html.

North, Joseph. *Literary Criticism: A Concise Political History.* Cambridge: Harvard University Press, 2017.

Obama, Barack. "State of the Union Address." Washington, DC, January 24, 2012: https://obamawhitehouse.archives.gov/the-press-office/2012/01/24/remarks-president-state-union-address.

O'Dair, Sharon. *Class, Critics, and Shakespeare: Bottom Lines on the Culture Wars*. Ann Arbor: University of Michigan Press, 2000.

———. "Superserviceable Subordinates, Universal Access, and Prestige-Driven Research." In *Over Ten Million Served: Gendered Service in Language and Literature Workplaces*, edited by Michelle A. Massé and Katie J. Hogan, 35–53. Albany: SUNY Press, 2010.

Ong, Walter. "Latin Language Study as a Renaissance Puberty Rite." *Studies in Philology* 61, no. 2 (1959):103–124.

Ostovich, Helen. "'Teach You Our Princess English?': Equivocal Translation of the French in *Henry V*." In *Gender Rhetorics: Postures of Dominance and Submission in History*, edited by Richard C. Trexler, 147–161. Binghamton, NY: Medieval and Renaissance Texts & Studies, 1994.

Ovid. *Ovid's Metamorphoses: The Arthur Golding Translation, 1567*, edited by John Frederick Nims. Philadelphia: Paul Dry Books, Inc., 2000.

Patterson, Annabel. *Censorship and Interpretation: The Conditions of Reading and Writing in Elizabethan* England. Madison: University of Wisconsin, 1984.

———. *Shakespeare and the Popular Voice.* Oxford: Basil Blackwell, 1989.

Payne, Ruby K. *A Framework for Understanding Poverty: A Cognitive Approach.* Highlands, TX: Aha! Process, Inc., 2013.

Peden, Wilson. "Upward Mobility Through Higher Education: Can We Get Back on Track?" *Association of American Colleges and Universities*, Washington, DC, September 3, 2015: https://www.aacu.org/leap/liberal-education-nation-blog/upward-mobility-through-higher-education-can-we-get-back-track.

Peters, Stephen. "America's Poorest Cities." *24/7 Wall Street*, October 7, 2016: http://247wallst.com/special-report/2016/10/07/americas-poorest cities-3/.

Petrilli, Michael J. "Kid, I'm Sorry, but You're Just Not College Material." *Slate*, March 18, 2014: http://www.slate.com/articles/life/education/2014/03/college_isn_t_for_everyone_let_s_stop_pretending_it_is.html.

Piketty, Thomas. *Capital in the Twenty-First Century*, translated by Arthur Goldhammer. Cambridge: Harvard University Press, 2014.

Pinsker, Joe. "Rich Kids Study English." *The Atlantic*, July 6, 2015: http://www.theatlantic.com/business/archive/2015/07/college-major-rich-families-liberal-arts/397439/.

Pollock, Linda. "'Teach Her to Live Under Obedience': The Making of Women in the Upper Ranks of Early Modern England." *Continuity and Change* 4, no. 2 (1989): 231–258.

Potter, Ursula. "The Naming of Holofernes *in Love's Labour's Lost.*" *English Language Notes* 38, no. 2 (December 2000): 11–23.

Piper, Andrew, and Chad Mellon. "How the Academic Elite Reproduces Itself." *The Chronicle Review*, October 8, 2017: https://www.chronicle.com/article/How-the-Academic-Elite/241374.

Puccio, Gerard and Susan Keller-Mathers, "Enhancing Thinking and Leadership Skills through Creative Problem Solving." In *Creativity: A Handbook for Teachers*, edited by Al-Girl Tan, 281–301. Singapore: World Scientific Publishing Co. 2007.

Puttenham, George. *The Art of English Poesy: A Critical Edition*, edited by Frank Whigham and Wayne A. Rebhorn. Ithaca: Cornell University Press, 2007.

Quintilian. *Institutes of Oratory*, translated by H.E. Butler. Cambridge: Harvard University Press, 1969.

Readings, Bill. "Dwelling in the Ruins." *University of Toronto Quarterly* 66, no. 4 (1997): 583–592.

———. *The University in Ruins*. Cambridge: Harvard University Press, 1997.

Rees, Jonathan. "Higher Education Is Not Available à la Carte." *More or Less Bunk*: http://moreorlessbunk.wordpress.com/2014/02/24/higher-education-is-not-available-a-la-carte.

Reich, Robert. "Why College Isn't (and Shouldn't Have to Be) for Everyone." *Bill Moyers*, March 26, 2015: http://billmoyers.com/2015/03/26/college-isnt-shouldnt-everyone/.

Reisman Diagnostic Creativity Assessment (RDCA). Apple iTunes/iPhone App, 2010.

Richards, Hunter. "Burning Bridges." *The Harvard Independent*, April 9, 2017: https://www.harvardindependent.com/2017/04/burning-bridges/.

Rich, Barnabe. *My Ladies Looking Glasse*. London, 1616, sig. F1v.

Robbins, Bruce. "Discipline and Parse: The Politics of Close Reading." Review of *Literary Criticism: A Concise Political History*, by Joseph North. *Los Angeles Review of Books*, May 14, 2017: https://lareviewofbooks.org/article/discipline-and-parse-the-politics-of-close-reading/#!.

Robertson, Tom. *Frostburg*. Charleston, SC: Arcadia Publishing, 2002.

Rossiter, A.P. *Angel With Horns: Fifteen Lecture on Shakespeare*. New York: Longman, 1957.

Roy, Andrew. *Recollections of A Prisoner of War*. 2nd ed., revised. Columbus, OH: J. L. Trauger Printing Co., 1909.

Ruiter, David. "Harry's (In)human Face." In *Spiritual Shakespeares*, edited by Ewan Fernie, 50–72. New York: Routledge, 2005.

Ruston, Roger. "Does It Matter What We Do with Our Money?" *Priests & People* (1993): 171–177.

Sabin, Margery. "The Debate: Seductions and Betrayals in Literary Studies." Review of *Professional Correctness*, by Stanley Fish, *The Rise and Fall of English*, by Robert Scholes, and *The Academic Postmodern and the Rule of Literature*, by David Simpson. *Raritan* 19, no. 1 (1999): 122–140.

Scheidel, Walter. *The Great Leveler: Violence and the History of Inequality from the Stone Age to the Twenty-First Century*. Princeton: Princeton University Press, 2017.

Schlosser, Eric. *Fast Food Nation: The Dark Side of the All-American Meal*. Boston: Houghton Mifflin Harcourt, 2001.

Schwartz, Robert, and Nancy Hoffman. "Pathways to Upward Mobility." *National Affairs* 37 (2015): http://www.nationalaffairs.com/publications/detail/pathways-to-upward-mobility.

Sebek, Barbara, and Stephen Deng, eds. *Global Traffic: Discourses and Practices of Trade in English Literature and Culture from 1550 to 1700*. New York: Springer, 2016.

Shakespeare, William. *The Riverside Shakespeare*, edited by G. Blakemore Evans. Boston: Houghton Mifflin Co., 1974.

———. *Love's Labour's Lost*, edited by G.R. Hibbard. Oxford: Oxford University Press, 1990.

———. *Coriolanus*, edited by R.B. Parker. Oxford: Oxford University Press, 1998.

———. *King Henry VI, Part II*, edited by Ronald Knowles. London: Thomson Learning, 1999.

———. *The Tempest*, edited by Virginia Mason Vaughan and Alden T. Vaughan. London: Thomson Learning, 1999.

———. *King Henry IV, Part 1*, edited by David Scott Kastan. New York: Bloomsbury, 2002.

———. *Hamlet*, edited by Ann Thompson and Neil Taylor. London: Arden, 2006.

———. *The Complete Works of Shakespeare*, 6th ed., edited by David Bevington. New York: Pearson, 2009.

———. *The Tempest*, edited by Virginia Mason Vaughan and Alden T. Vaughan. London: Arden, 2011.

———. *Troilus and Cressida*, edited by David Bevington. New York: Bloombury, 2015.

———. *The Norton Shakespeare*, 3rd ed., edited by Stephen Greenblatt et al. New York: W. W. Norton, 2015.

Shapiro, James, ed. *Shakespeare in America: An Anthology from the Revolution to Now.* New York: Literary Classics of the United States, 2014.

Sherman, Erik. "Wealthy Kids 8 Times More Likely to Graduate College Than Poor." *Forbes*, February 5, 2015: http://www.forbes.com/sites/eriksherman/2015/02/05/wealthy-college-kids-8-times-more-likely-to-graduate-than-poor/#38d790fd5727.

Sinfield, Alan. *Faultlines: Cultural Materialism and the Politics of Dissident Reading.* Berkeley: Univesity of California Press, 1992.

Singh, Jyotsna G., ed. *A Companion to the Global Renaissance: English Literature and Culture in the Era of Expansion.* Oxford: Wiley, 2009.

Skopcal, Theda. "The Lasting Effects of Occupy Wall Street, Five Years Later." *Time*, September 16, 2016: http://time.com/money/4495707/occupy-wall-street-anniversary-effects/.

Sloterdijk, Peter. *A Critique of Cynical Reason*, translated by Michael Eldred. Minneapolis: University of Minnesota Press, 1988.

Smith, Hallett. "Introduction to *Cymbeline*," In *The Riverside Shakespeare*, edited by G.B. Evans, 1520. Boston: Houghton Mifflin, 1974.

Smith, Sidonie. "The English Major as Social Action." *Profession* (2010): 196–206.

Smith, Thomas. *De Republica Anglorum: A Discourse on the Commonwealth of England*, edited by L. Alston. Cambridge: Cambridge University Press, 1906.

Sowards, J.K. "Erasmus and the Education of Women." *The Sixteenth Century Journal* 13, no. 4 (1982): 77–89.

Stegmaier, Harry I., Jr., David M. Dean, Gordon E. Kershaw, and John B. Wiseman. *Allegany County: A History.* Parsons, WV: McClain Printing Co., 1976.

Steinsaltz, David. "The Politics of French Language in Shakespeare's History Plays." *Studies in English Literatue* 42, no. 2 (2002): 317–334.

Stewart, Matthew. "The 9.9 Percent Is the New American Aristocracy." *The Atlantic*, June 2018: https://www.theatlantic.com/magazine/archive/2018/06/the-birth-of-a-new-american-aristocracy/559130/.

Stiglitz, Joseph E. "Of the 1%, by the 1% for the 1%." *Vanity Fair*, March 31, 2011: https://www.vanityfair.com/news/2011/05/top-one-percent-201105.

Strier, Richard. "'I Am Power': Normal and Magical Politics in *The Tempest.*" In *Writing and Political Engagement in Seventeenth-Century England*, edited by Derek Hirst and Richard Strier, 10–30. Cambridge: Cambridge University Press, 1999.

Sturgess, Kim C. *Shakespeare and the American Nation.* Cambridge: Cambridge University Press, 2004.

Stupnisky, R.H., M.B. Weaver-Hightower, and Y. Kartoshkina. "Exploring and Testing the Predictors of New Faculty Success: A Mixed Methods Study." *Studies in Higher Education* 40, no. 2 (2015): 368–390.

Styles, Amber. "New Reports Calls for an Admissions Preference for Low-Income Students." *Jack Kent Cooke Foundation*, January 11, 2016: http://blog.jkcf.org/welcome-to-the-jack-kent-cooke-foundation-blog/new-report-calls-for-an-admissions-preference-for-low-income-students.

Tate, Emily. "Uneven Access, Equal Success." *Inside Higher Ed*, January 19, 2017: https://www.insidehighered.com/news/2017/01/19/rich-students-flock-elite-colleges-study-finds-graduating-college-levels-playing.

Teague, Frances. *Shakespeare and the American Popular Stage.* New York: Cambridge University Press, 2006.

Teskey, Gordon. "Recent Studies in the English Renaissance." *Studies in English Literature, 1500–1900* 50, no. 1 (2010): 205–258.

Tillyard, E.M.W. *Shakespeare's History Plays.* London: Chatto & Windus, 1944.

Torrance, E. Paul. "Creative Positives of Disadvantaged Children and Youth." *Gifted Children Quarterly* 1 (June 1969): 71–81, http://journals.sagepub.com/doi/abs/10.1177/001698626901300201.

Trotman, Carroll-Ann, and Betsy E. Brown. "Faculty Recruitment and Retention: Concerns of Early and Mid-Career Faculty." *TIAA-CREF Research Dialogue* 86 (2005): 1–10.

Twain, Mark. *The Adventures of Huckleberry Finn.* 1884. Reprint, New York: Penguin, 1985.

———. *Is Shakespeare Dead? From My Autobiography.* New York: Harper & Brothers, 1909.

Vaghul, Kayva, and Marshall Steinbaum. "How the Student Debt Crisis Affects African Americans and Latinos." Washington, DC: Washington Center for Equitable Growth, 2016.

Vance, J.D. *Hillbilly Elegy: A Memoir of a Family and Culture in Crisis.* New York: HarperCollins, 2016.

Vaughan, Alden T., and Virginia Mason Vaughan. *Shakespeare in America.* Oxford: Oxford University Press, 2012.

Vives, Juan Luis. *A Very Fruteful and Pleasant Boke Called Instruction of a Christen Woman*, edited by Richard Hyrde. London, 1547, sigs. C4v, D.

Wall, Wendy. *Staging Domesticity: Household Work and English Identity in Early Modern Drama.* Cambridge: Cambridge University Press, 2002.

Warner, Michael. *Publics and Counter Publics.* Cambridge: MIT Press, 2002.

Warner, William B., and Clifford Siskin. "Stopping Cultural Studies." *Profession* (2008): 94–107.

Weinstein, Adam. "'We Are the 99 Percent' Creators Revealed." *Mother Jones*, October 7, 2011: https://www.motherjones.com/politics/2011/10/we-are-the-99-percent-creators/.

Wells, Stanley, ed. *American Shakespeare Travesties (1852–1888).* Vol. 5 of *Nineteenth-Century Shakespeare Burlesques.* Wilmington, DE: Michael Glazier, Inc., 1978.

Wescott, David. "Is This Economist Too Far Ahead of His Time?" *The Chronicle of Higher Education*, October 16, 2016: http://www.chronicle.com/article/Is-This-Economist-Too-Far/238050.

Wexler, Ellen. "Subscription Scare Fuels Worries Over Who Controls Data That Scholars Need." *The Chronicle of Higher Education*, October 30, 2015: https://www.chronicle.com/article/Subscription-Scare-Fuels/234003.

White, Gillian B. "In D.C., White Families Are on Average 81 Times Richer Than Black Ones." *The Atlantic*, November 26, 2016: https://www.theatlantic.com/business/archive/2016/11/racial-wealth-gap-dc/508631/.

Whittle, Jane. "Lords and Tenants in Kett's Rebellion." *Past and Present* 27, no. 1 (2010): 3–52.

Wilbers, Jens, and Reinders Duit. "Post-Festum and Heuristic Analogies." In *Metaphor and Analogy in Science Education*, edited by Peter J. Aubusson, Allan G. Harrison, and Stephen M. Ritchie, 38–49. Dordrecht: Springer, 2006.

Wilcox, Lance. "Katherine of France: Victim and Bride." *Shakespeare Studies* 17 (1985): 61–76.

Willis, Paul. *Learning to Labour: How Working Class Kids Get Working Class Jobs.* New York: Columbia University Press, 1981.

Woolf, Virginia. Mrs. Dalloway, with a foreword by Maureen Howard (New York: Harcourt, Inc., 1981).

Index

S. O'Dair and T. Francisco (eds.), *Shakespeare and the 99%*, https://doi.org/10.1007/978-3-030-03883-0

CPSIA information can be obtained
at www.ICGtesting.com
Printed in the USA
LVHW061740260319
611865LV00011BB/624/P

9 783030 038823